GREEN LANTERN

SECRET ORIGIN

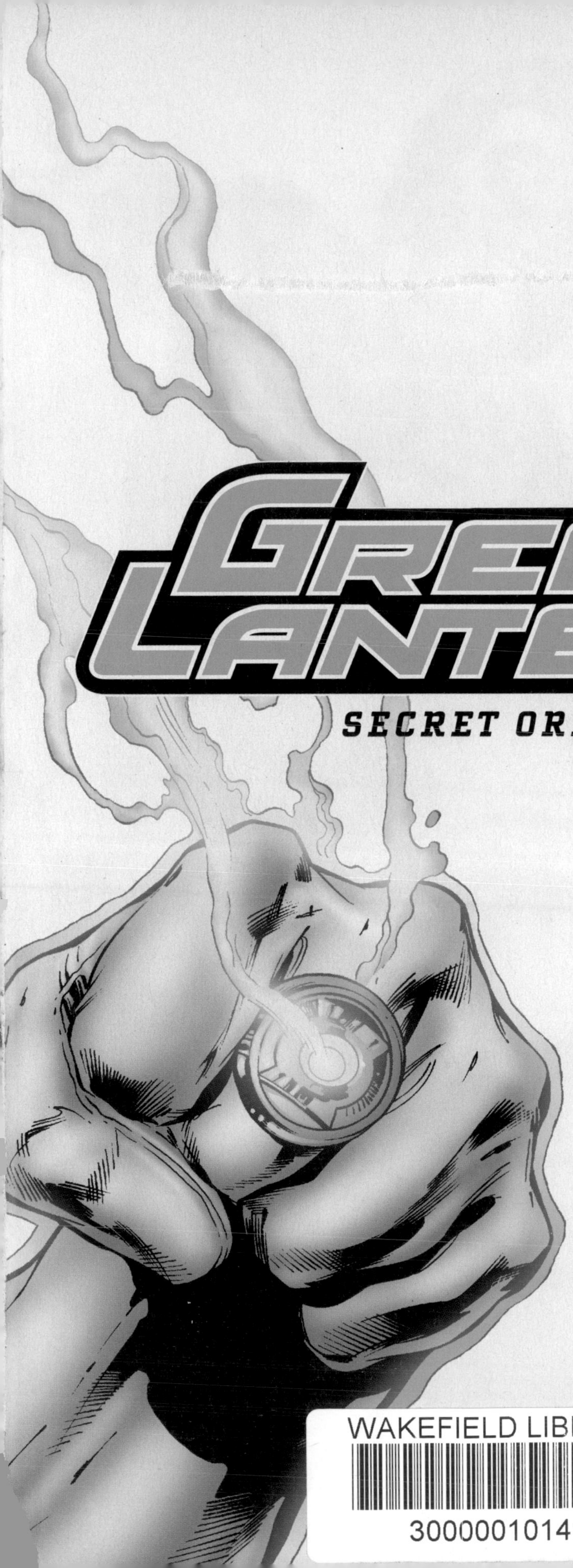

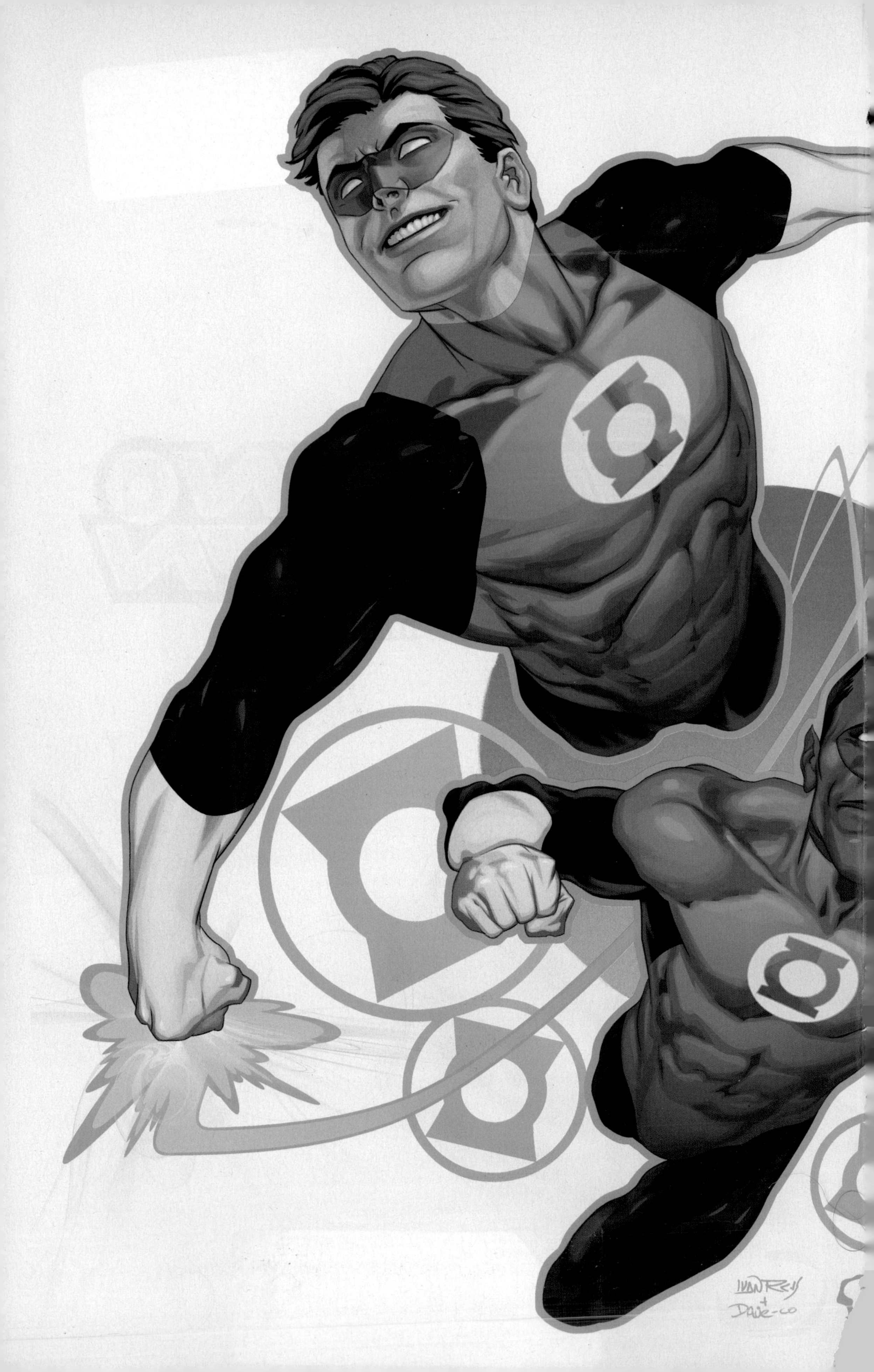

SECRET ORIGIN

Geoff Johns
Writer

Ivan Reis
Penciller

Oclair Albert
Inker

Randy Mayor
Colors

Rob Leigh
Letters

With
Julio Ferreira Partial Inker Book 3
Ivan Reis Partial Inker Book 6

Original Series Covers by **Ivan Reis** and **Dave McCaig**

DC COMICS

Dan DiDio Senior VP-Executive Editor
Eddie Berganza Editor-original series
Adam Schlagman Assistant Editor-original series
Bob Joy Editor-collected edition
Robbin Brosterman Senior Art Director
Paul Levitz President & Publisher
Georg Brewer VP-Design & DC Direct Creative
Richard Bruning Senior VP-Creative Director
Patrick Caldon Executive VP-Finance & Operations
Chris Caramalis VP-Finance
John Cunningham VP-Marketing
Terri Cunningham VP-Managing Editor
Amy Genkins Senior VP-Business & Legal Affairs
Alison Gill VP-Manufacturing
David Hyde VP-Publicity
Hank Kanalz VP-General Manager, WildStorm
Jim Lee Editorial Director-WildStorm
Gregory Noveck Senior VP-Creative Affairs
Sue Pohja VP-Book Trade Sales
Steve Rotterdam Senior VP-Sales & Marketing
Cheryl Rubin Senior VP-Brand Management
Alysse Soll VP-Advertising & Custom Publishing
Jeff Trojan VP-Business Development, DC Direct
Bob Wayne VP-Sales

Cover art by Ivan Reis and Dave McCaig

GREEN LANTERN: SECRET ORIGIN

Published by DC Comics. Cover and compilation
Copyright © 2008 DC Comics. All Rights Reserved.

Originally published in single magazine form in
GREEN LANTERN 29-35 Copyright © 2008
DC Comics. All Rights Reserved. All characters,
their distinctive likenesses and related elements
featured in this publication are trademarks of
DC Comics. The stories, characters and incidents
featured in this publication are entirely fictional.
DC Comics does not read or accept unsolicited
submissions of ideas, stories or artwork.

DC Comics, 1700 Broadway, New York, NY 10019
A Warner Bros. Entertainment Company
Printed by Worldcolor Press, Inc., Dubuque, IA. USA.
6/16/10. Second Printing.

ISBN: 978-1-4012-2017-4

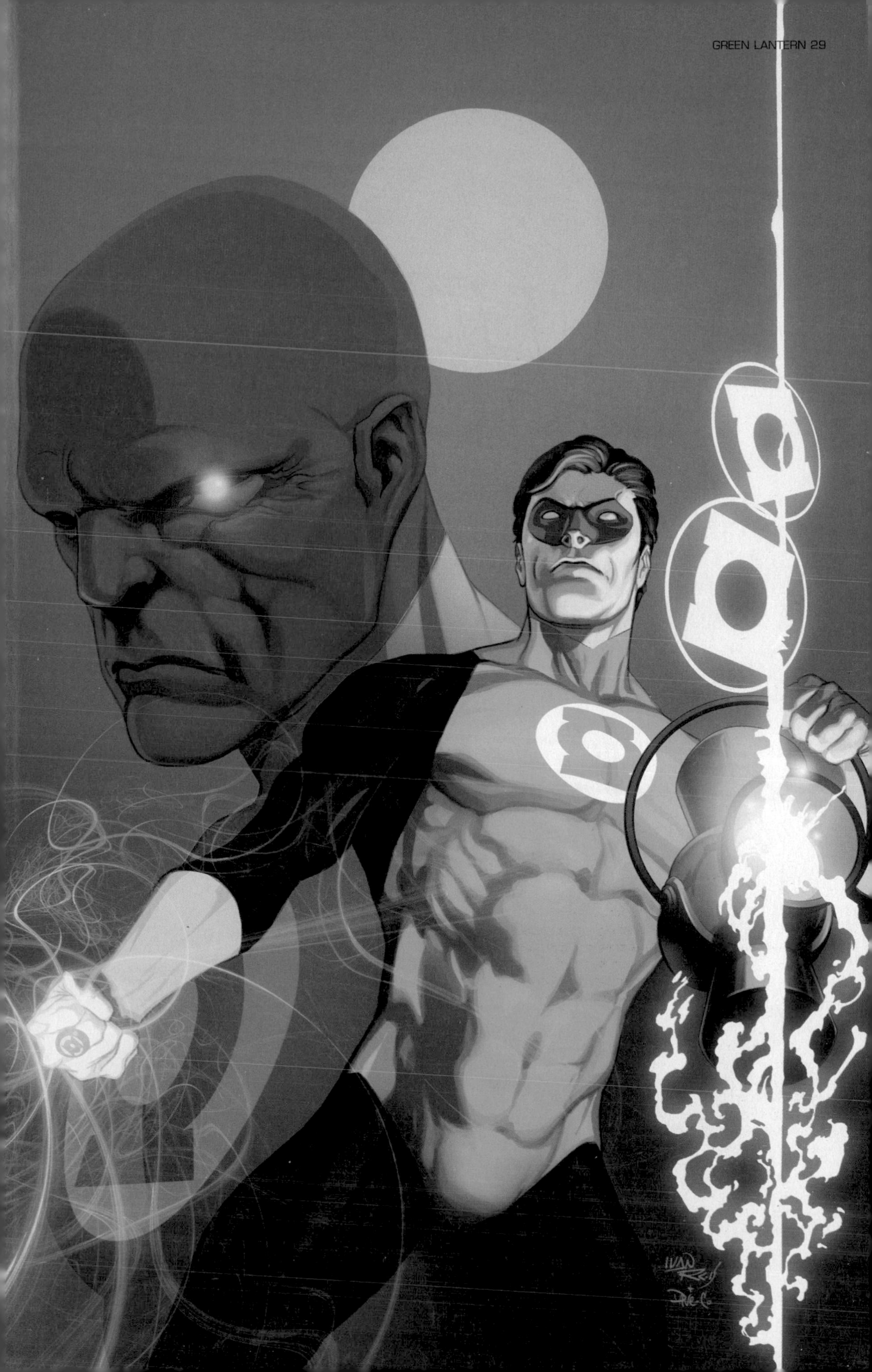

SECRET ORIGIN

BOOK ONE

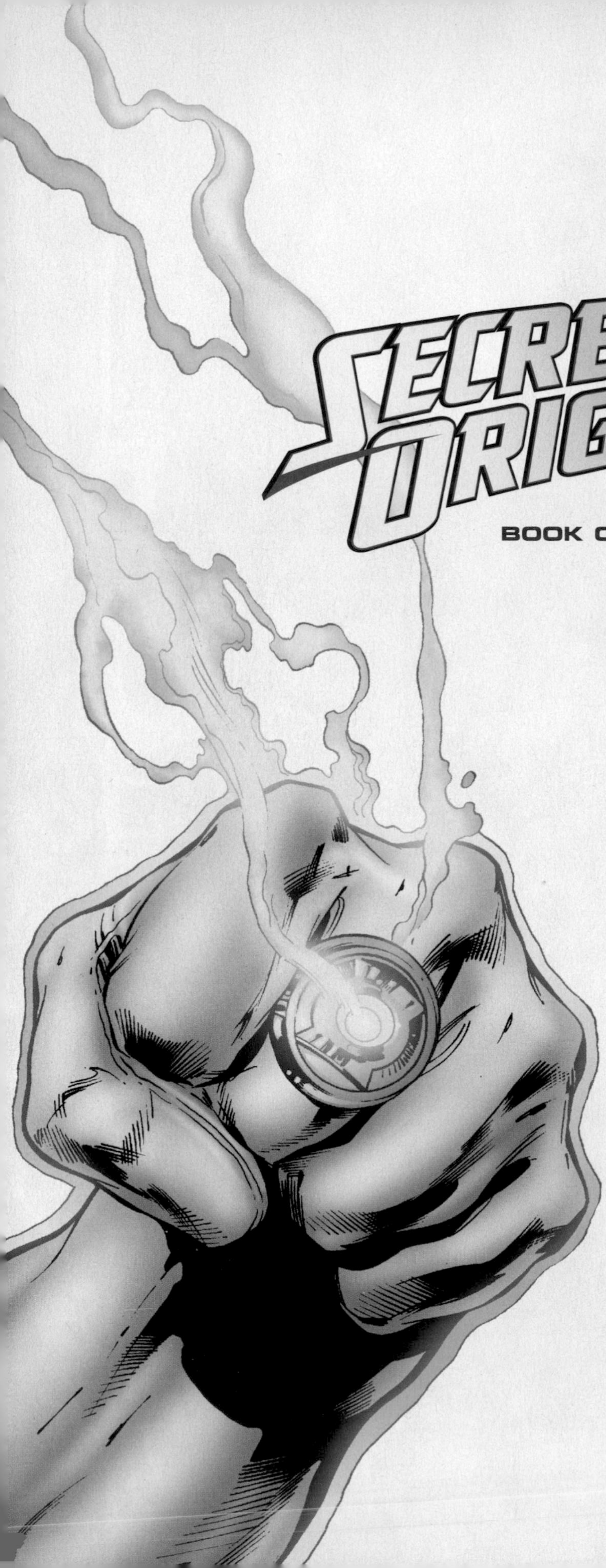

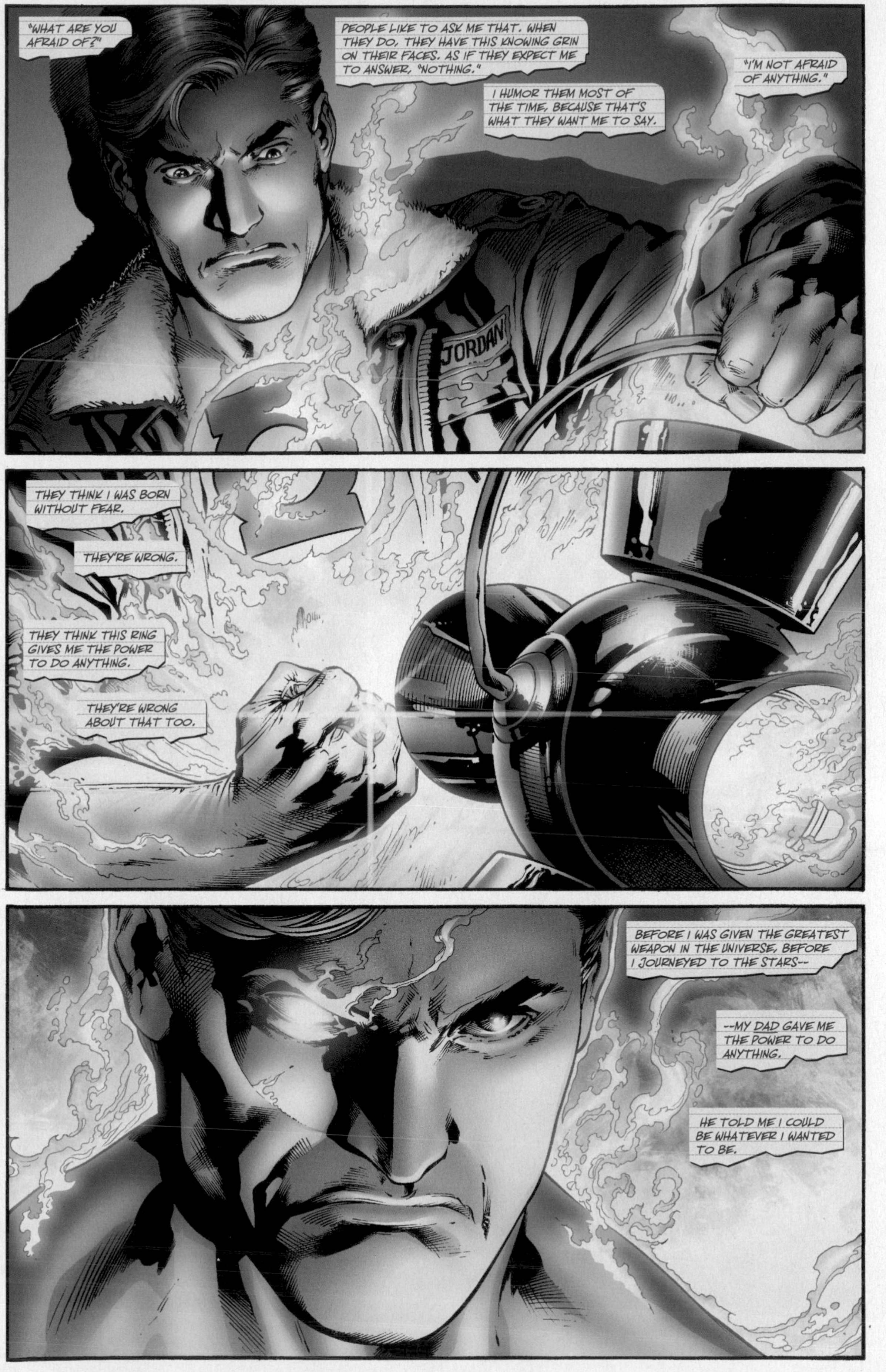
"WHAT ARE YOU AFRAID OF?"
PEOPLE LIKE TO ASK ME THAT. WHEN THEY DO, THEY HAVE THIS KNOWING GRIN ON THEIR FACES. AS IF THEY EXPECT ME TO ANSWER, "NOTHING."
I HUMOR THEM MOST OF THE TIME, BECAUSE THAT'S WHAT THEY WANT ME TO SAY.
"I'M NOT AFRAID OF ANYTHING."
JORDAN
THEY THINK I WAS BORN WITHOUT FEAR.
THEY'RE WRONG.
THEY THINK THIS RING GIVES ME THE POWER TO DO ANYTHING.
THEY'RE WRONG ABOUT THAT TOO.
BEFORE I WAS GIVEN THE GREATEST WEAPON IN THE UNIVERSE, BEFORE I JOURNEYED TO THE STARS--
--MY DAD GAVE ME THE POWER TO DO ANYTHING.
HE TOLD ME I COULD BE WHATEVER I WANTED TO BE.

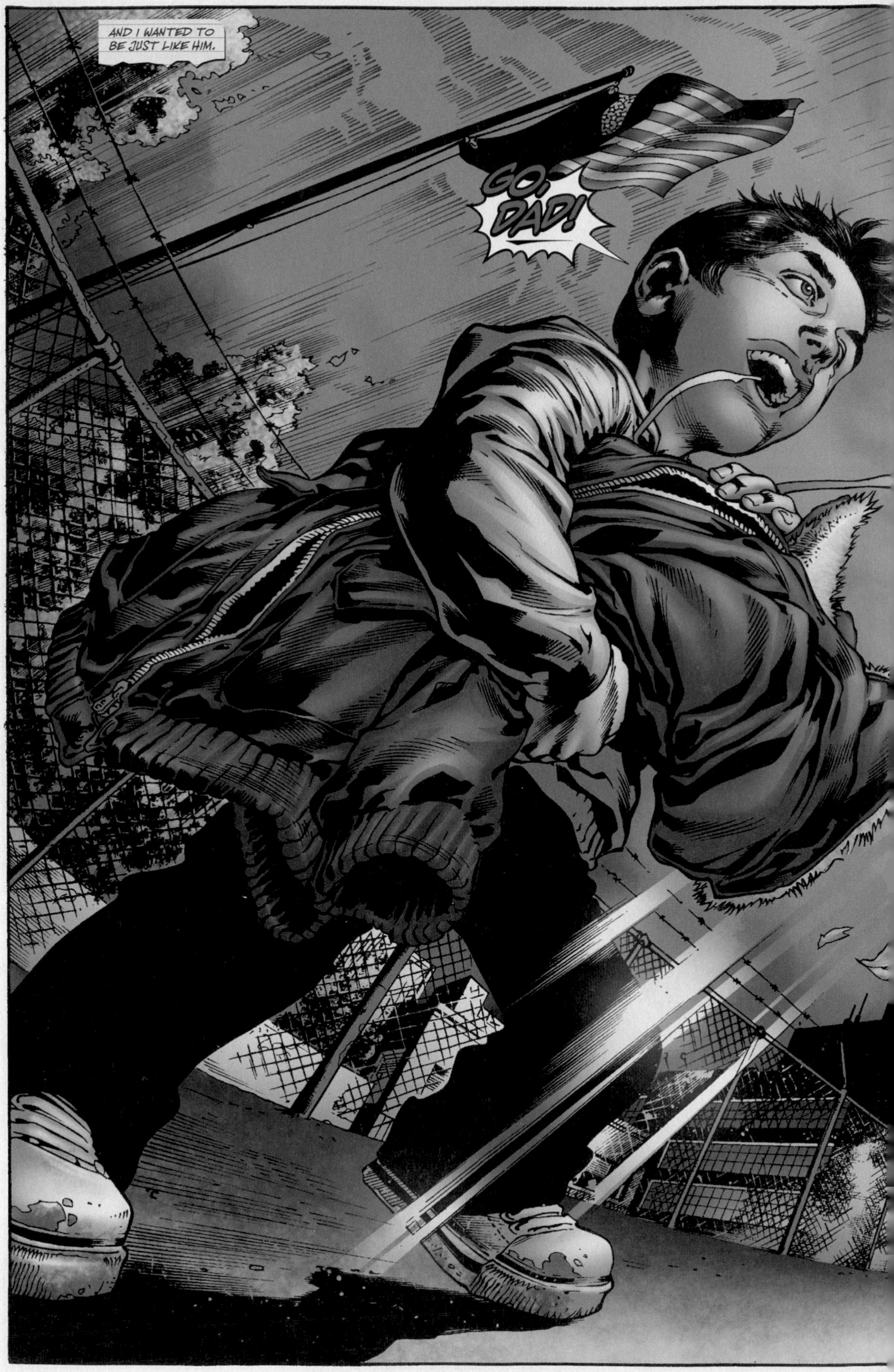

AND I WANTED TO BE JUST LIKE HIM.
GO, DAD!

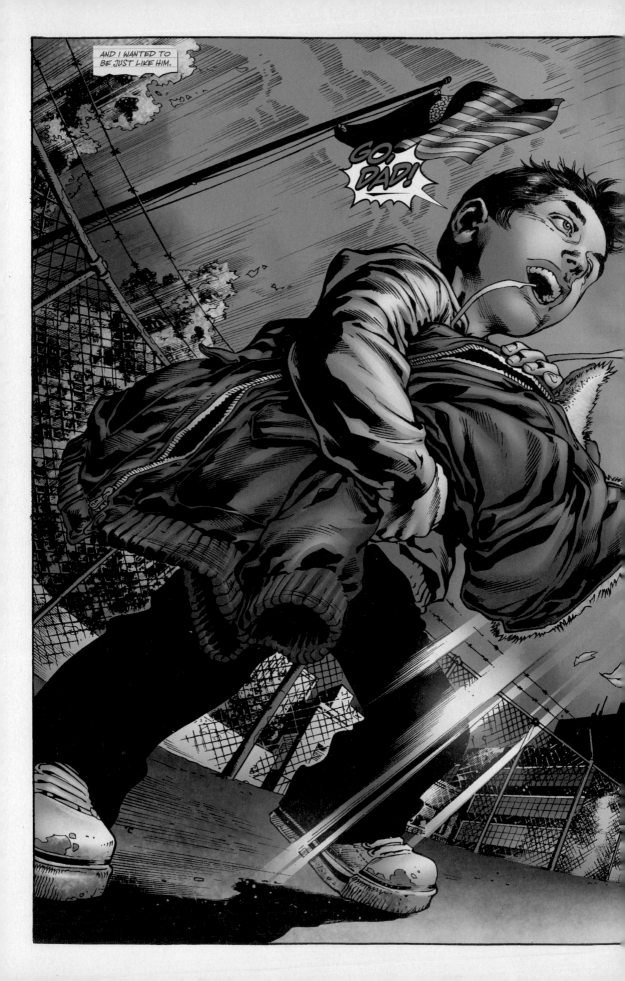

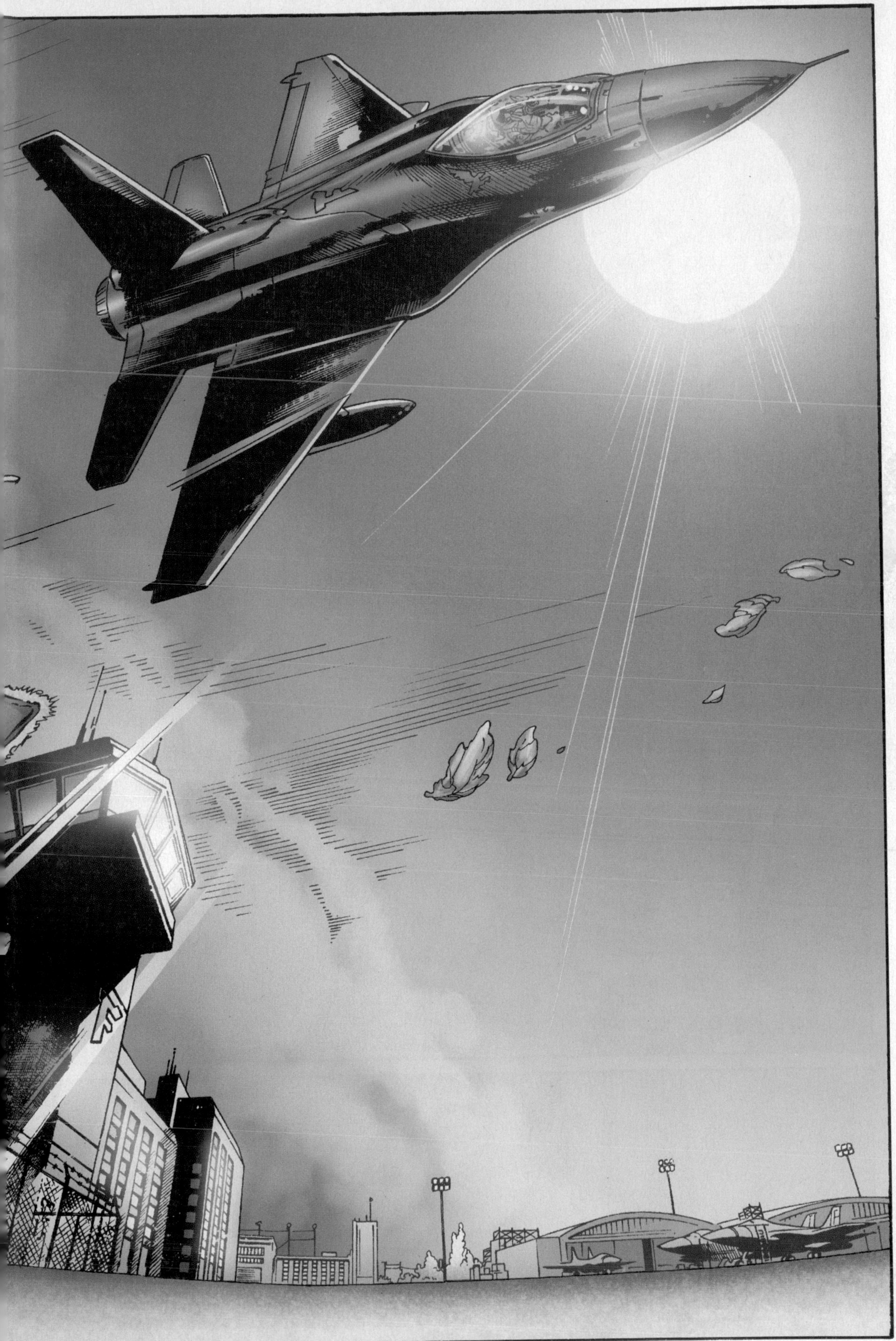

DAMMIT. I'M HAVING SOME PROBLEMS HERE, FERRIS. OIL'S GETTIN' EATEN UP QUICK. I THINK THE LAST OF MY TORQUE PINS JUST FAILED.

I THOUGHT THIS WAS SENT TO I-LEVEL REPAIR.

IT *WAS.*

DADDY! DADDY, THAT BOY IS BREAKING THE *RULES!*

ONE MINUTE, HONEY, OKAY?

I NEED TO BRING IT IN. AWAY FROM THE CROWD.

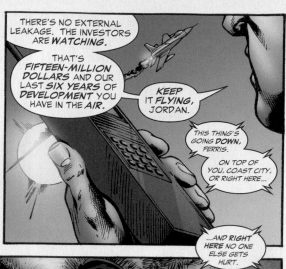

THERE'S NO EXTERNAL LEAKAGE. THE INVESTORS ARE *WATCHING.*

THAT'S *FIFTEEN-MILLION DOLLARS* AND OUR LAST *SIX YEARS* OF *DEVELOPMENT* YOU HAVE IN THE *AIR.*

KEEP IT *FLYING,* JORDAN.

THIS THING'S GOING *DOWN,* FERRIS.

ON TOP OF YOU, COAST CITY, OR RIGHT HERE...

...AND *RIGHT HERE* NO ONE ELSE GETS HURT.

WHEN YOUR WORST FEAR HAPPENS IN FRONT OF YOUR EYES—

DAD.

—I THOUGHT THERE WAS NOTHING *LEFT* TO BE *AFRAID* OF.

MOM THOUGHT THERE WAS EVERYTHING.

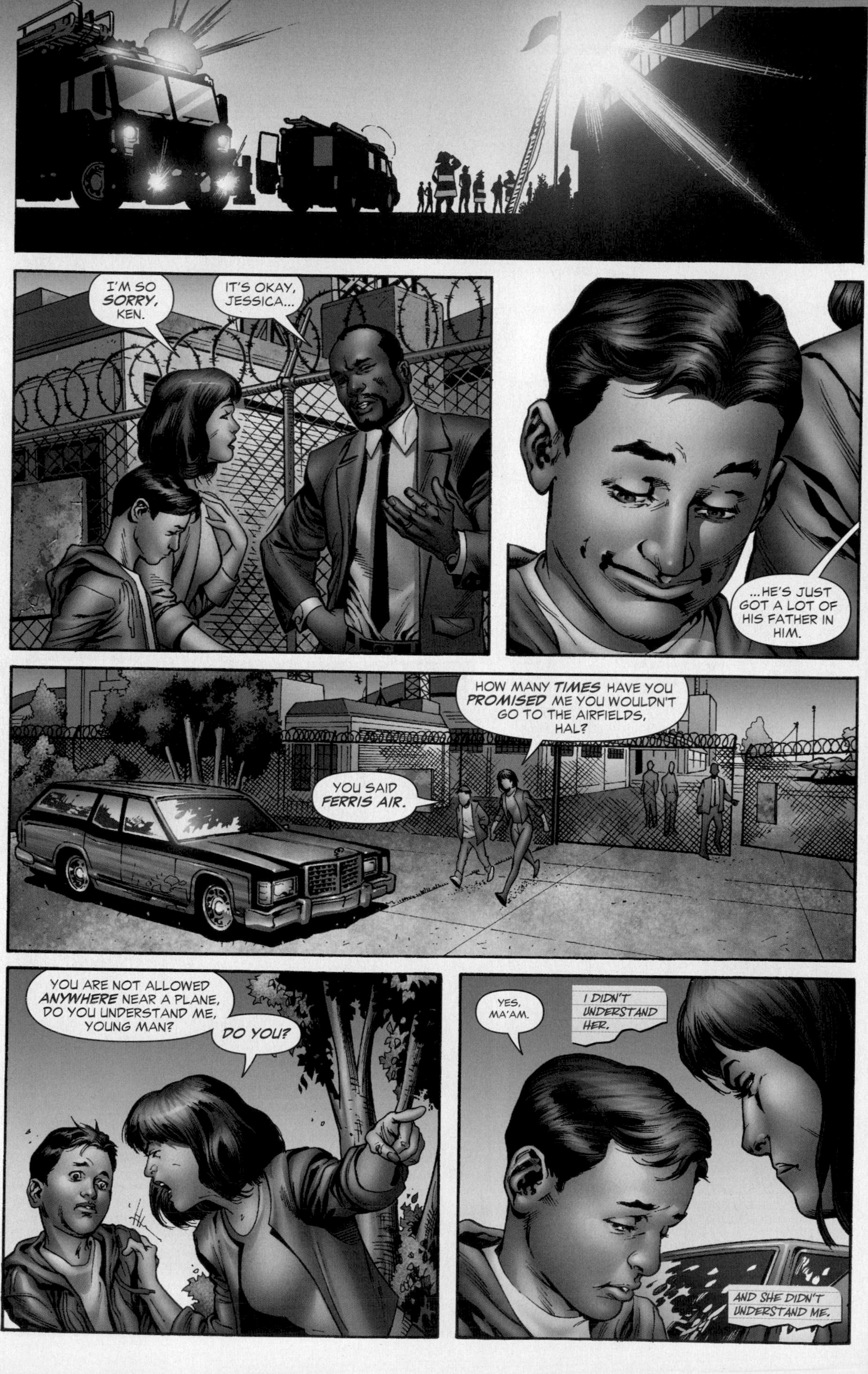
I'M SO SORRY, KEN.
IT'S OKAY, JESSICA...
...HE'S JUST GOT A LOT OF HIS FATHER IN HIM.
HOW MANY TIMES HAVE YOU PROMISED ME YOU WOULDN'T GO TO THE AIRFIELDS, HAL?
YOU SAID FERRIS AIR.
YOU ARE NOT ALLOWED ANYWHERE NEAR A PLANE, DO YOU UNDERSTAND ME, YOUNG MAN?
DO YOU?
YES, MA'AM.
I DIDN'T UNDERSTAND HER.
AND SHE DIDN'T UNDERSTAND ME.

NO ONE DID.

NICE GOING, *JERK*.

SHUT *UP*, JACK.

MOM WAS *FREAKING OUT* WHEN MR. ARDEN CALLED. SHE ALMOST HAD A HEART ATTACK!

OW.

YOU SCARE MOM LIKE THAT AGAIN AND THERE'S PLENTY MORE.

DON'T FIGHT! DON'T FIGHT!

WE'RE *NOT*, JIM.

WE AREN'T MOVING.

BUCKLE UP.

BETTER SAFE THAN SORRY. MOM SAYS SO.

BUCKLE UP.

BEFORE MOM HAS TO TELL YOU TO.

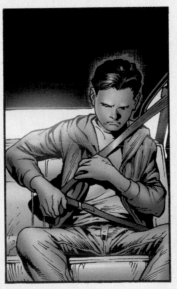

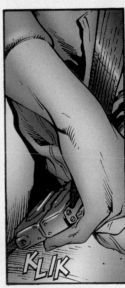

KLIK

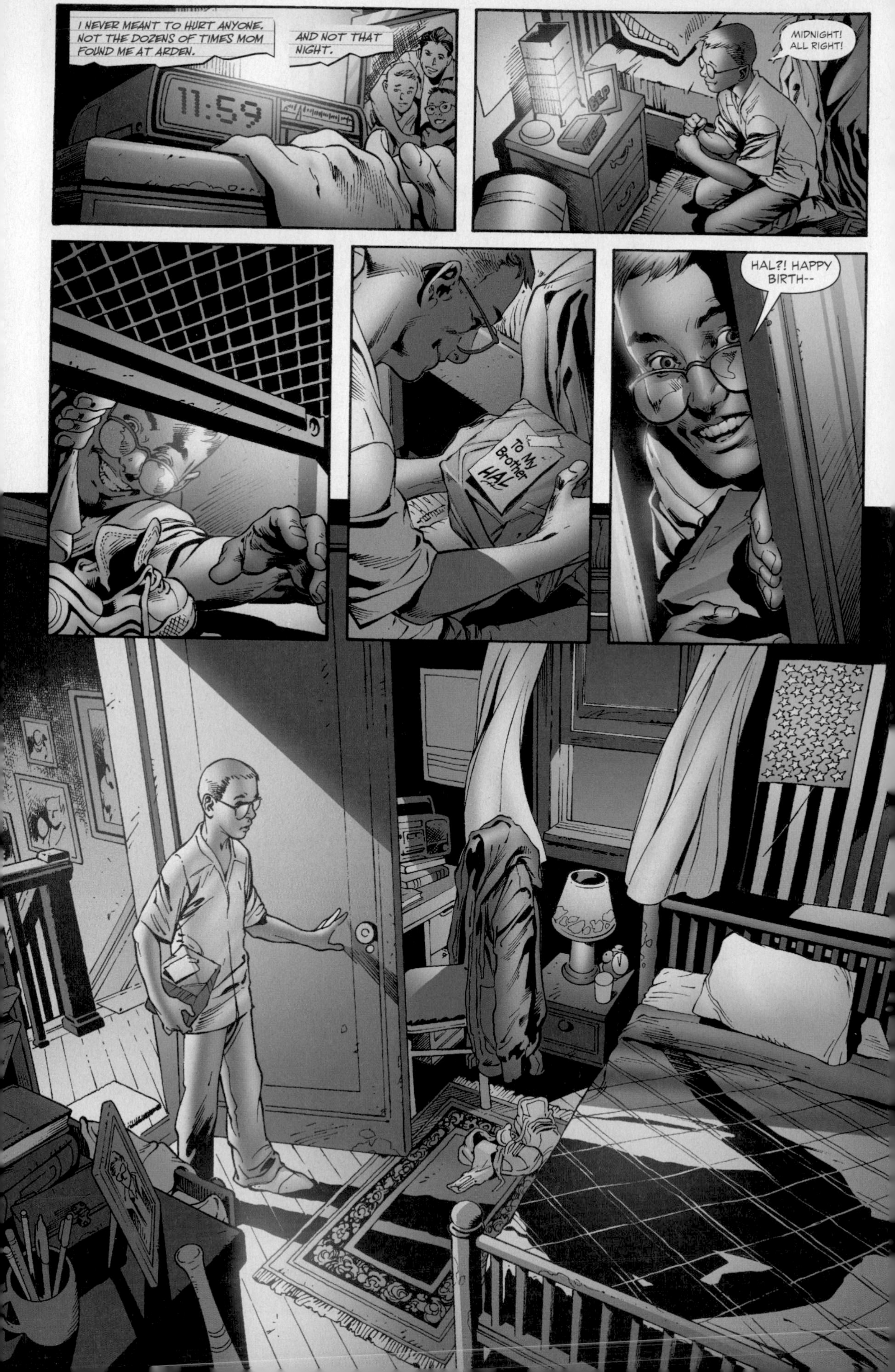

I NEVER MEANT TO HURT ANYONE. NOT THE DOZENS OF TIMES MOM FOUND ME AT ARDEN.
AND NOT THAT NIGHT.
11:59
MIDNIGHT! ALL RIGHT!
To My Brother HAL
HAL?! HAPPY BIRTH--

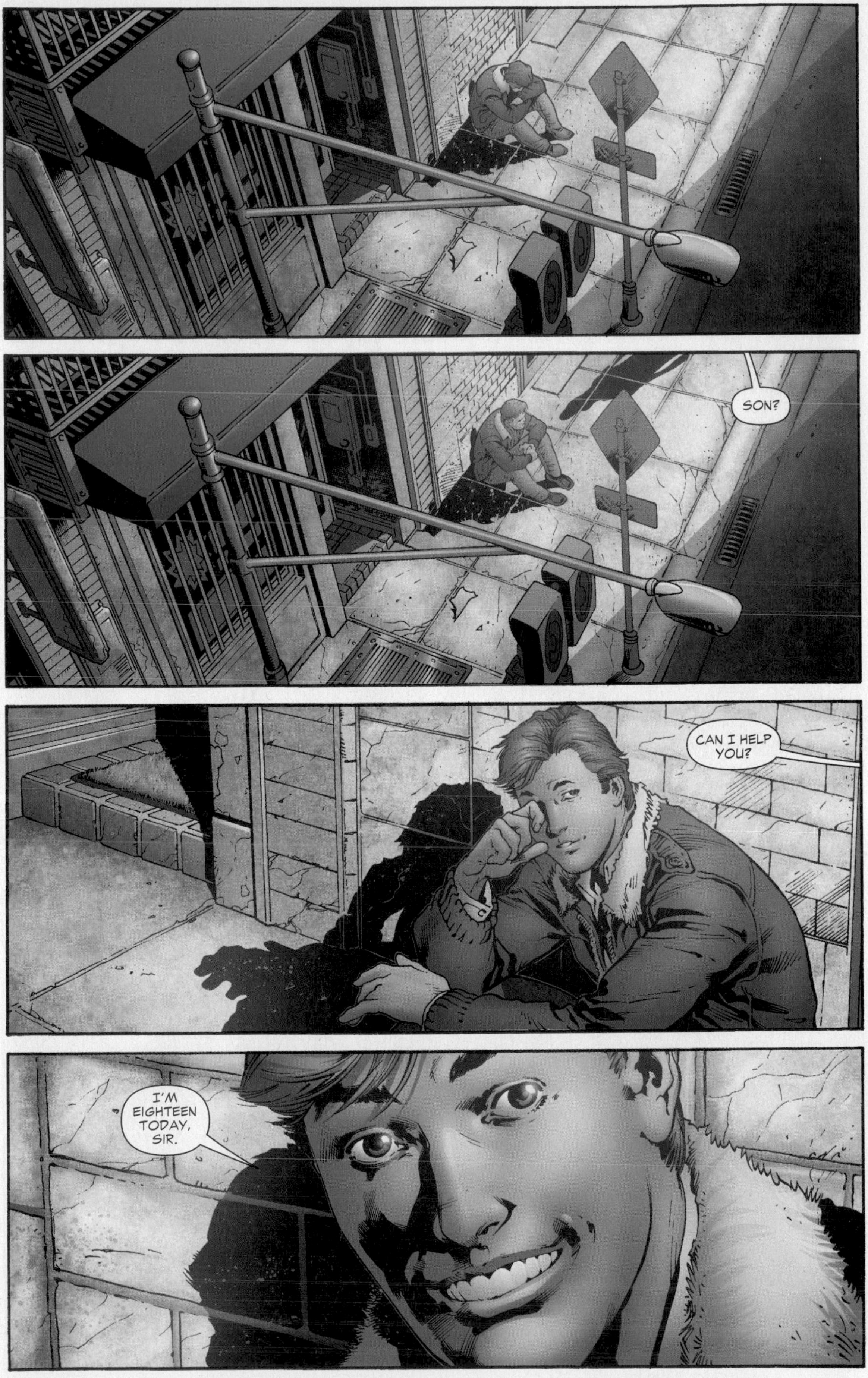
SON?
CAN I HELP YOU?
I'M EIGHTEEN TODAY, SIR.

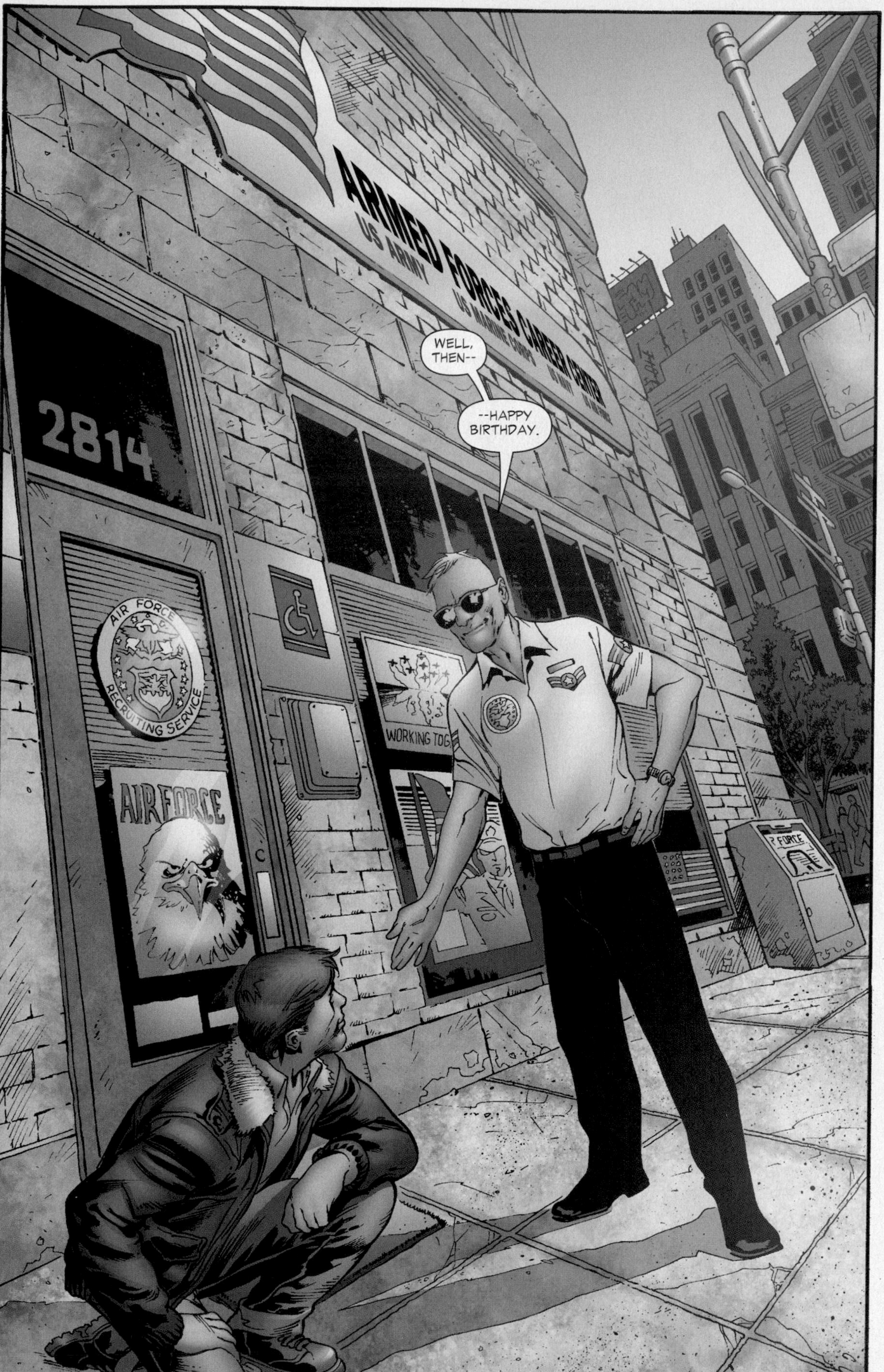
ARMED FORCES CAREER CENTER
US ARMY
2814
AIR FORCE RECRUITING SERVICE
AIR FORCE
WORKING TOG
WELL, THEN--
--HAPPY BIRTHDAY.

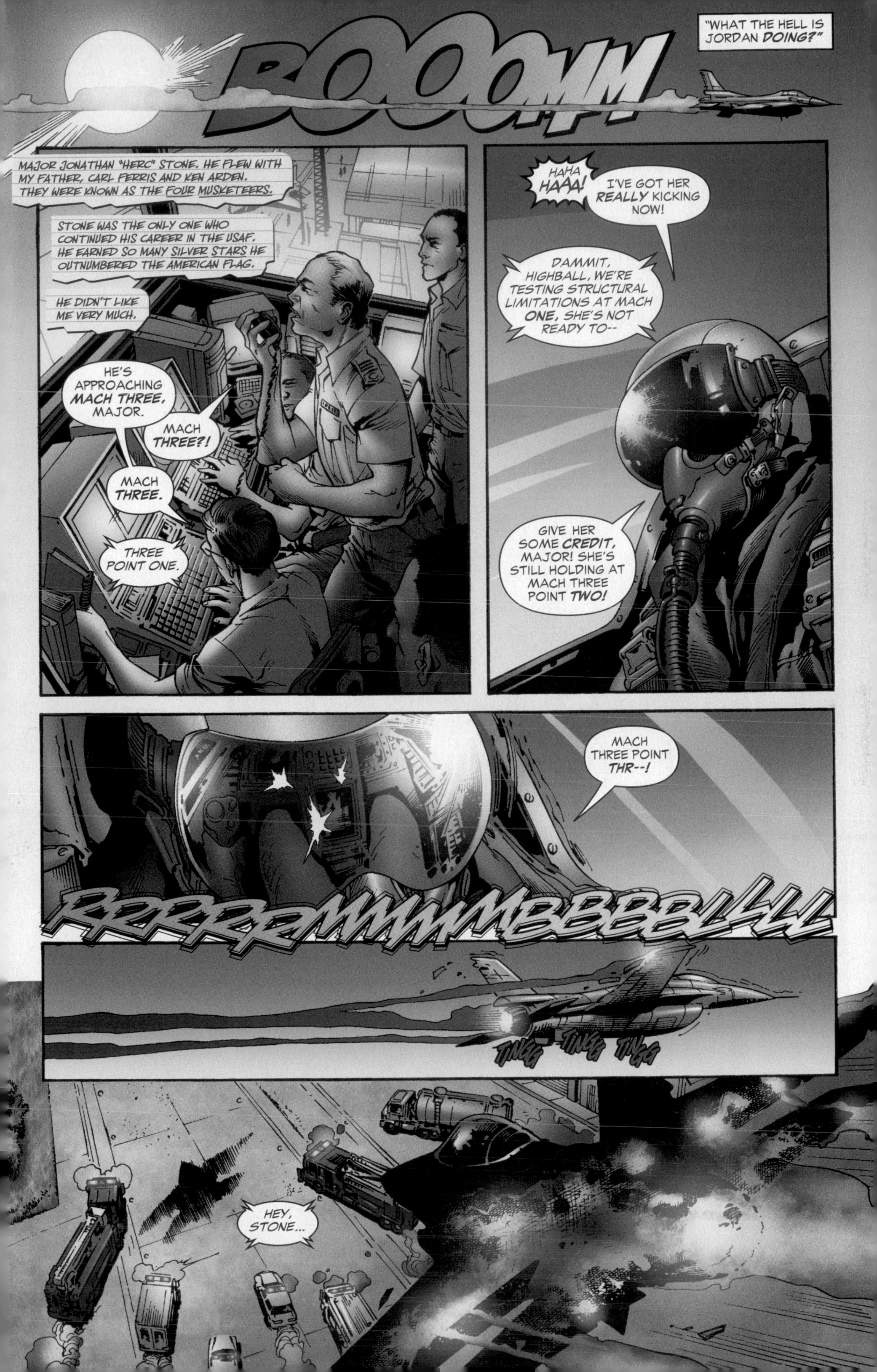
"WHAT THE HELL IS JORDAN DOING?"
BOOOMM
MAJOR JONATHAN "HERC" STONE. HE FLEW WITH MY FATHER, CARL FERRIS AND KEN ARDEN. THEY WERE KNOWN AS THE FOUR MUSKETEERS.
STONE WAS THE ONLY ONE WHO CONTINUED HIS CAREER IN THE USAF. HE EARNED SO MANY SILVER STARS HE OUTNUMBERED THE AMERICAN FLAG.
HE DIDN'T LIKE ME VERY MUCH.
HE'S APPROACHING MACH THREE, MAJOR.
MACH THREE?!
MACH THREE.
THREE POINT ONE.
HAHA HAAA!
I'VE GOT HER REALLY KICKING NOW!
DAMMIT, HIGHBALL, WE'RE TESTING STRUCTURAL LIMITATIONS AT MACH ONE. SHE'S NOT READY TO--
GIVE HER SOME CREDIT, MAJOR! SHE'S STILL HOLDING AT MACH THREE POINT TWO!
MACH THREE POINT THR--!
RRRRRMMMMMBBBBBLLLL
TINGG TINGG TINGG
HEY, STONE...

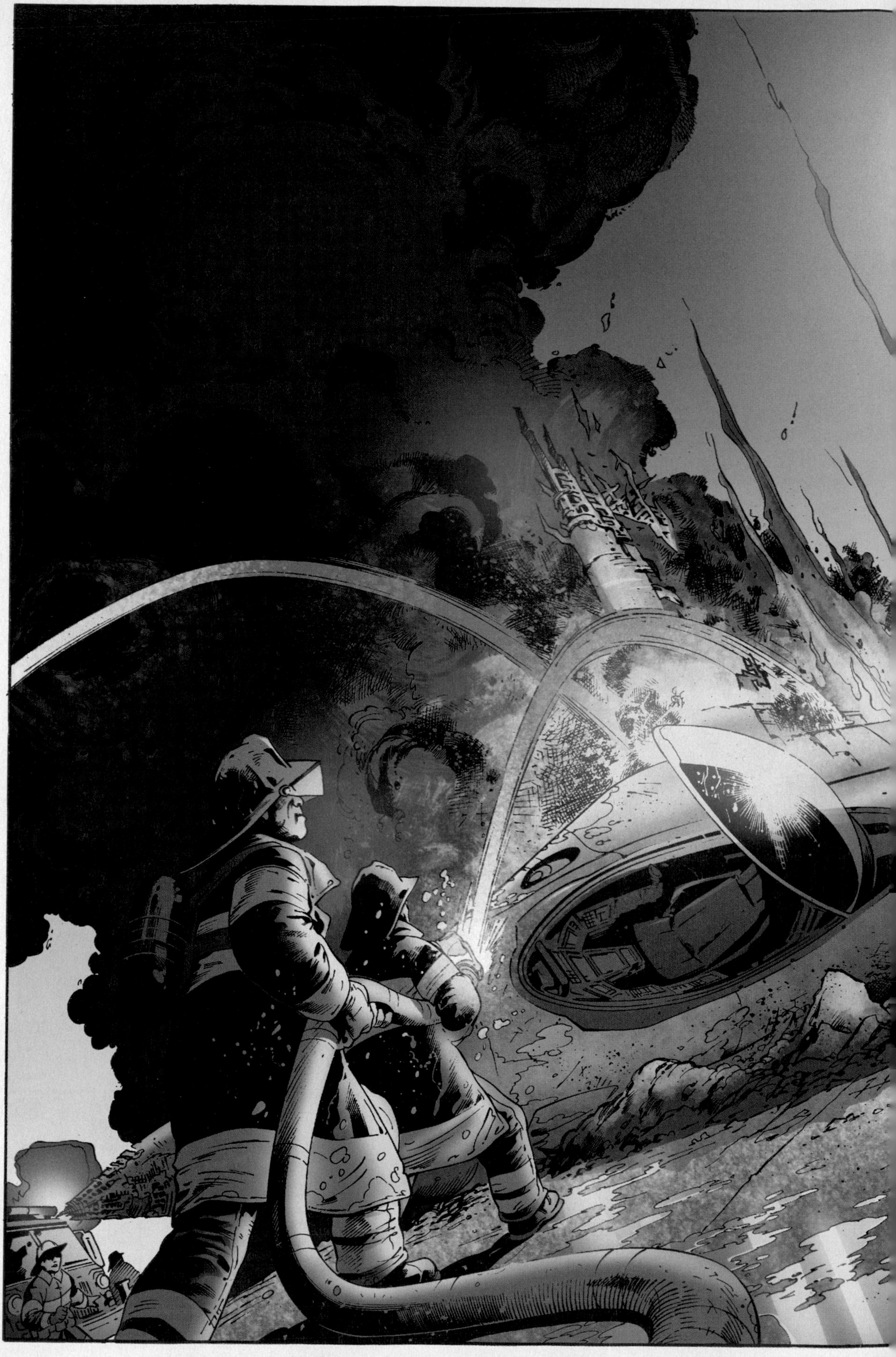

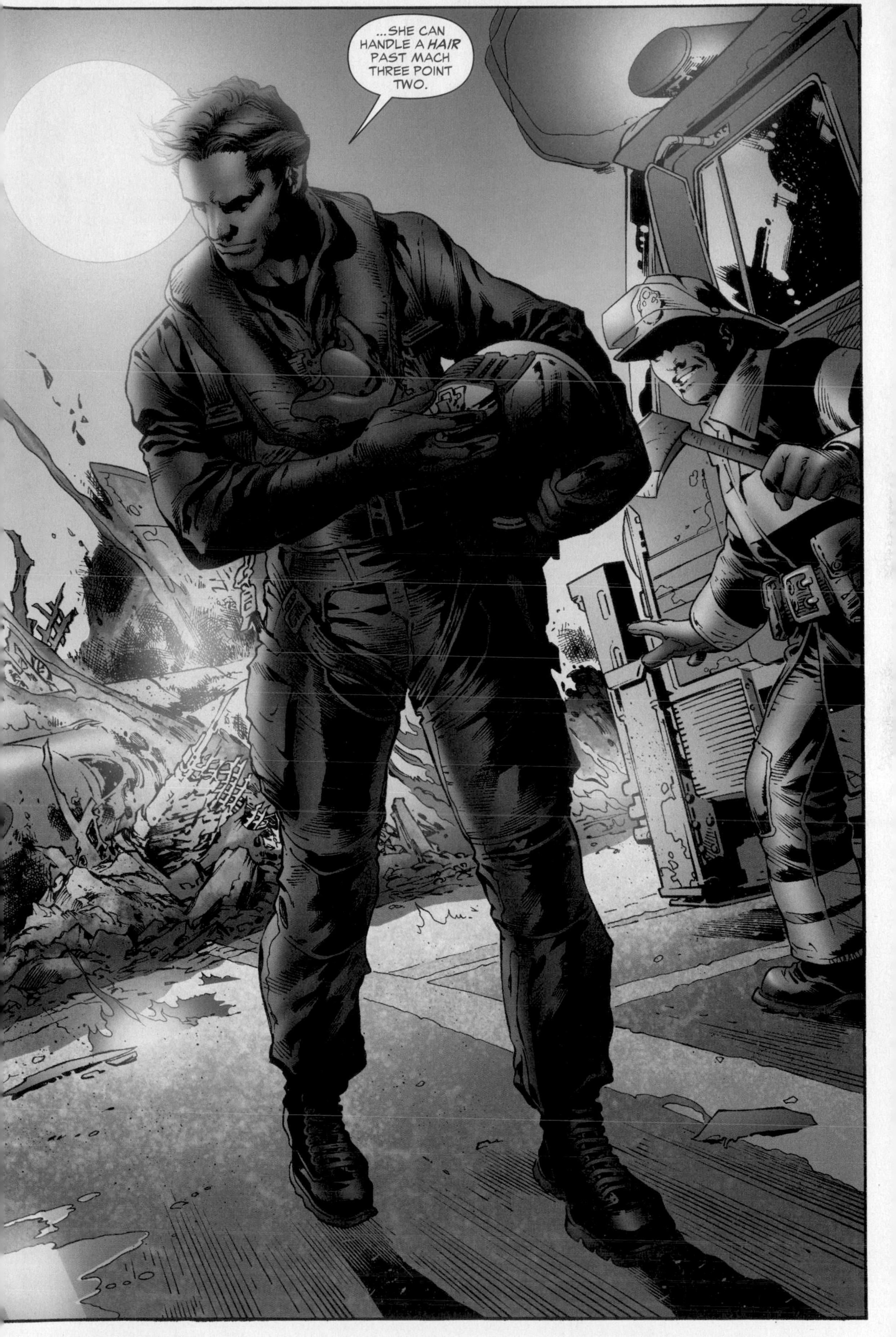
...SHE CAN HANDLE A HAIR PAST MACH THREE POINT TWO.

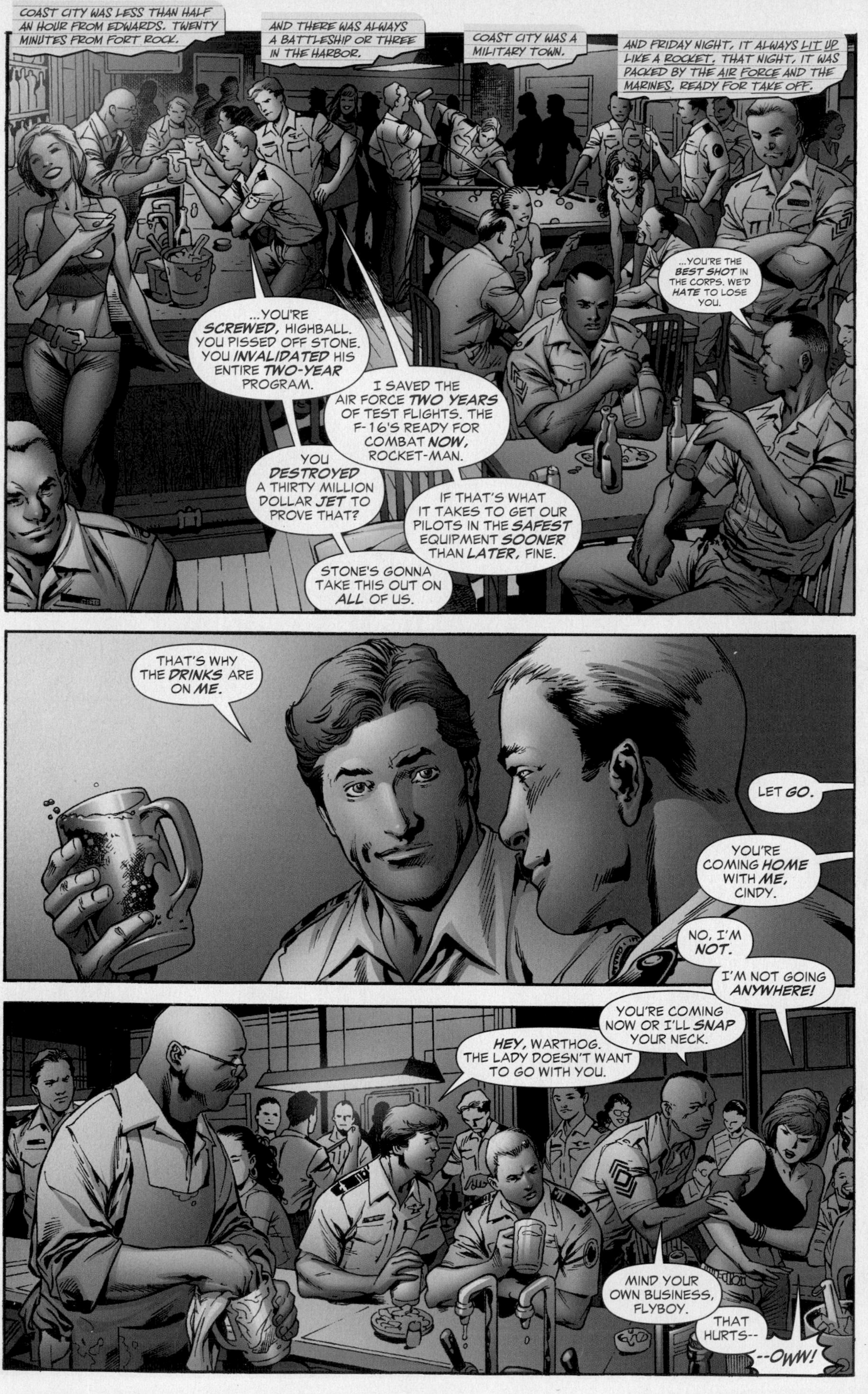
COAST CITY WAS LESS THAN HALF AN HOUR FROM EDWARDS. TWENTY MINUTES FROM FORT ROCK.
AND THERE WAS ALWAYS A BATTLESHIP OR THREE IN THE HARBOR.
COAST CITY WAS A MILITARY TOWN.
AND FRIDAY NIGHT, IT ALWAYS LIT UP LIKE A ROCKET. THAT NIGHT, IT WAS PACKED BY THE AIR FORCE AND THE MARINES. READY FOR TAKE OFF.
...YOU'RE THE BEST SHOT IN THE CORPS. WE'D HATE TO LOSE YOU.
...YOU'RE SCREWED, HIGHBALL. YOU PISSED OFF STONE. YOU INVALIDATED HIS ENTIRE TWO-YEAR PROGRAM.
I SAVED THE AIR FORCE TWO YEARS OF TEST FLIGHTS. THE F-16'S READY FOR COMBAT NOW, ROCKET-MAN.
YOU DESTROYED A THIRTY MILLION DOLLAR JET TO PROVE THAT?
IF THAT'S WHAT IT TAKES TO GET OUR PILOTS IN THE SAFEST EQUIPMENT SOONER THAN LATER, FINE.
STONE'S GONNA TAKE THIS OUT ON ALL OF US.
THAT'S WHY THE DRINKS ARE ON ME.
LET GO.
YOU'RE COMING HOME WITH ME, CINDY.
NO, I'M NOT.
I'M NOT GOING ANYWHERE!
YOU'RE COMING NOW OR I'LL SNAP YOUR NECK.
HEY, WARTHOG. THE LADY DOESN'T WANT TO GO WITH YOU.
MIND YOUR OWN BUSINESS, FLYBOY.
THAT HURTS--
--OWW!

YOU SEE THAT, STEWART? THAT *JET JOCKEY* JUST KNOCKED DOWN ONE OF *OURS.*

HERE WE GO.

HERE WE GO.

WHEN IT COMES TO WAR, WE MIGHT ALL BE ON THE SAME SIDE. BUT IF YOU THINK THERE'S NO INTERSERVICE RIVALRY BETWEEN THE AMERICAN ARMED FORCES--

--YOU'RE AS SHARP AS A JARHEAD.

YOU SHOULD BE *HAPPY.*

THIS IS MORE *FIGHTING* THAN THE AIR FORCE WILL SHOW YOU ALL YEAR.

THEN I BETTER MAKE IT *COUNT.*

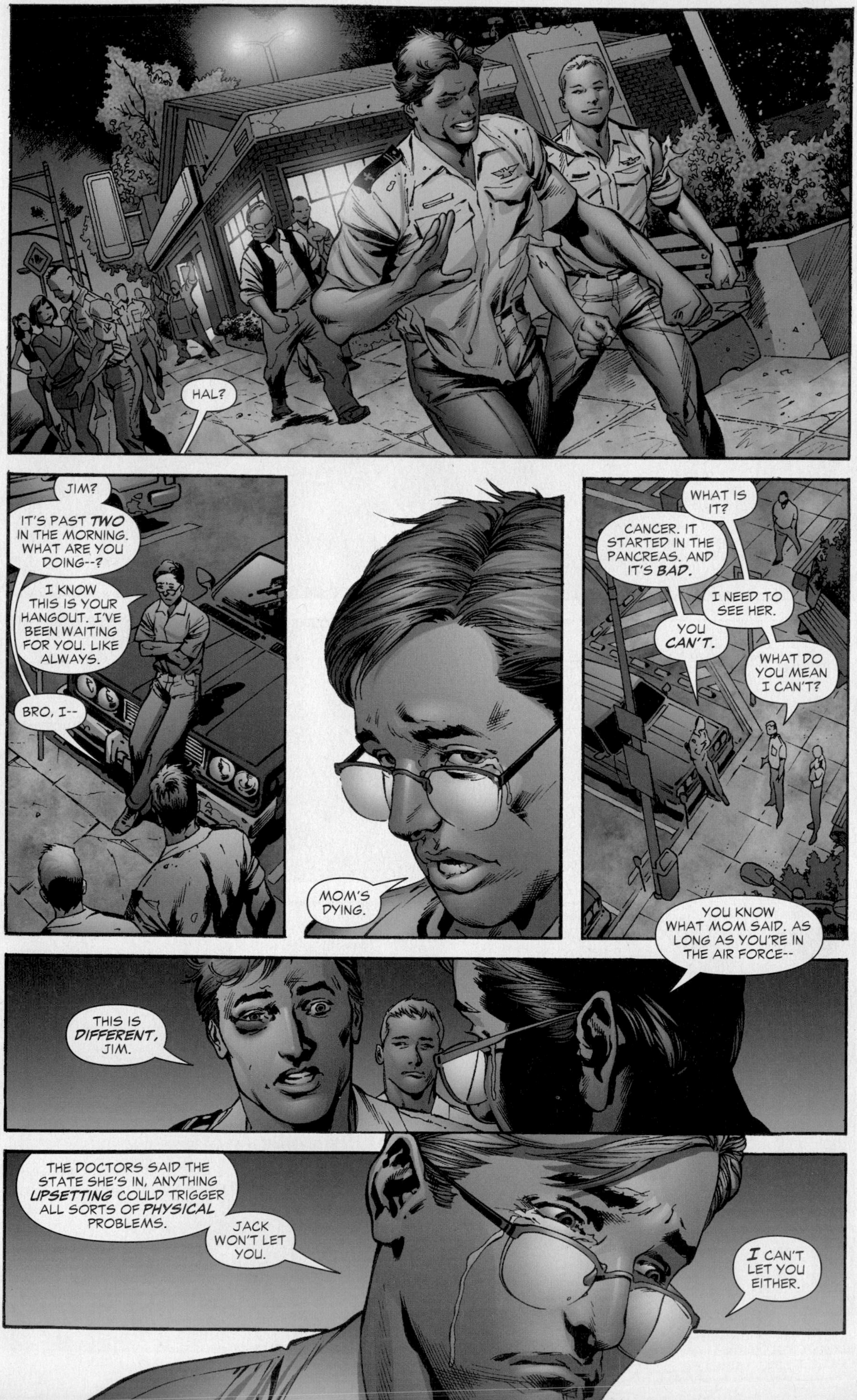
HAL?
JIM?
IT'S PAST TWO IN THE MORNING. WHAT ARE YOU DOING--?
I KNOW THIS IS YOUR HANGOUT. I'VE BEEN WAITING FOR YOU. LIKE ALWAYS.
BRO, I--
MOM'S DYING.
WHAT IS IT?
CANCER. IT STARTED IN THE PANCREAS. AND IT'S BAD.
I NEED TO SEE HER.
YOU CAN'T.
WHAT DO YOU MEAN I CAN'T?
YOU KNOW WHAT MOM SAID. AS LONG AS YOU'RE IN THE AIR FORCE--
THIS IS DIFFERENT, JIM.
THE DOCTORS SAID THE STATE SHE'S IN, ANYTHING UPSETTING COULD TRIGGER ALL SORTS OF PHYSICAL PROBLEMS.
JACK WON'T LET YOU.
I CAN'T LET YOU EITHER.

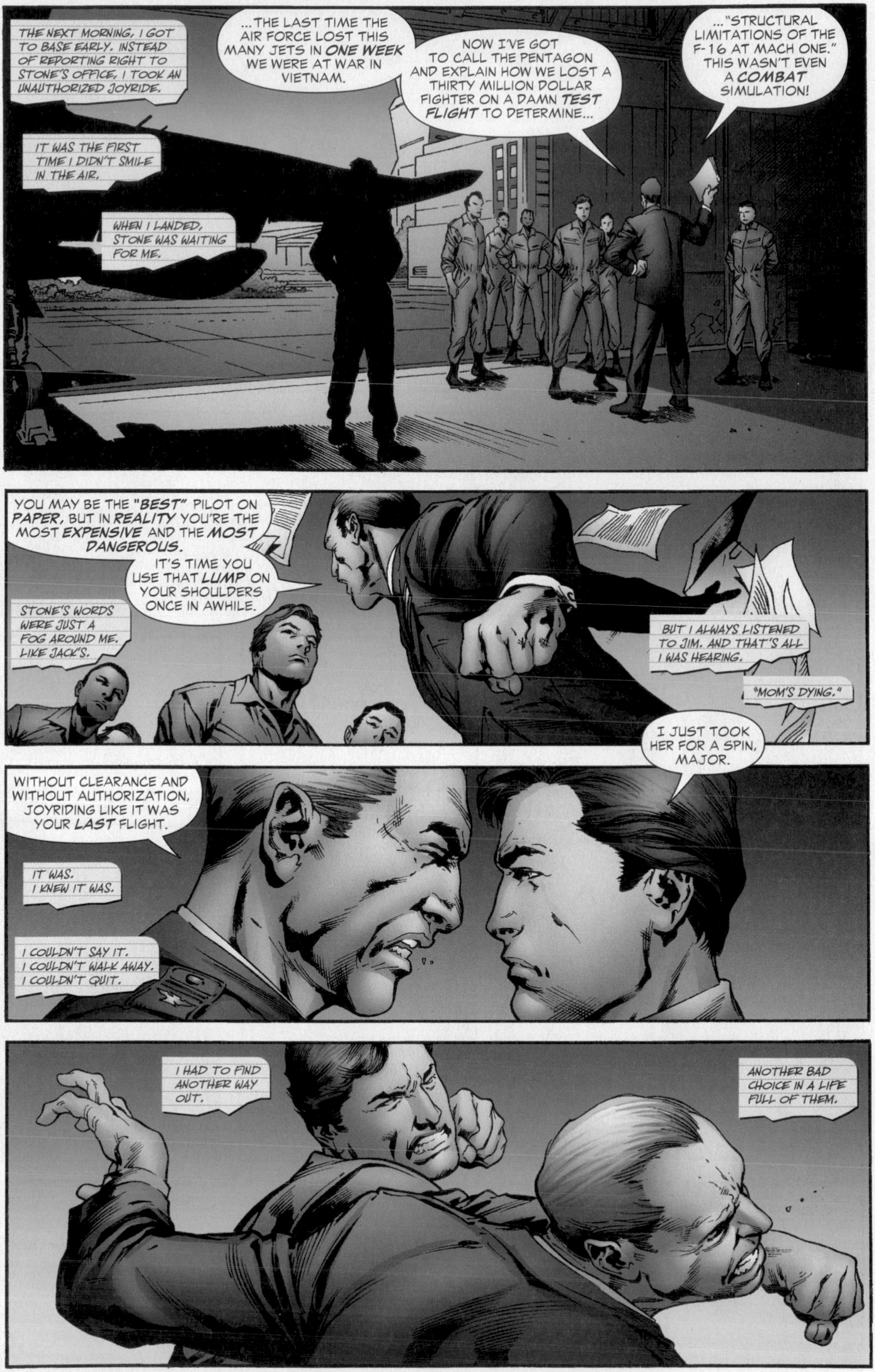
THE NEXT MORNING, I GOT TO BASE EARLY. INSTEAD OF REPORTING RIGHT TO STONE'S OFFICE, I TOOK AN UNAUTHORIZED JOYRIDE.
...THE LAST TIME THE AIR FORCE LOST THIS MANY JETS IN ONE WEEK WE WERE AT WAR IN VIETNAM.
NOW I'VE GOT TO CALL THE PENTAGON AND EXPLAIN HOW WE LOST A THIRTY MILLION DOLLAR FIGHTER ON A DAMN TEST FLIGHT TO DETERMINE...
..."STRUCTURAL LIMITATIONS OF THE F-16 AT MACH ONE." THIS WASN'T EVEN A COMBAT SIMULATION!
IT WAS THE FIRST TIME I DIDN'T SMILE IN THE AIR.
WHEN I LANDED, STONE WAS WAITING FOR ME.
YOU MAY BE THE "BEST" PILOT ON PAPER, BUT IN REALITY YOU'RE THE MOST EXPENSIVE AND THE MOST DANGEROUS.
IT'S TIME YOU USE THAT LUMP ON YOUR SHOULDERS ONCE IN AWHILE.
STONE'S WORDS WERE JUST A FOG AROUND ME. LIKE JACK'S.
BUT I ALWAYS LISTENED TO JIM. AND THAT'S ALL I WAS HEARING.
"MOM'S DYING."
I JUST TOOK HER FOR A SPIN, MAJOR.
WITHOUT CLEARANCE AND WITHOUT AUTHORIZATION, JOYRIDING LIKE IT WAS YOUR LAST FLIGHT.
IT WAS. I KNEW IT WAS.
I COULDN'T SAY IT. I COULDN'T WALK AWAY. I COULDN'T QUIT.
I HAD TO FIND ANOTHER WAY OUT.
ANOTHER BAD CHOICE IN A LIFE FULL OF THEM.

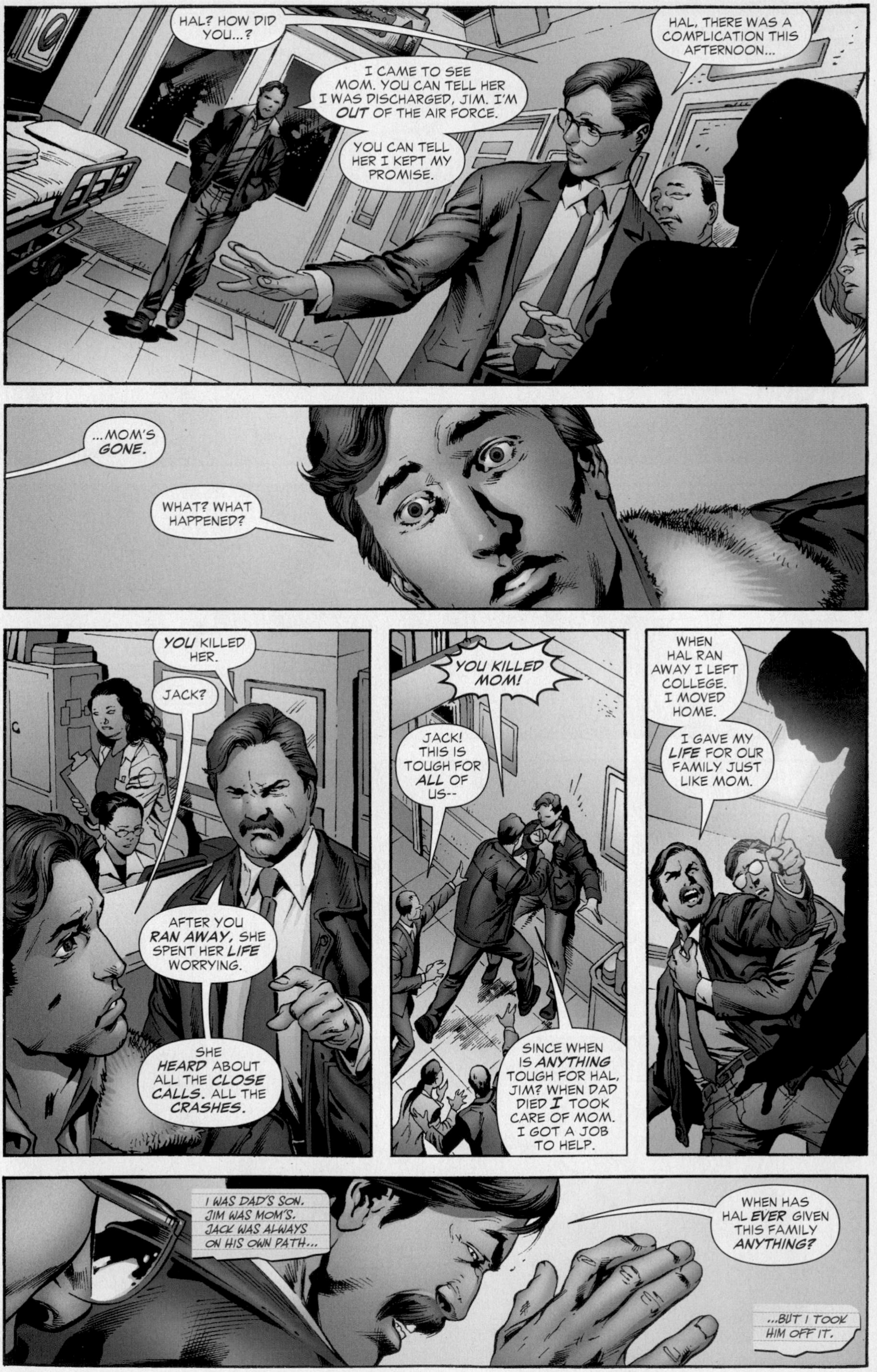
HAL? HOW DID YOU...?
I CAME TO SEE MOM. YOU CAN TELL HER I WAS DISCHARGED, JIM. I'M OUT OF THE AIR FORCE.
YOU CAN TELL HER I KEPT MY PROMISE.
HAL, THERE WAS A COMPLICATION THIS AFTERNOON...
...MOM'S GONE.
WHAT? WHAT HAPPENED?
YOU KILLED HER.
JACK?
AFTER YOU RAN AWAY, SHE SPENT HER LIFE WORRYING.
SHE HEARD ABOUT ALL THE CLOSE CALLS. ALL THE CRASHES.
YOU KILLED MOM!
JACK! THIS IS TOUGH FOR ALL OF US--
SINCE WHEN IS ANYTHING TOUGH FOR HAL, JIM? WHEN DAD DIED I TOOK CARE OF MOM. I GOT A JOB TO HELP.
WHEN HAL RAN AWAY I LEFT COLLEGE. I MOVED HOME.
I GAVE MY LIFE FOR OUR FAMILY JUST LIKE MOM.
I WAS DAD'S SON. JIM WAS MOM'S. JACK WAS ALWAYS ON HIS OWN PATH...
WHEN HAS HAL EVER GIVEN THIS FAMILY ANYTHING?
...BUT I TOOK HIM OFF IT.

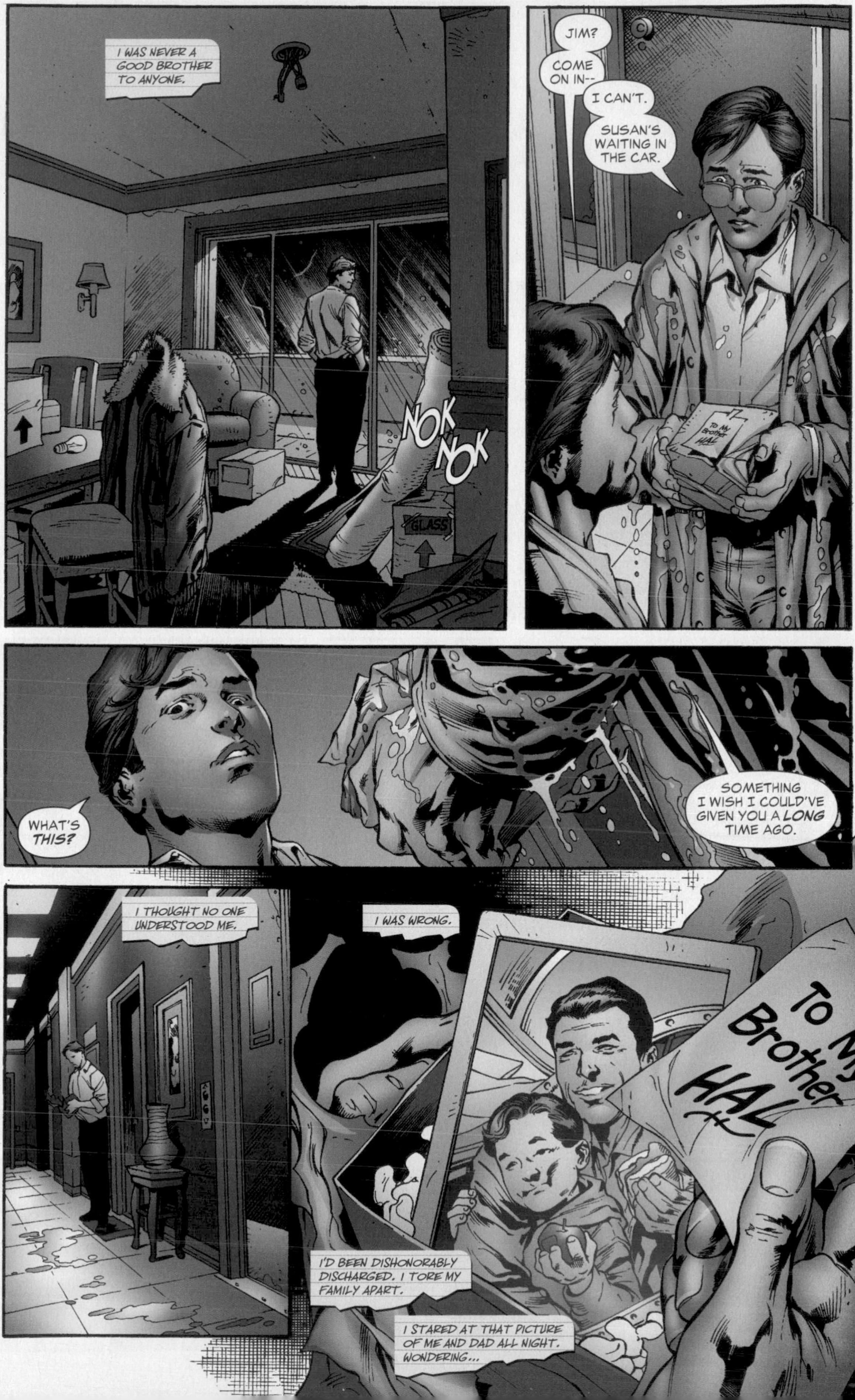

I WAS NEVER A GOOD BROTHER TO ANYONE.
NOK NOK
GLASS
JIM?
COME ON IN--
I CAN'T.
SUSAN'S WAITING IN THE CAR.
To My Brother HAL
WHAT'S THIS?
SOMETHING I WISH I COULD'VE GIVEN YOU A LONG TIME AGO.
I THOUGHT NO ONE UNDERSTOOD ME.
I WAS WRONG.
To My Brother HAL
I'D BEEN DISHONORABLY DISCHARGED. I TORE MY FAMILY APART.
I STARED AT THAT PICTURE OF ME AND DAD ALL NIGHT. WONDERING...

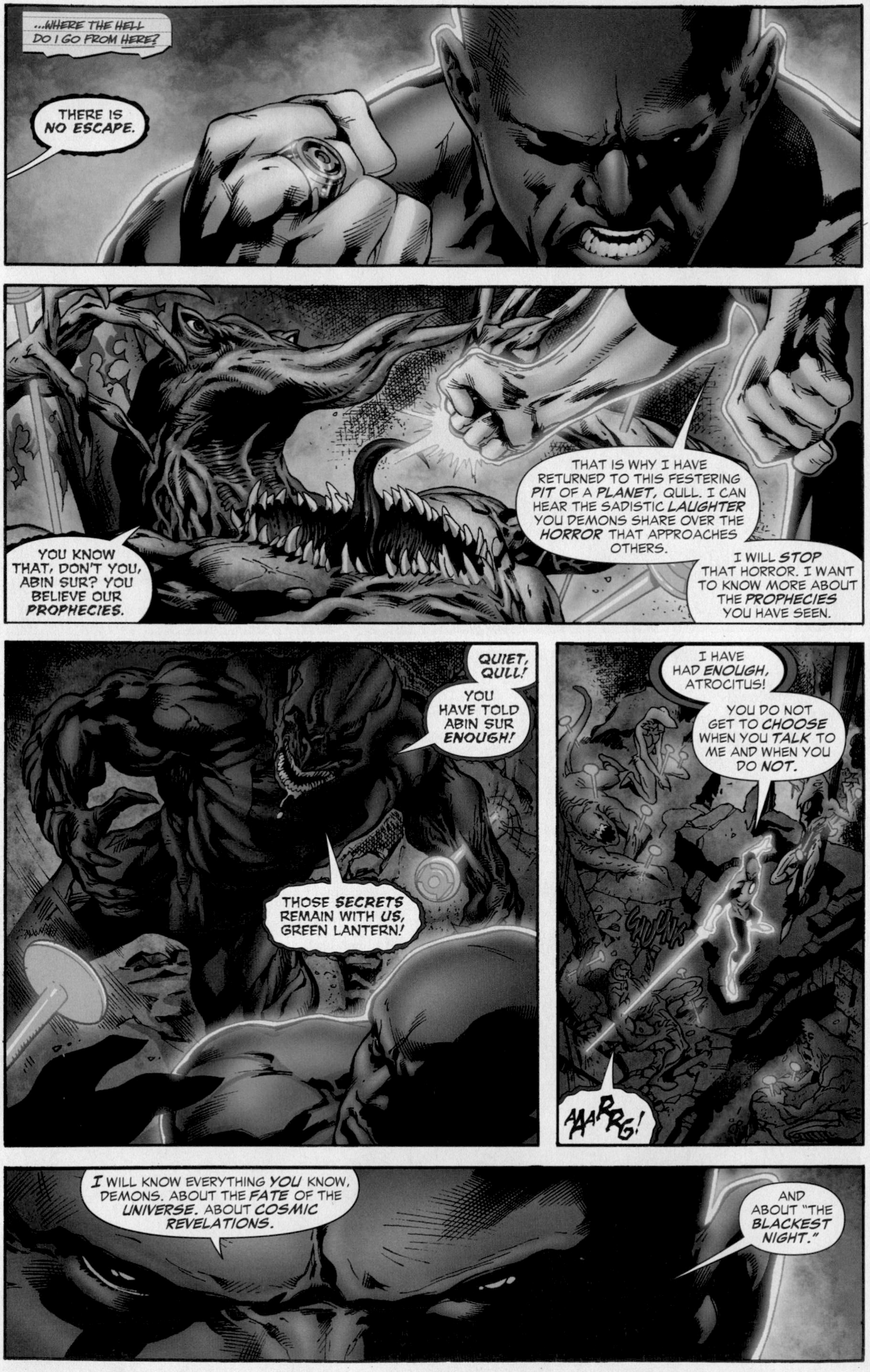
...WHERE THE HELL DO I GO FROM HERE?
THERE IS NO ESCAPE.
THAT IS WHY I HAVE RETURNED TO THIS FESTERING PIT OF A PLANET, QULL. I CAN HEAR THE SADISTIC LAUGHTER YOU DEMONS SHARE OVER THE HORROR THAT APPROACHES OTHERS.
YOU KNOW THAT, DON'T YOU, ABIN SUR? YOU BELIEVE OUR PROPHECIES.
I WILL STOP THAT HORROR. I WANT TO KNOW MORE ABOUT THE PROPHECIES YOU HAVE SEEN.
QUIET, QULL!
YOU HAVE TOLD ABIN SUR ENOUGH!
THOSE SECRETS REMAIN WITH US, GREEN LANTERN!
I HAVE HAD ENOUGH, ATROCITUS!
YOU DO NOT GET TO CHOOSE WHEN YOU TALK TO ME AND WHEN YOU DO NOT.
AAARRG!
I WILL KNOW EVERYTHING YOU KNOW, DEMONS. ABOUT THE FATE OF THE UNIVERSE. ABOUT COSMIC REVELATIONS.
AND ABOUT "THE BLACKEST NIGHT."

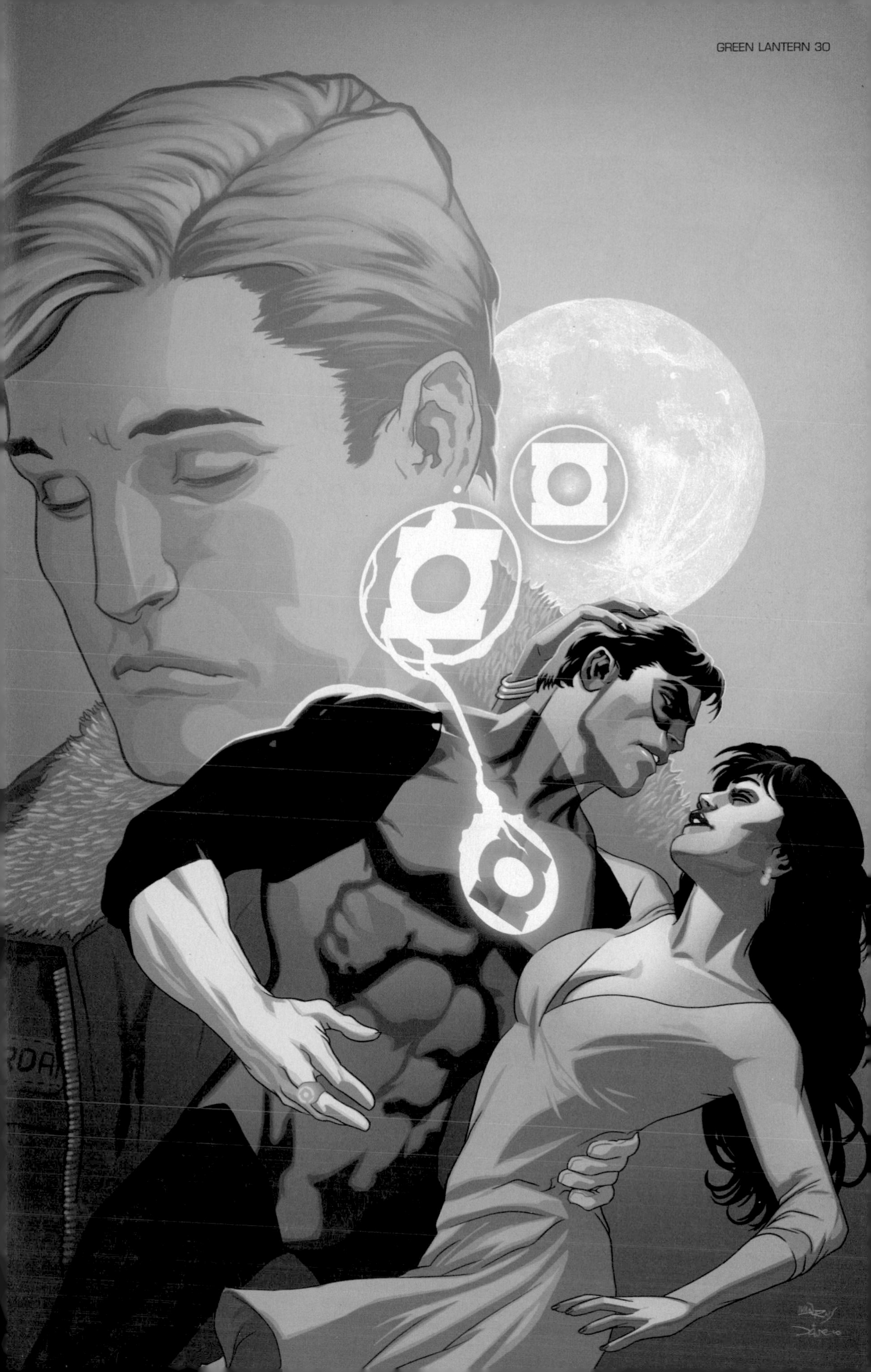

SECRET ORIGIN

BOOK TWO

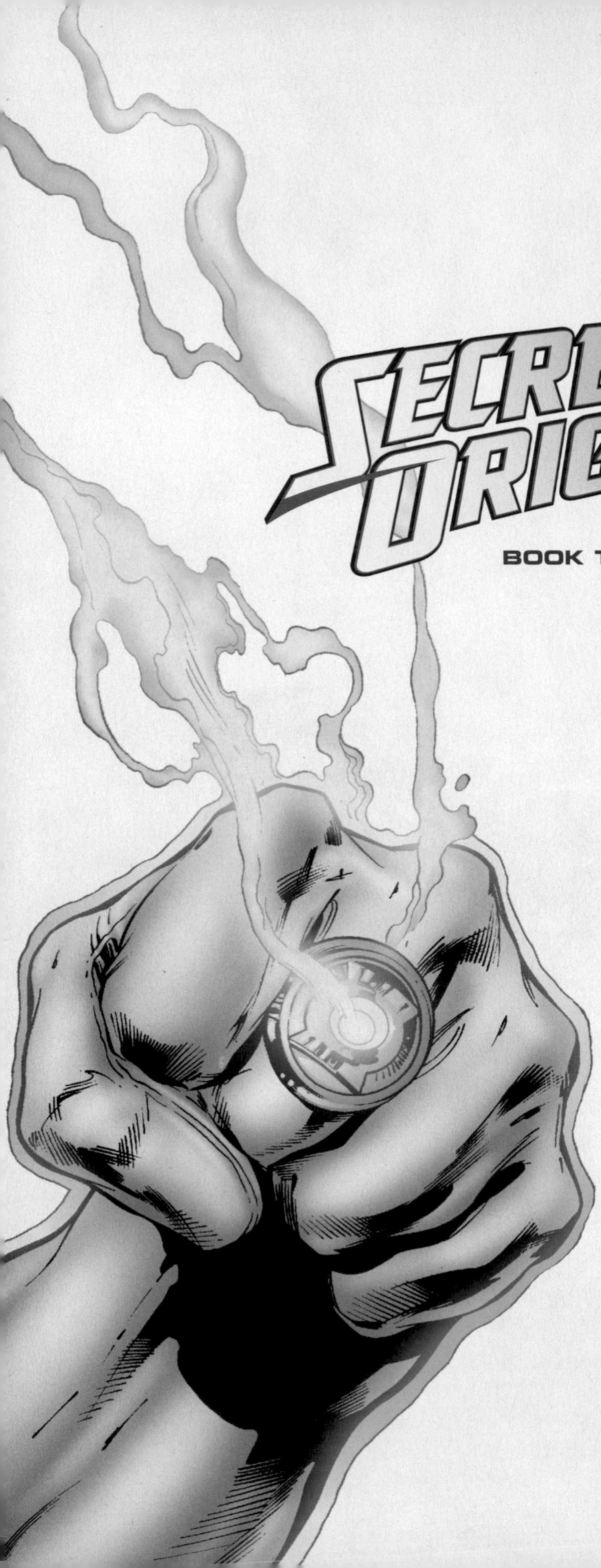

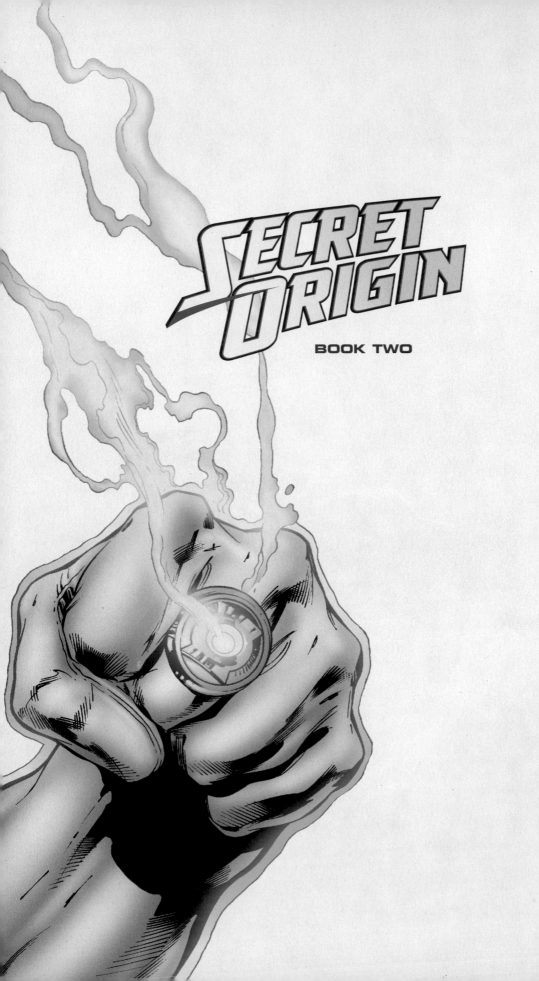

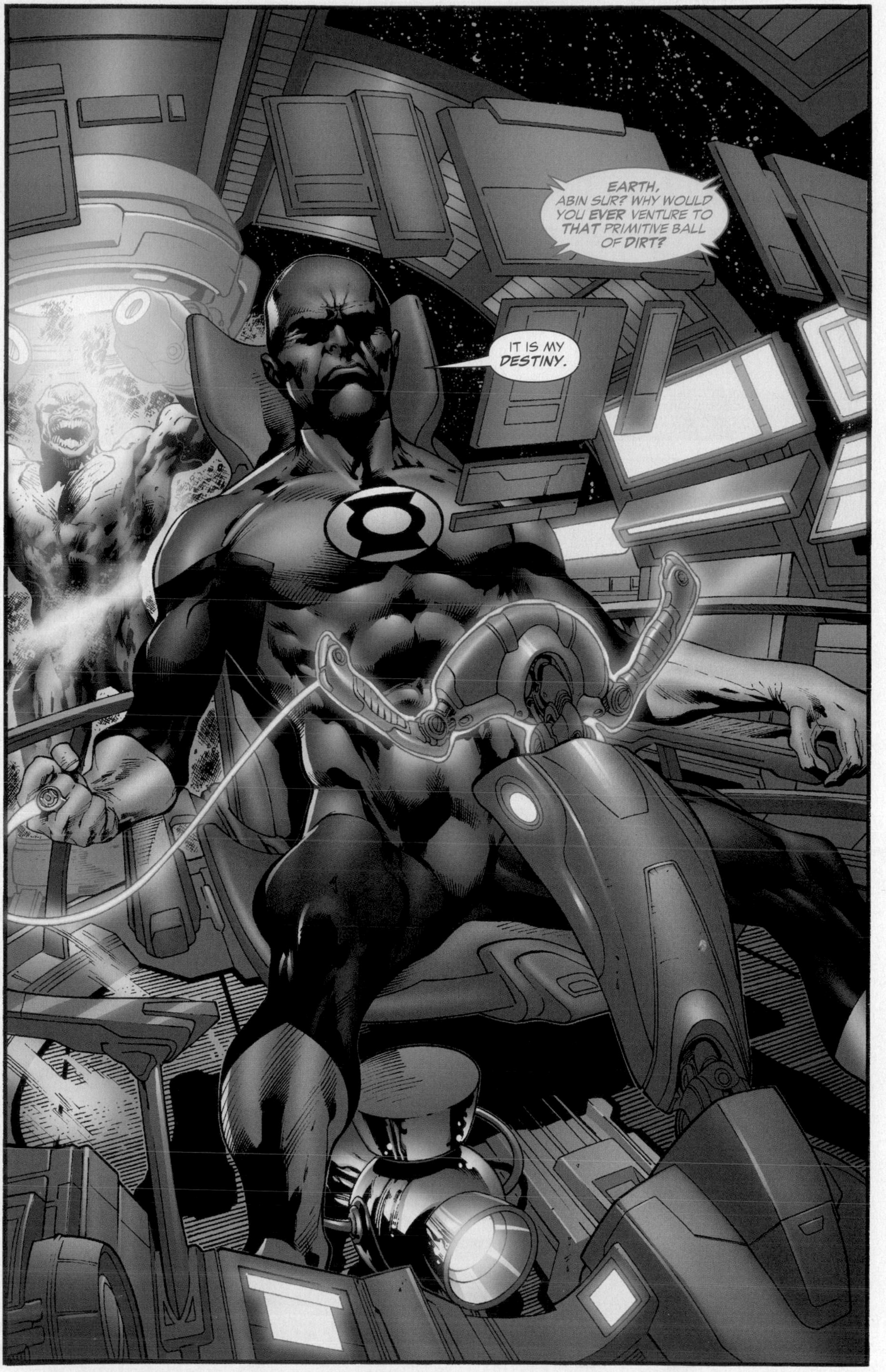
EARTH, ABIN SUR? WHY WOULD YOU EVER VENTURE TO THAT PRIMITIVE BALL OF DIRT?
IT IS MY DESTINY.

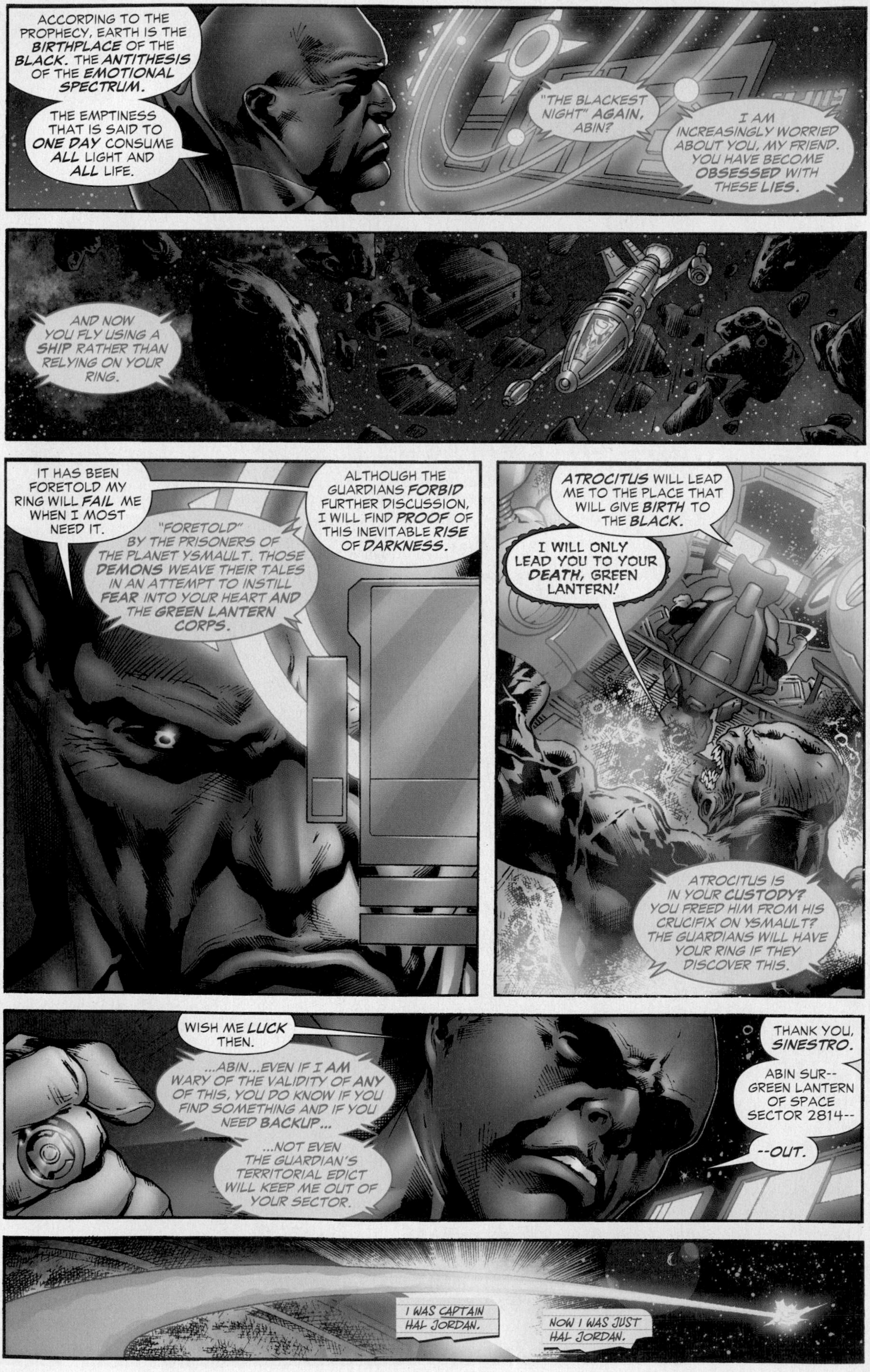
ACCORDING TO THE PROPHECY, EARTH IS THE BIRTHPLACE OF THE BLACK. THE ANTITHESIS OF THE EMOTIONAL SPECTRUM.
THE EMPTINESS THAT IS SAID TO ONE DAY CONSUME ALL LIGHT AND ALL LIFE.
"THE BLACKEST NIGHT" AGAIN, ABIN?
I AM INCREASINGLY WORRIED ABOUT YOU, MY FRIEND. YOU HAVE BECOME OBSESSED WITH THESE LIES.
AND NOW YOU FLY USING A SHIP RATHER THAN RELYING ON YOUR RING.
IT HAS BEEN FORETOLD MY RING WILL FAIL ME WHEN I MOST NEED IT.
"FORETOLD" BY THE PRISONERS OF THE PLANET YSMAULT. THOSE DEMONS WEAVE THEIR TALES IN AN ATTEMPT TO INSTILL FEAR INTO YOUR HEART AND THE GREEN LANTERN CORPS.
ALTHOUGH THE GUARDIANS FORBID FURTHER DISCUSSION, I WILL FIND PROOF OF THIS INEVITABLE RISE OF DARKNESS.
ATROCITUS WILL LEAD ME TO THE PLACE THAT WILL GIVE BIRTH TO THE BLACK.
I WILL ONLY LEAD YOU TO YOUR DEATH, GREEN LANTERN!
ATROCITUS IS IN YOUR CUSTODY? YOU FREED HIM FROM HIS CRUCIFIX ON YSMAULT? THE GUARDIANS WILL HAVE YOUR RING IF THEY DISCOVER THIS.
WISH ME LUCK THEN.
...ABIN...EVEN IF I AM WARY OF THE VALIDITY OF ANY OF THIS, YOU DO KNOW IF YOU FIND SOMETHING AND IF YOU NEED BACKUP...
...NOT EVEN THE GUARDIAN'S TERRITORIAL EDICT WILL KEEP ME OUT OF YOUR SECTOR.
THANK YOU, SINESTRO.
ABIN SUR-- GREEN LANTERN OF SPACE SECTOR 2814--
--OUT.
I WAS CAPTAIN HAL JORDAN.
NOW I WAS JUST HAL JORDAN.

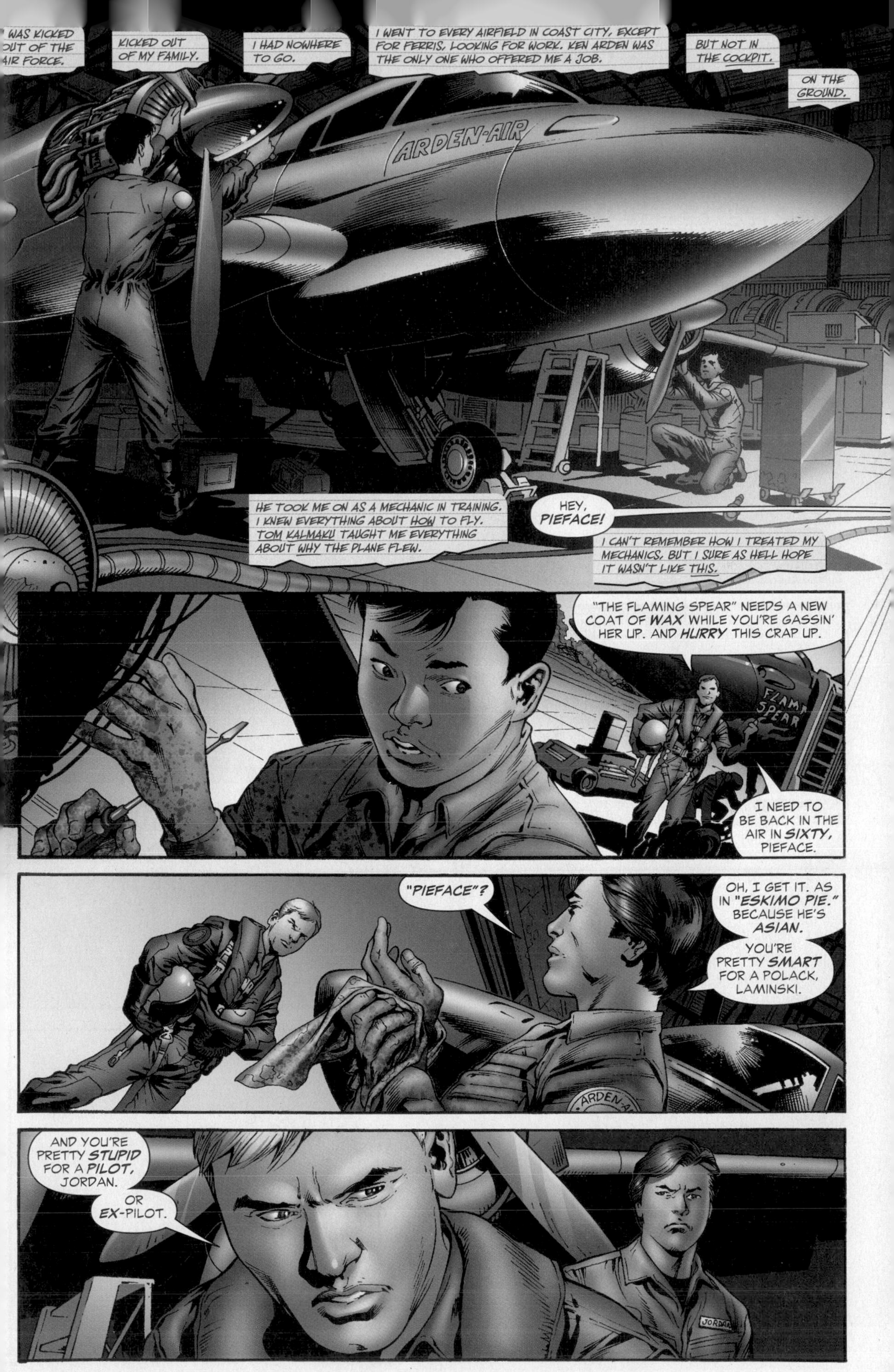
I WAS KICKED OUT OF THE AIR FORCE.
KICKED OUT OF MY FAMILY.
I HAD NOWHERE TO GO.
I WENT TO EVERY AIRFIELD IN COAST CITY, EXCEPT FOR FERRIS, LOOKING FOR WORK. KEN ARDEN WAS THE ONLY ONE WHO OFFERED ME A JOB.
BUT NOT IN THE COCKPIT.
ON THE GROUND.
ARDEN-AIR
HE TOOK ME ON AS A MECHANIC IN TRAINING. I KNEW EVERYTHING ABOUT HOW TO FLY. TOM KALMAKU TAUGHT ME EVERYTHING ABOUT WHY THE PLANE FLEW.
HEY, PIEFACE!
I CAN'T REMEMBER HOW I TREATED MY MECHANICS, BUT I SURE AS HELL HOPE IT WASN'T LIKE THIS.
"THE FLAMING SPEAR" NEEDS A NEW COAT OF WAX WHILE YOU'RE GASSIN' HER UP. AND HURRY THIS CRAP UP.
I NEED TO BE BACK IN THE AIR IN SIXTY, PIEFACE.
"PIEFACE"?
OH, I GET IT. AS IN "ESKIMO PIE." BECAUSE HE'S ASIAN.
YOU'RE PRETTY SMART FOR A POLACK, LAMINSKI.
AND YOU'RE PRETTY STUPID FOR A PILOT, JORDAN.
OR EX-PILOT.

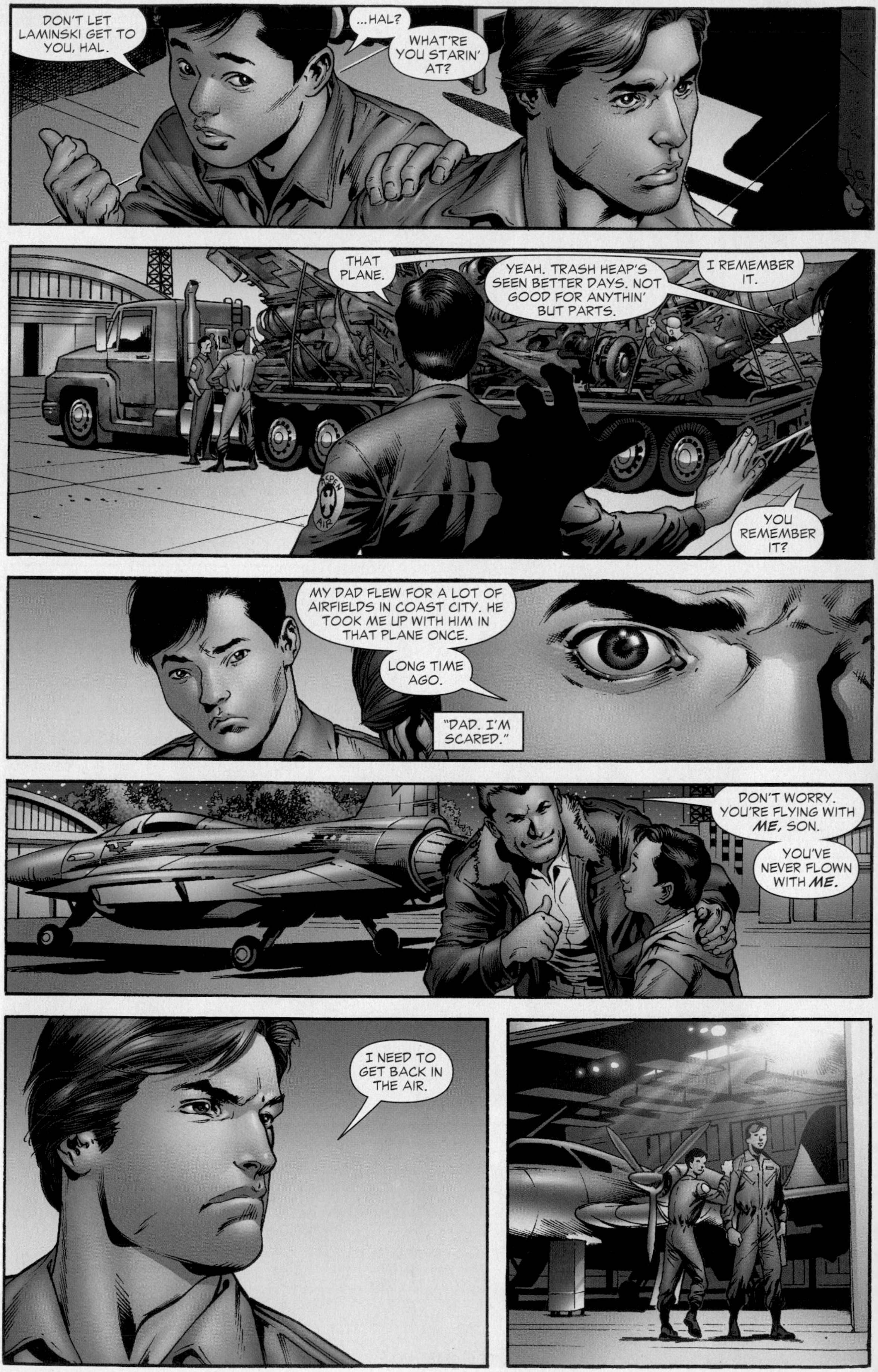
DON'T LET LAMINSKI GET TO YOU, HAL.
...HAL?
WHAT'RE YOU STARIN' AT?
THAT PLANE.
YEAH. TRASH HEAP'S SEEN BETTER DAYS. NOT GOOD FOR ANYTHIN' BUT PARTS.
I REMEMBER IT.
YOU REMEMBER IT?
MY DAD FLEW FOR A LOT OF AIRFIELDS IN COAST CITY. HE TOOK ME UP WITH HIM IN THAT PLANE ONCE.
LONG TIME AGO.
"DAD. I'M SCARED."
DON'T WORRY. YOU'RE FLYING WITH ME, SON.
YOU'VE NEVER FLOWN WITH ME.
I NEED TO GET BACK IN THE AIR.

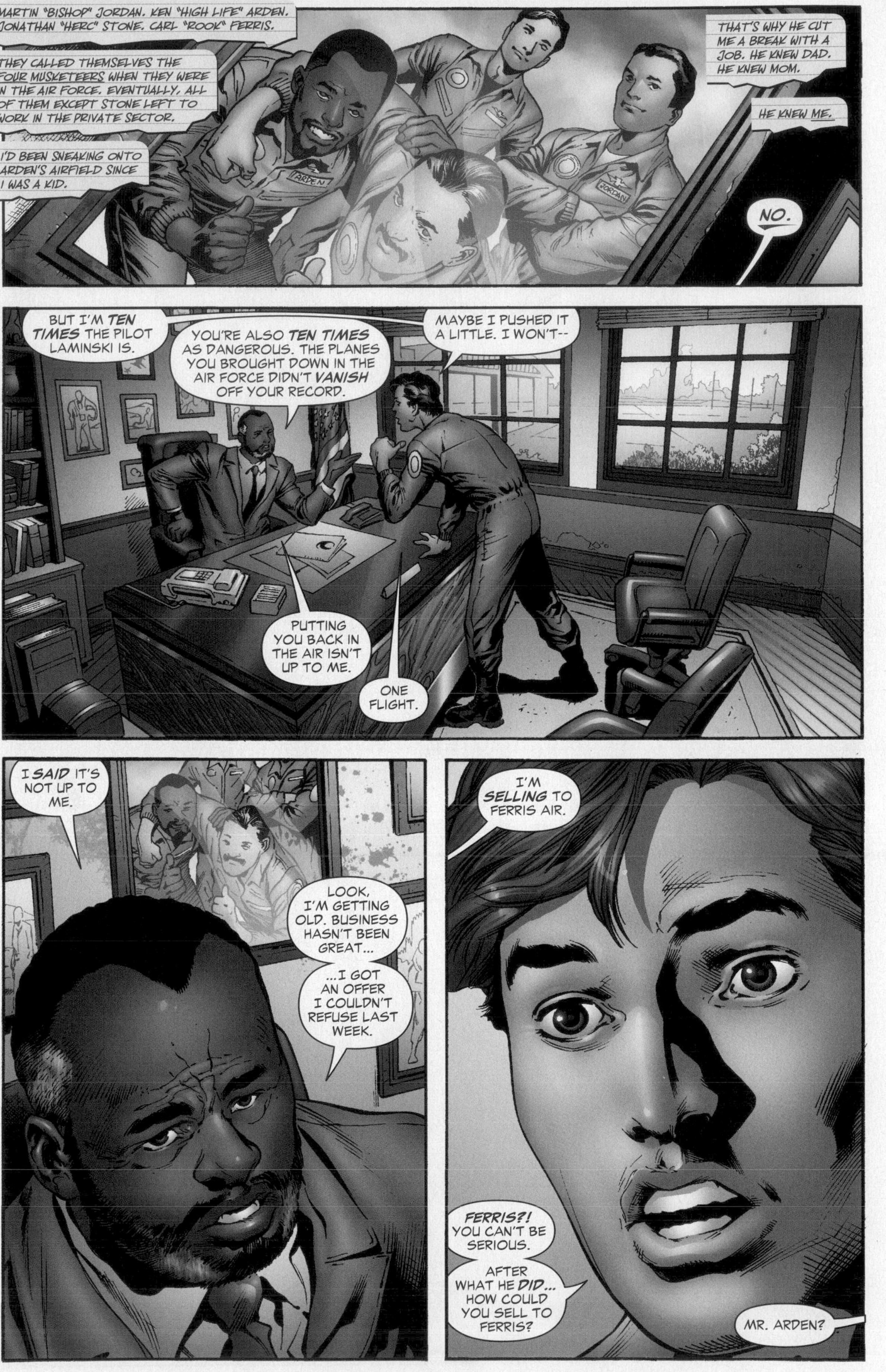
MARTIN "BISHOP" JORDAN. KEN "HIGH LIFE" ARDEN. JONATHAN "HERC" STONE. CARL "ROOK" FERRIS.
THEY CALLED THEMSELVES THE FOUR MUSKETEERS WHEN THEY WERE IN THE AIR FORCE. EVENTUALLY, ALL OF THEM EXCEPT STONE LEFT TO WORK IN THE PRIVATE SECTOR.
I'D BEEN SNEAKING ONTO ARDEN'S AIRFIELD SINCE I WAS A KID.
ARDEN
JORDAN
THAT'S WHY HE CUT ME A BREAK WITH A JOB. HE KNEW DAD. HE KNEW MOM.
HE KNEW ME.
NO.
BUT I'M TEN TIMES THE PILOT LAMINSKI IS.
YOU'RE ALSO TEN TIMES AS DANGEROUS. THE PLANES YOU BROUGHT DOWN IN THE AIR FORCE DIDN'T VANISH OFF YOUR RECORD.
MAYBE I PUSHED IT A LITTLE. I WON'T--
PUTTING YOU BACK IN THE AIR ISN'T UP TO ME.
ONE FLIGHT.
I SAID IT'S NOT UP TO ME.
LOOK, I'M GETTING OLD. BUSINESS HASN'T BEEN GREAT...
...I GOT AN OFFER I COULDN'T REFUSE LAST WEEK.
I'M SELLING TO FERRIS AIR.
FERRIS?! YOU CAN'T BE SERIOUS.
AFTER WHAT HE DID... HOW COULD YOU SELL TO FERRIS?
MR. ARDEN?

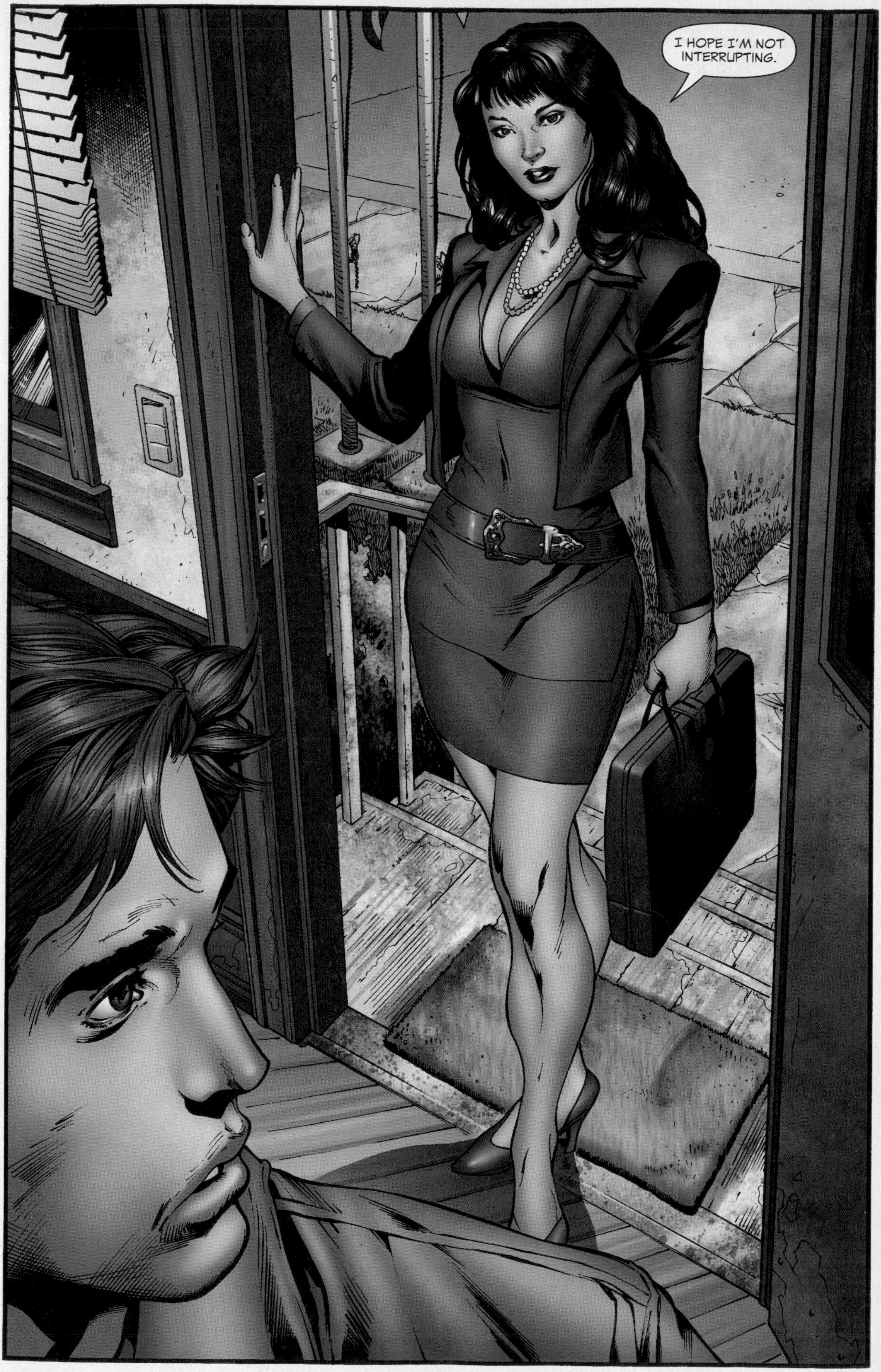
I HOPE I'M NOT INTERRUPTING.

I HAVE THE FINAL PAPERS. MY FATHER WOULD HAVE BROUGHT THEM HIMSELF, BUT APPARENTLY HE'S GOLFING THE GAME OF HIS *LIFE* IN PEBBLE BEACH.

IT'S *NICE* HE CAN ENJOY HIS GOLDEN YEARS.

CAROL. THIS IS HAL--

JORDAN. OF COURSE. IT'S BEEN A LONG TIME.

CAROL'S FATHER RETIRED A FEW YEARS AGO. SHE'S COME OUT OF THE COCKPIT TO RUN FERRIS AIR.

YOU'RE A PILOT?

I *WAS.* I HAVE MORE IMPORTANT THINGS TO DO.

LIKE *NOW,* MR. JORDAN.

HE'S A PROBLEM.

THE DEAL WAS YOU KEEP HIM ON.

MY FATHER'S NOT GOING TO LIKE THIS.

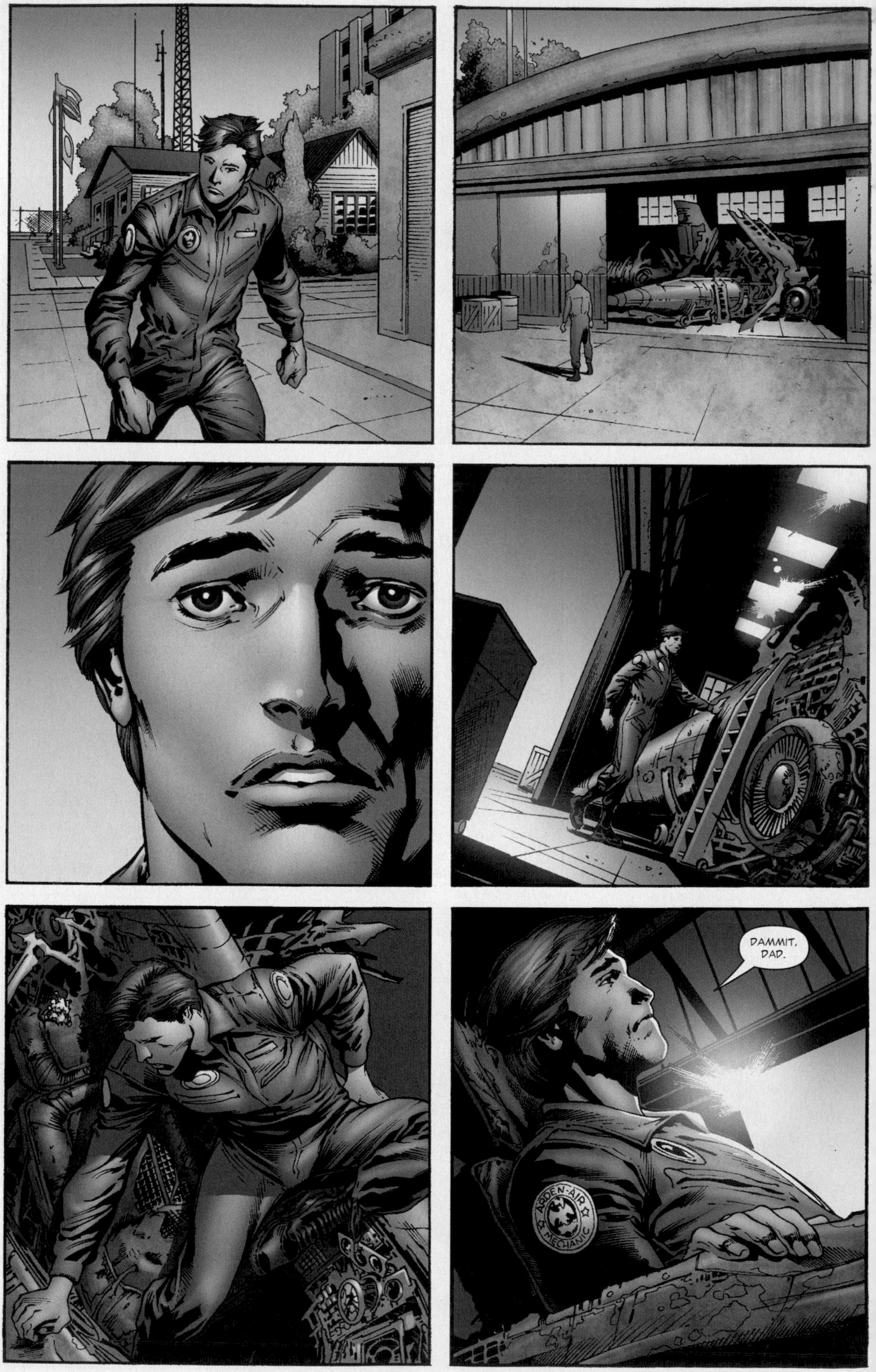
DAMMIT, DAD.
ARDEN-AIR MECHANIC

YOU CANNOT STOP "THE BLACKEST NIGHT," GREEN LANTERN. YOU CAN ONLY *FACE* IT.

LIKE YOUR OWN *DEATH*.

BUT YOU ARE *AFRAID*.

I AM NOT AFRAID OF DEATH, ATROCITUS.

WE HAVE SHARED OUR VISION OF YOUR RING *FAILING* YOU WHEN YOU NEEDED IT MOST.

NOW YOU FLY IN A SHIP. ARMED WITH WEAPONS.

I SIMPLY REMAIN *CAUTIOUS*.

YOUR *WEAKNESS* IN YOUR OWN WILLPOWER AND YOUR POWER RING--

YOUR FAITH IN YOUR POWER IS *WEAKENING*.

YOU'RE *AFRAID* TO RELY ON YOUR RING. YOU DON'T BELIEVE YOUR RING IS *STRONG* ENOUGH TO SAVE YOU.

--CARRIES THROUGH TO YOUR *CONSTRUCTS*.

YOU FEEL FEAR...

KRA KRAKK

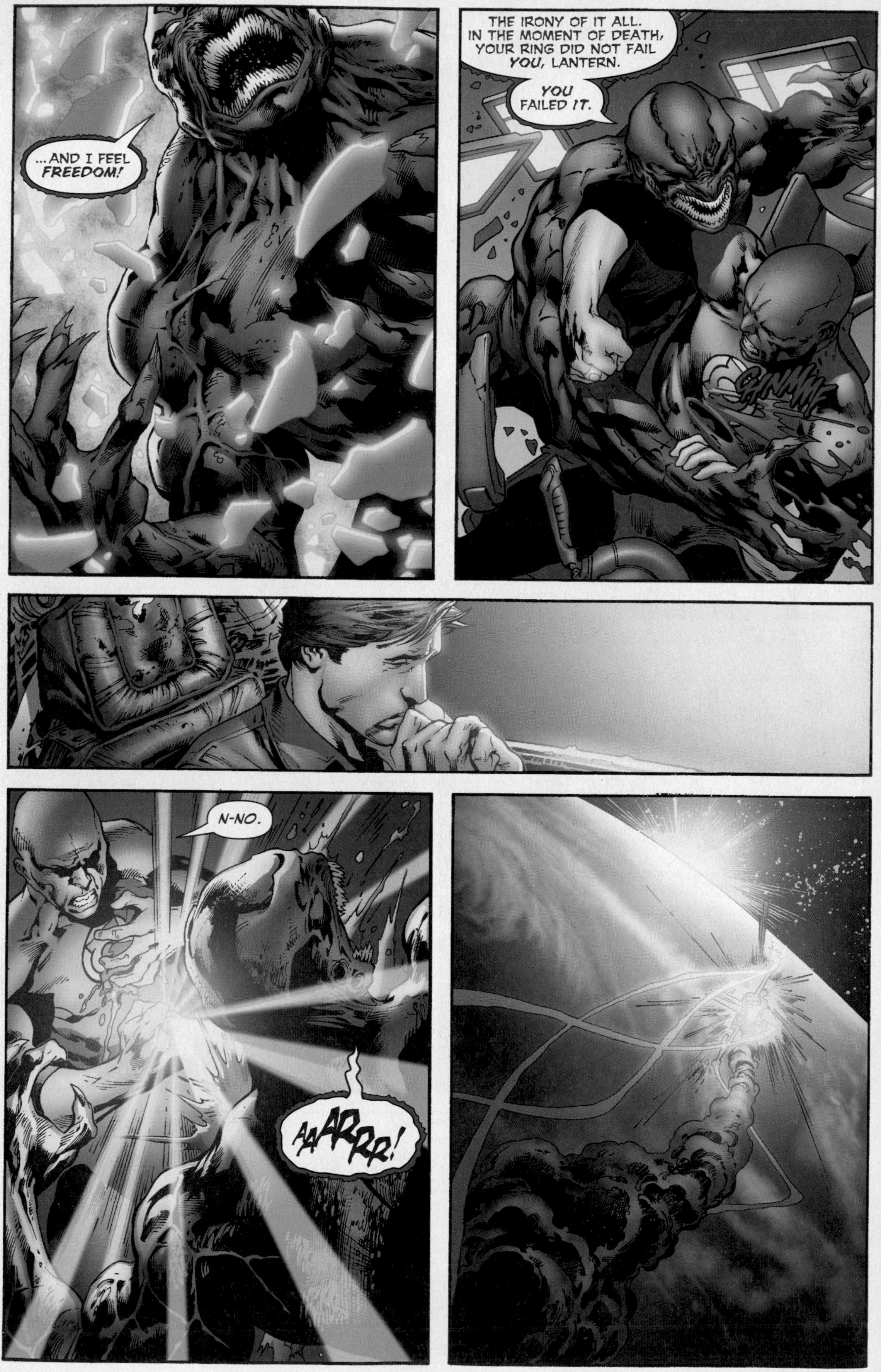
...AND I FEEL FREEDOM!
THE IRONY OF IT ALL. IN THE MOMENT OF DEATH, YOUR RING DID NOT FAIL YOU, LANTERN.
YOU FAILED IT.
N-NO.
AAARRR!

...RING. PREPARE MESSAGE AND FILE INFORMATION FOR SINESTRO. HE MUST CONTINUE MY MISSION. IT IS NOT ONE FOR A ROOKIE...*NNN*...

KAFF

SPACE SECTOR SCAN 2814 FOR REPLACEMENT SENTIENT INITIATED.

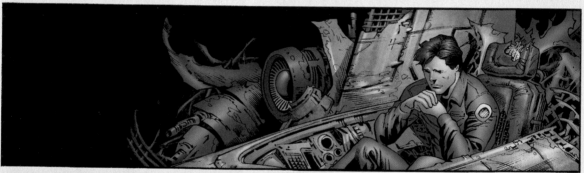

HAL JORDAN.

WHAT--?

YOU HAVE BEEN CHOSEN.

BOOOM

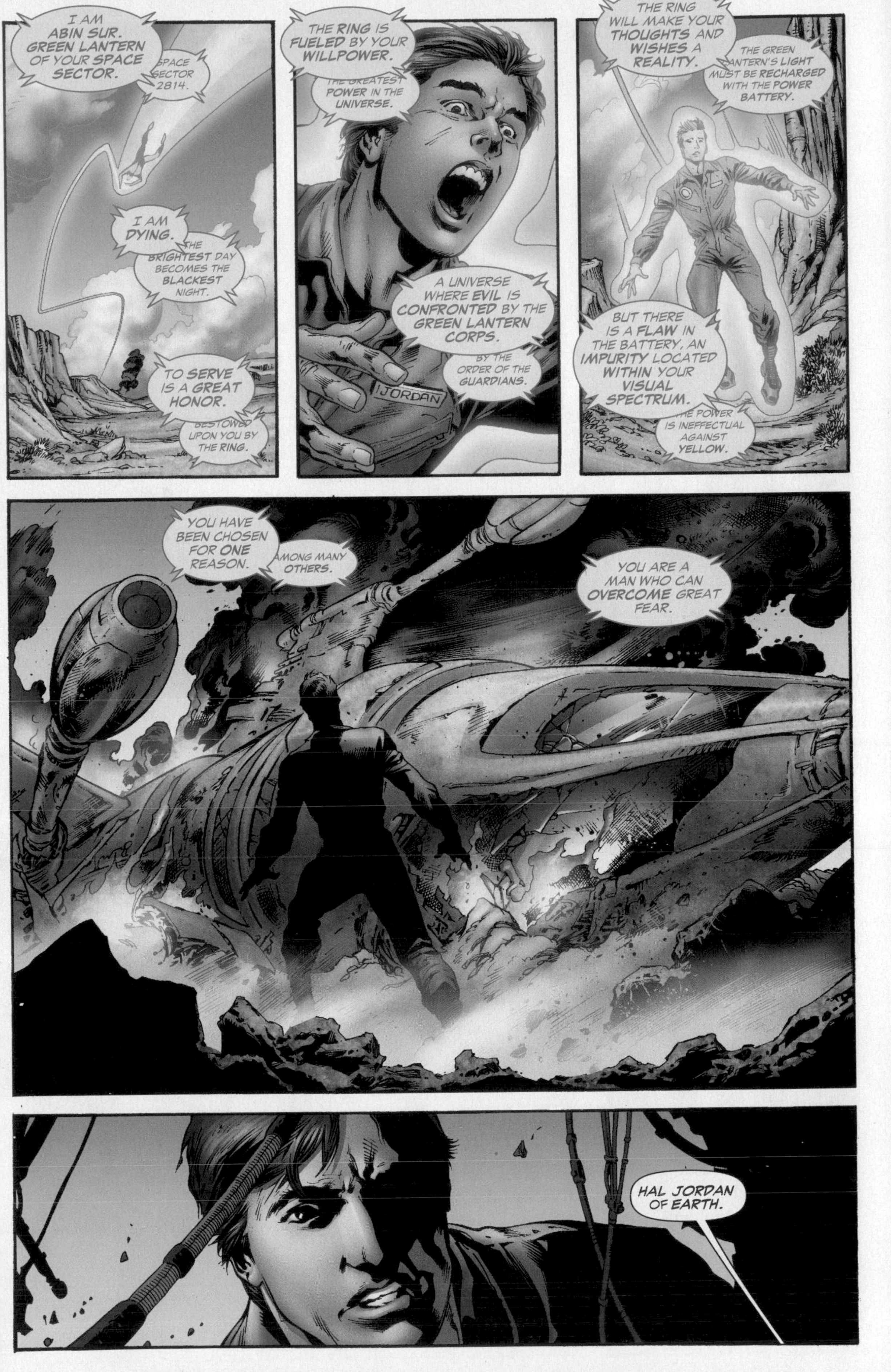
I AM ABIN SUR. GREEN LANTERN OF YOUR SPACE SECTOR.
SPACE SECTOR 2814.
I AM DYING.
THE BRIGHTEST DAY BECOMES THE BLACKEST NIGHT.
TO SERVE IS A GREAT HONOR.
BESTOWED UPON YOU BY THE RING.
THE RING IS FUELED BY YOUR WILLPOWER.
THE GREATEST POWER IN THE UNIVERSE.
A UNIVERSE WHERE EVIL IS CONFRONTED BY THE GREEN LANTERN CORPS.
BY THE ORDER OF THE GUARDIANS.
JORDAN
THE RING WILL MAKE YOUR THOUGHTS AND WISHES A REALITY.
THE GREEN LANTERN'S LIGHT MUST BE RECHARGED WITH THE POWER BATTERY.
BUT THERE IS A FLAW IN THE BATTERY, AN IMPURITY LOCATED WITHIN YOUR VISUAL SPECTRUM.
THE POWER IS INEFFECTUAL AGAINST YELLOW.
YOU HAVE BEEN CHOSEN FOR ONE REASON.
AMONG MANY OTHERS.
YOU ARE A MAN WHO CAN OVERCOME GREAT FEAR.
HAL JORDAN OF EARTH.

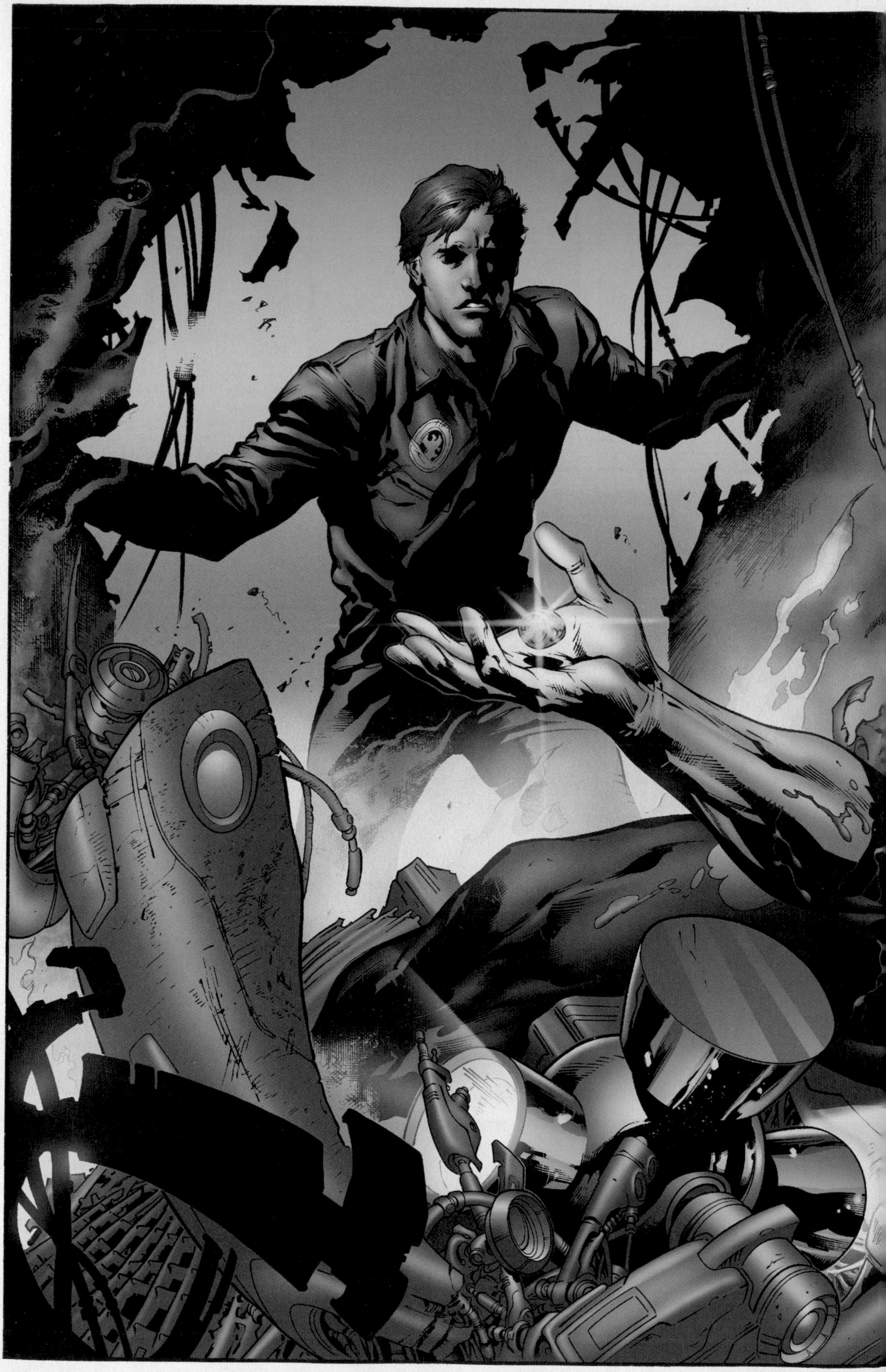

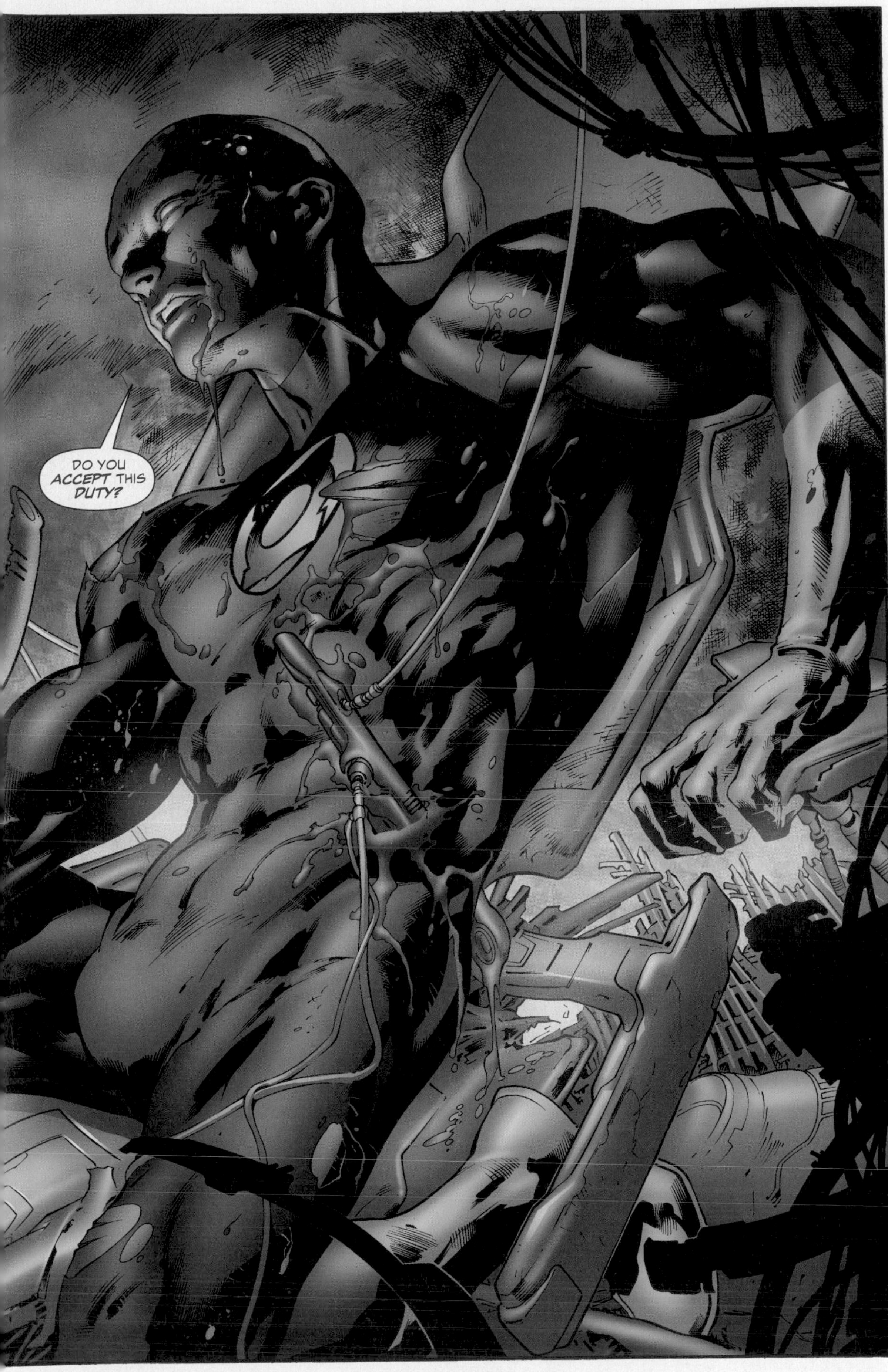
DO YOU ACCEPT THIS DUTY?

I WAS DISORIENTED. THE LIGHT BLINDED MY EYES.

THE SOUNDS ECHOED IN THE CRAFT.

IF I'M *NOT* DREAMING--

--ABSOLUTELY.

AN EARTHMAN... heh...

...I NEVER THOUGHT I'D *LIVE* TO SEE THE DAY...

HE EXHALED ONE LAST TIME. AND I HEARD HIS FINAL WORD.

...SINESTRO...

AN ALIEN WORD. I HAD NO IDEA WHAT IT MEANT.

I HAD NO IDEA WHAT ANY OF THIS MEANT.

HAL JORDAN OF EARTH.

YOU HAVE THE ABILITY TO OVERCOME GREAT FEAR.

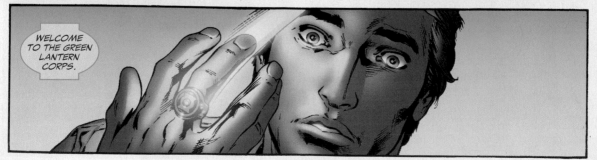

WELCOME TO THE GREEN LANTERN CORPS.

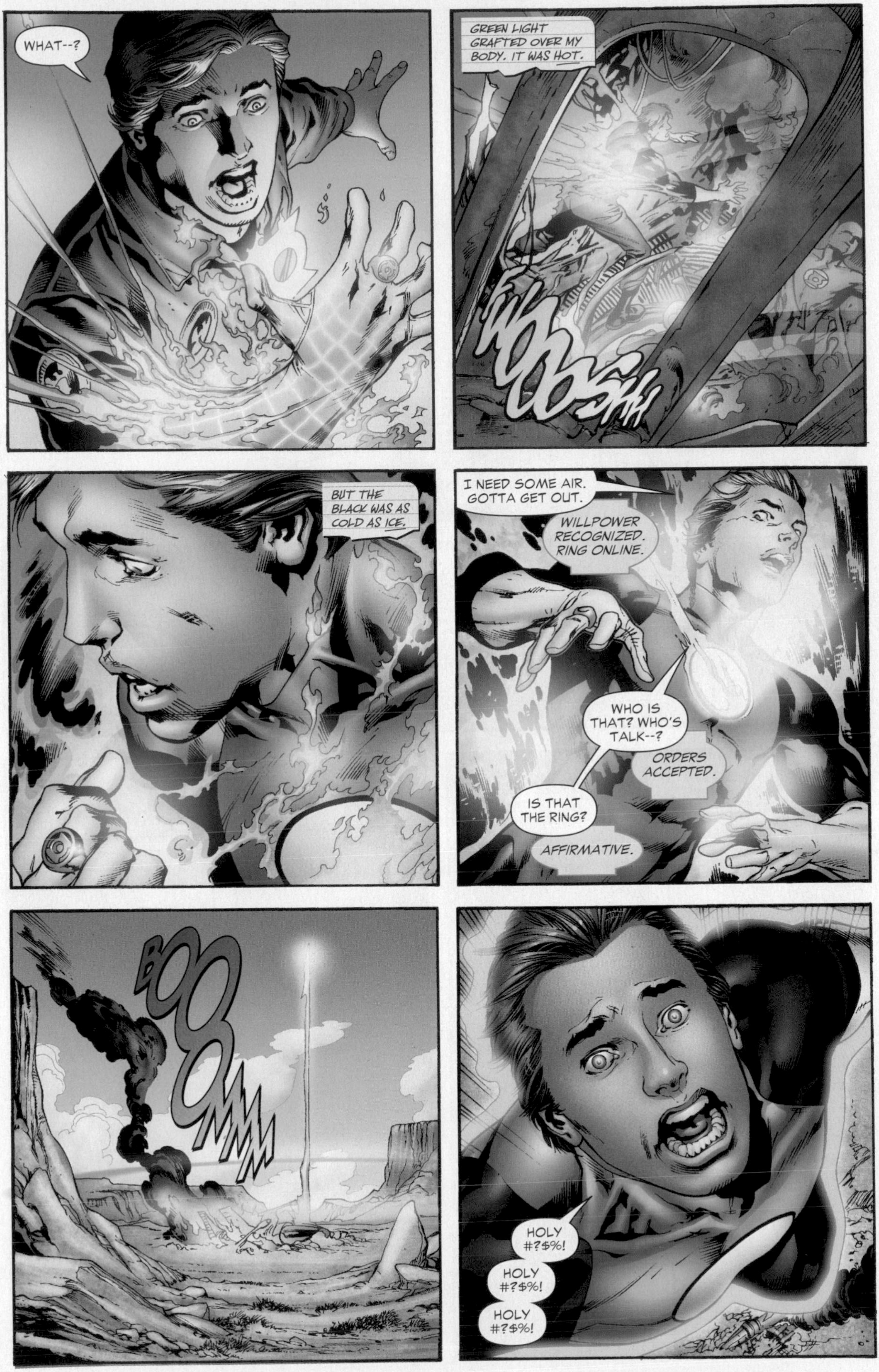
WHAT--?
GREEN LIGHT GRAFTED OVER MY BODY. IT WAS HOT.
FWOOOSHH
BUT THE BLACK WAS AS COLD AS ICE.
I NEED SOME AIR. GOTTA GET OUT.
WILLPOWER RECOGNIZED. RING ONLINE.
WHO IS THAT? WHO'S TALK--?
ORDERS ACCEPTED.
IS THAT THE RING?
AFFIRMATIVE.
BOOOMMM
HOLY #?$%!
HOLY #?$%!
HOLY #?$%!

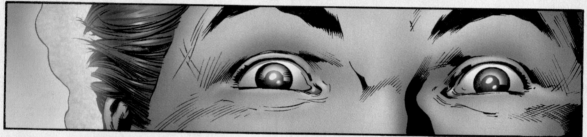

THERE WAS NO RUMBLING OF ANY ENGINE.

NO STICK TO PULL ON.

NO TOWER TO GET PERMISSION FROM.

IT WAS JUST ME.

ME AND THE RING.

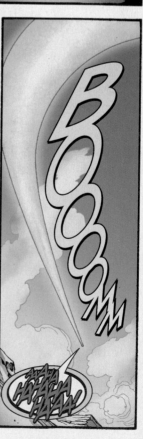

BOOOOMM

HAHAHA HAAH

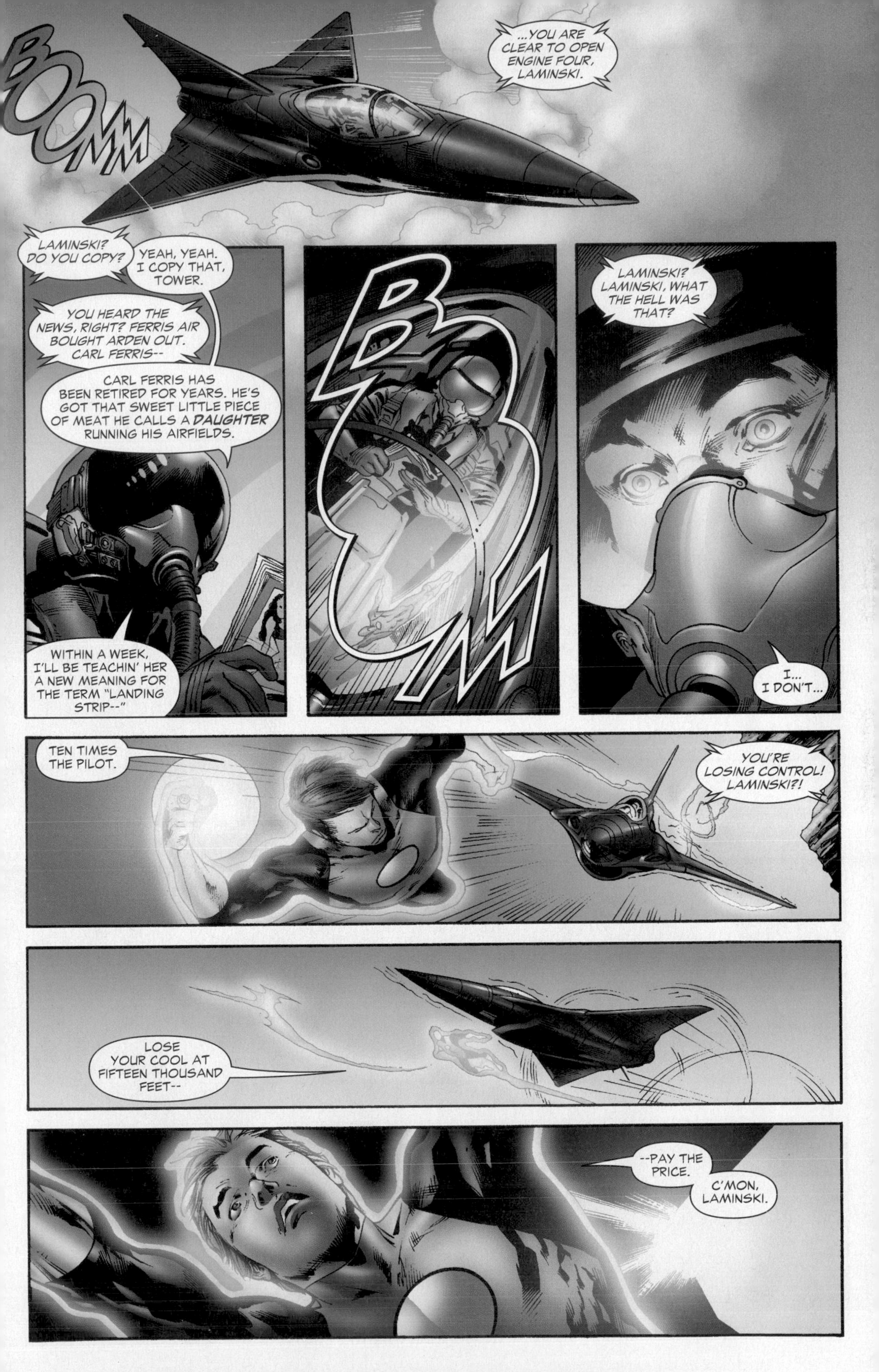
BOOMM
...YOU ARE CLEAR TO OPEN ENGINE FOUR, LAMINSKI.
LAMINSKI? DO YOU COPY?
YEAH, YEAH. I COPY THAT, TOWER.
YOU HEARD THE NEWS, RIGHT? FERRIS AIR BOUGHT ARDEN OUT. CARL FERRIS--
CARL FERRIS HAS BEEN RETIRED FOR YEARS. HE'S GOT THAT SWEET LITTLE PIECE OF MEAT HE CALLS A DAUGHTER RUNNING HIS AIRFIELDS.
WITHIN A WEEK, I'LL BE TEACHIN' HER A NEW MEANING FOR THE TERM "LANDING STRIP--"
BOOM
LAMINSKI? LAMINSKI, WHAT THE HELL WAS THAT?
I... I DON'T...
TEN TIMES THE PILOT.
YOU'RE LOSING CONTROL! LAMINSKI?!
LOSE YOUR COOL AT FIFTEEN THOUSAND FEET--
--PAY THE PRICE.
C'MON, LAMINSKI.

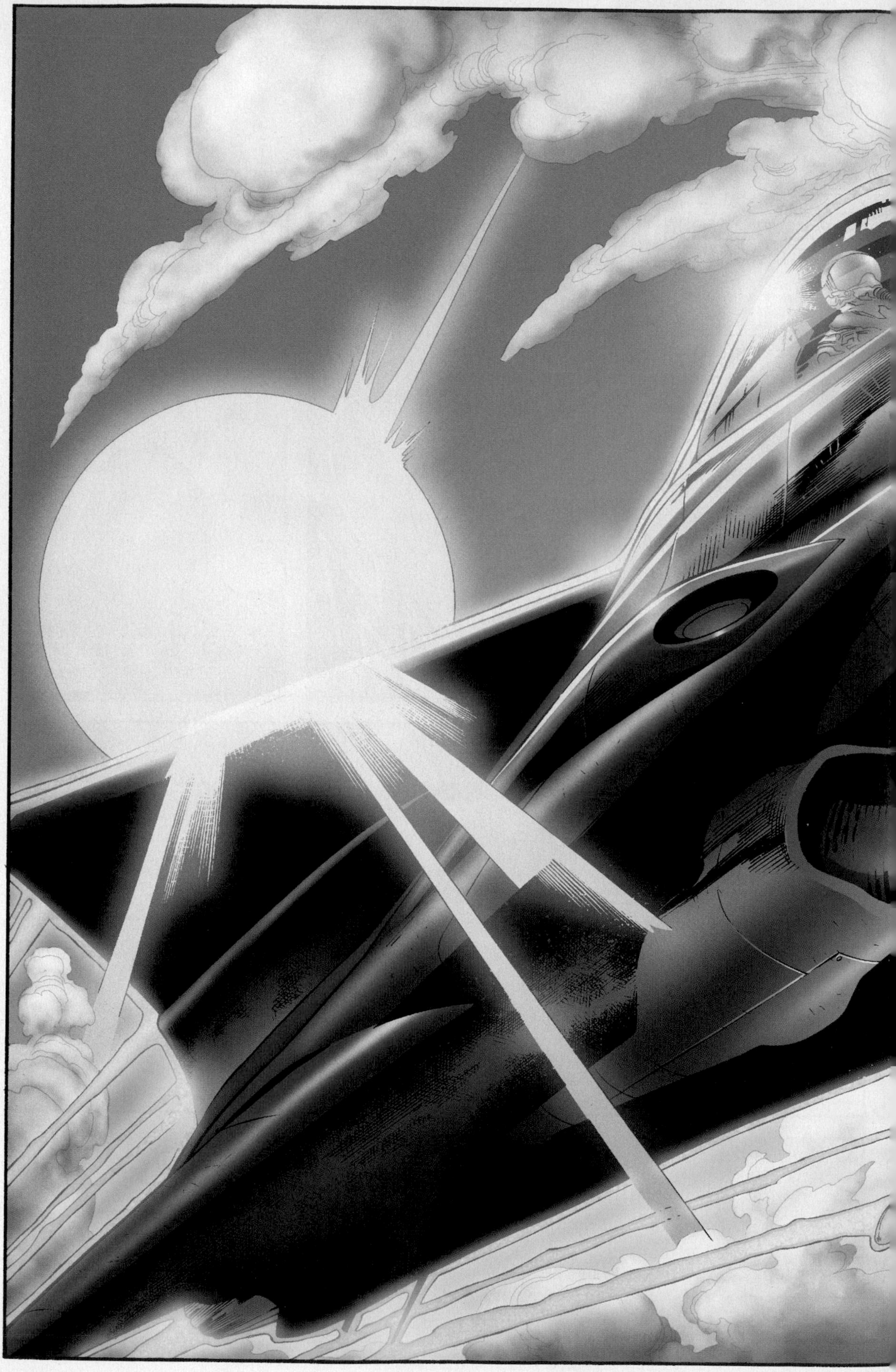

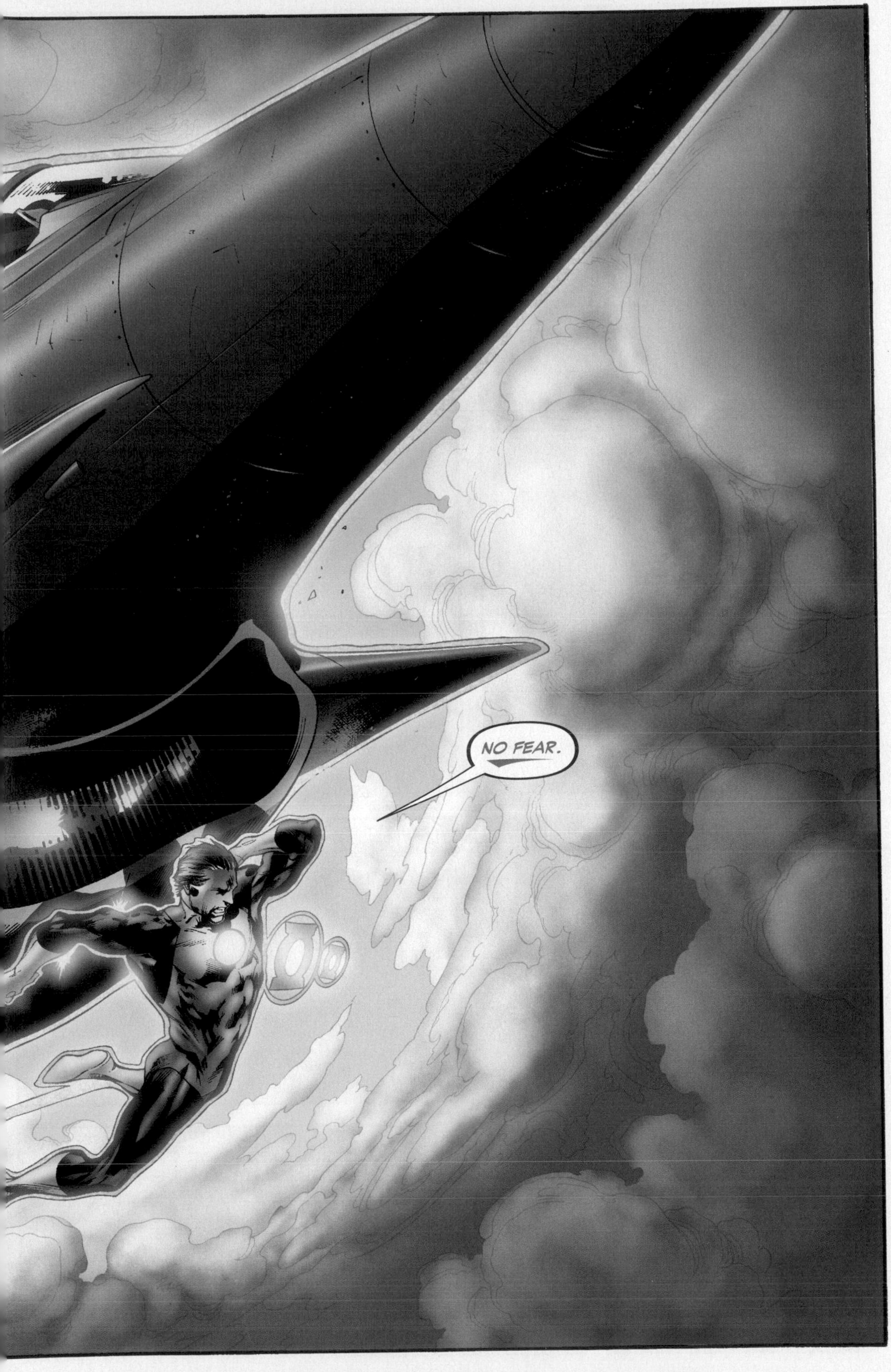
NO FEAR.

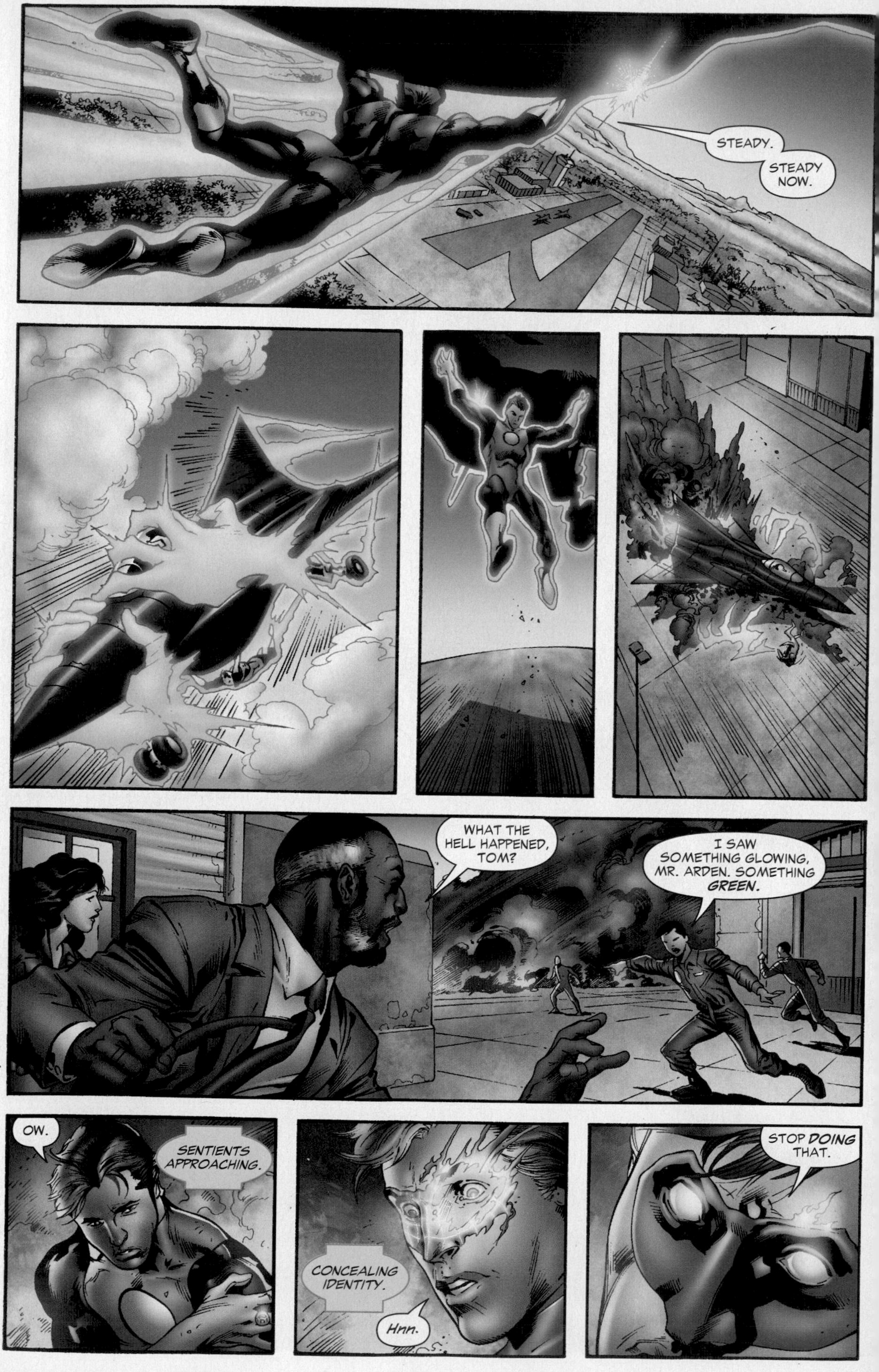
STEADY.
STEADY NOW.
WHAT THE HELL HAPPENED, TOM?
I SAW SOMETHING GLOWING, MR. ARDEN. SOMETHING GREEN.
OW.
SENTIENTS APPROACHING.
CONCEALING IDENTITY.
Hnn.
STOP DOING THAT.

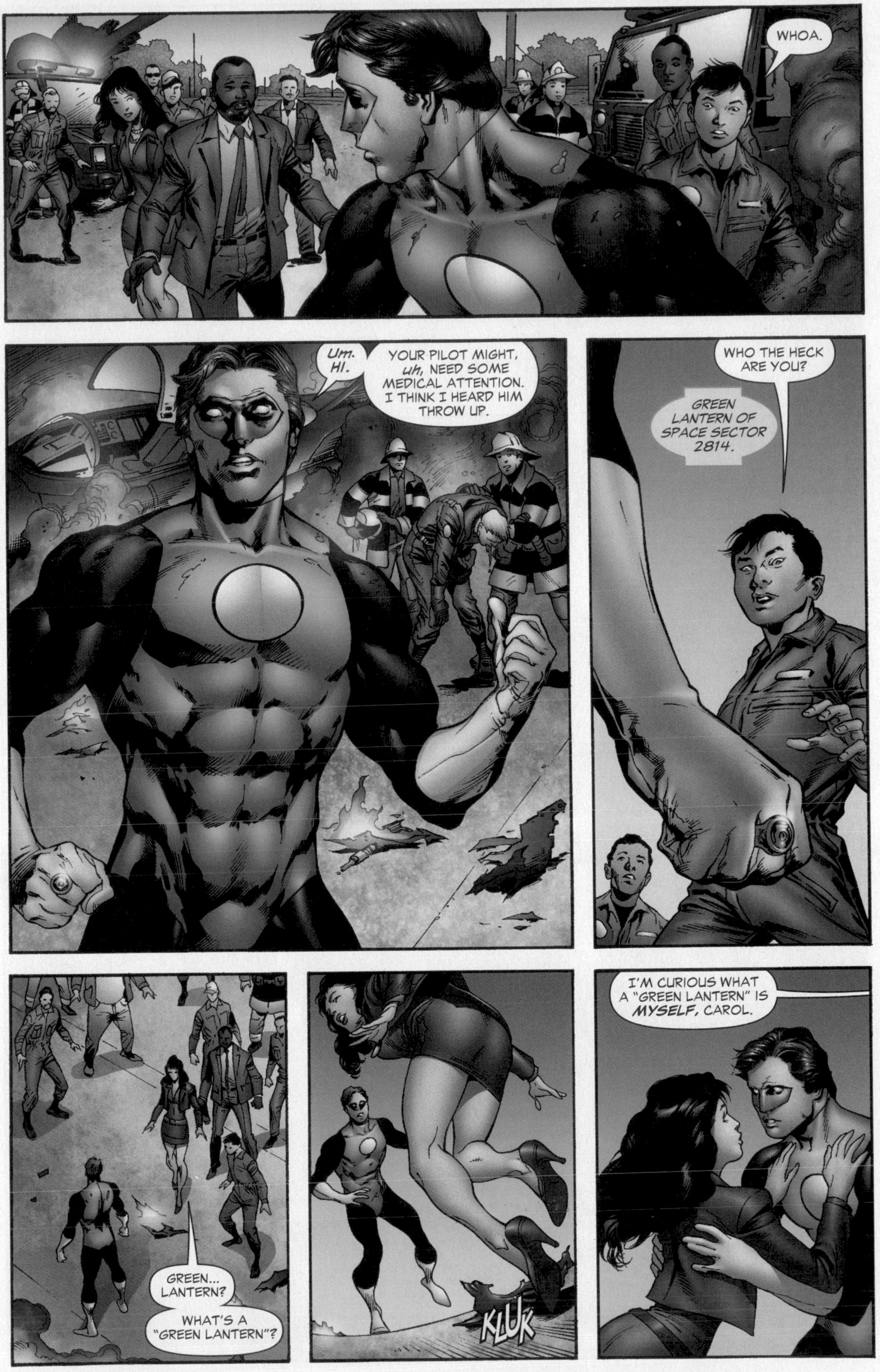
WHOA.
Um. HI.
YOUR PILOT MIGHT, uh, NEED SOME MEDICAL ATTENTION. I THINK I HEARD HIM THROW UP.
WHO THE HECK ARE YOU?
GREEN LANTERN OF SPACE SECTOR 2814.
GREEN... LANTERN?
WHAT'S A "GREEN LANTERN"?
KLUK
I'M CURIOUS WHAT A "GREEN LANTERN" IS MYSELF, CAROL.

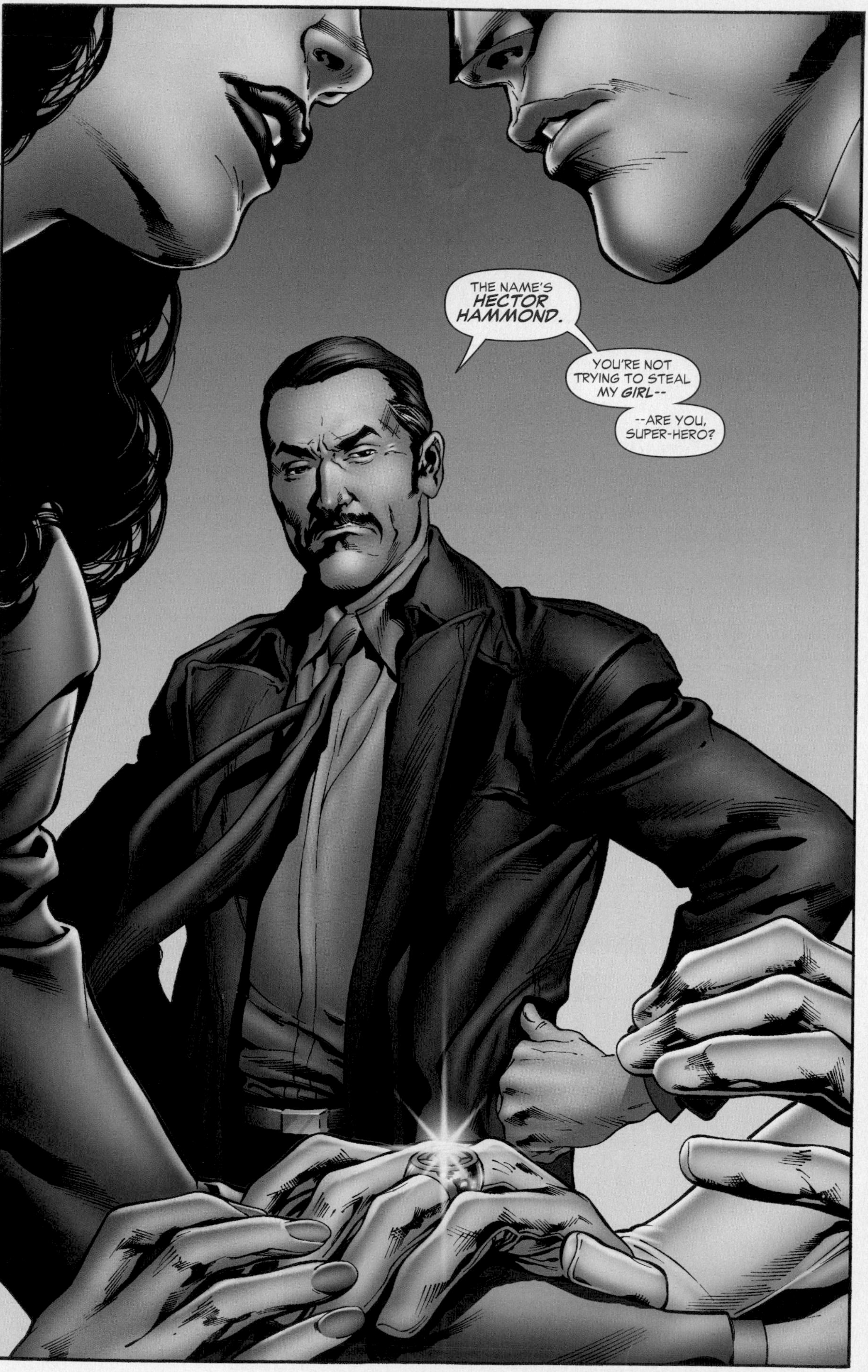
THE NAME'S HECTOR HAMMOND.
YOU'RE NOT TRYING TO STEAL MY GIRL--
--ARE YOU, SUPER-HERO?

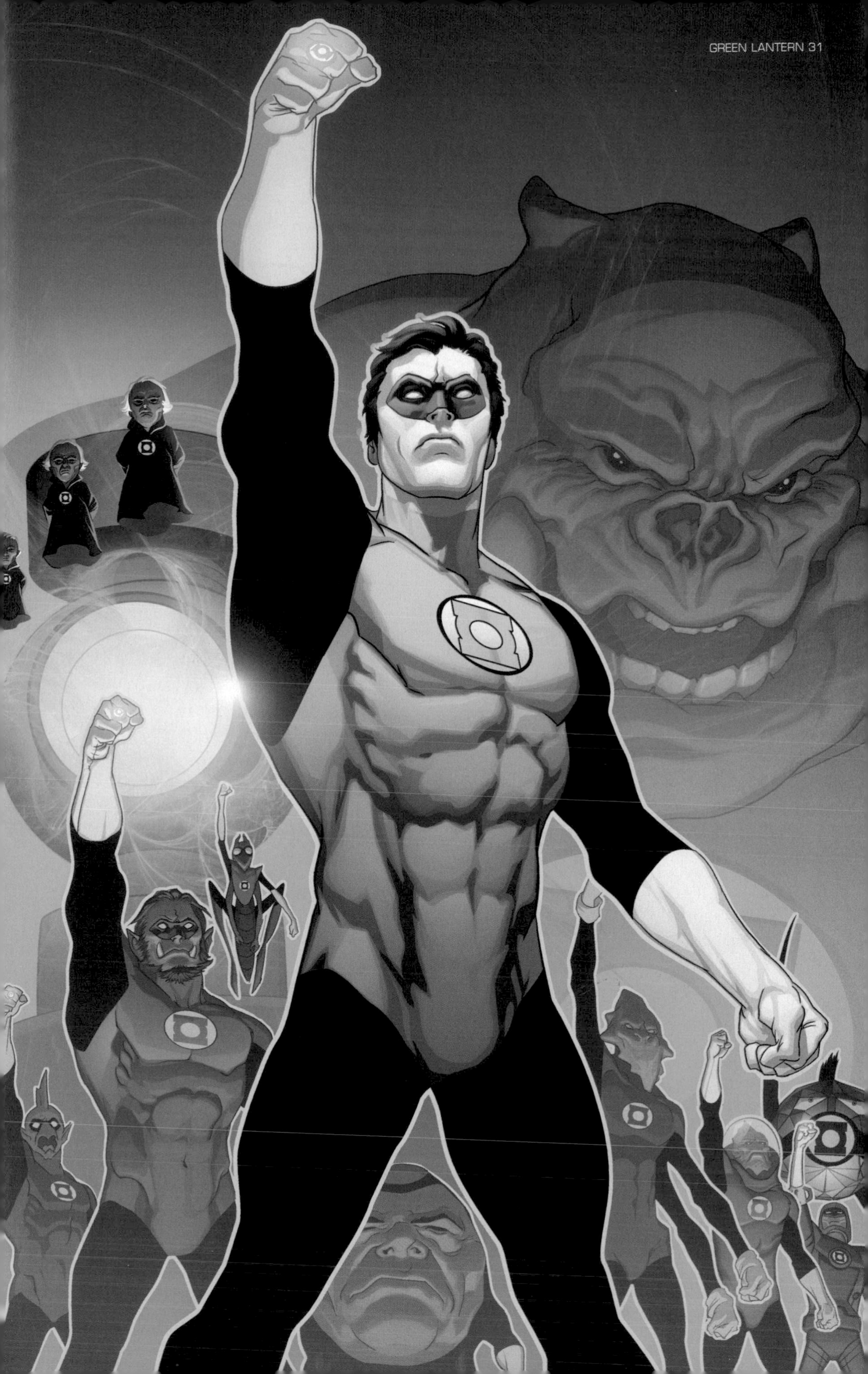

SECRET ORIGIN

BOOK THREE

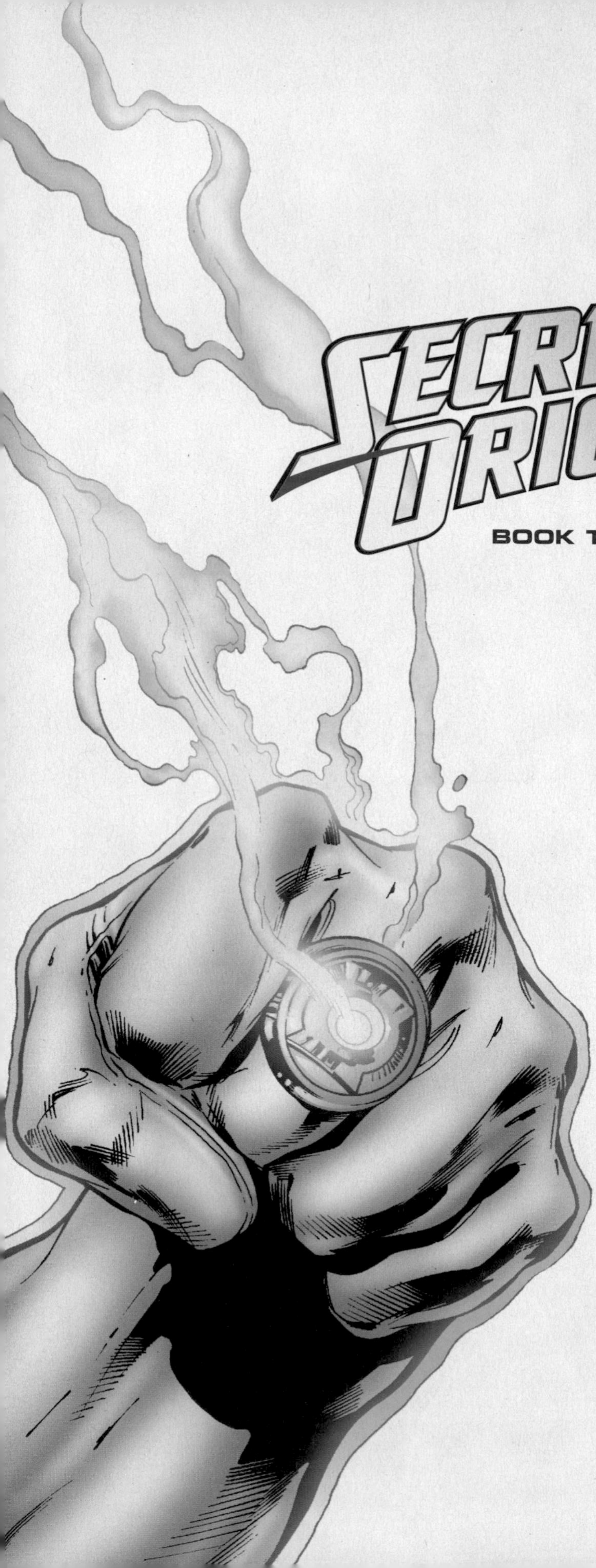

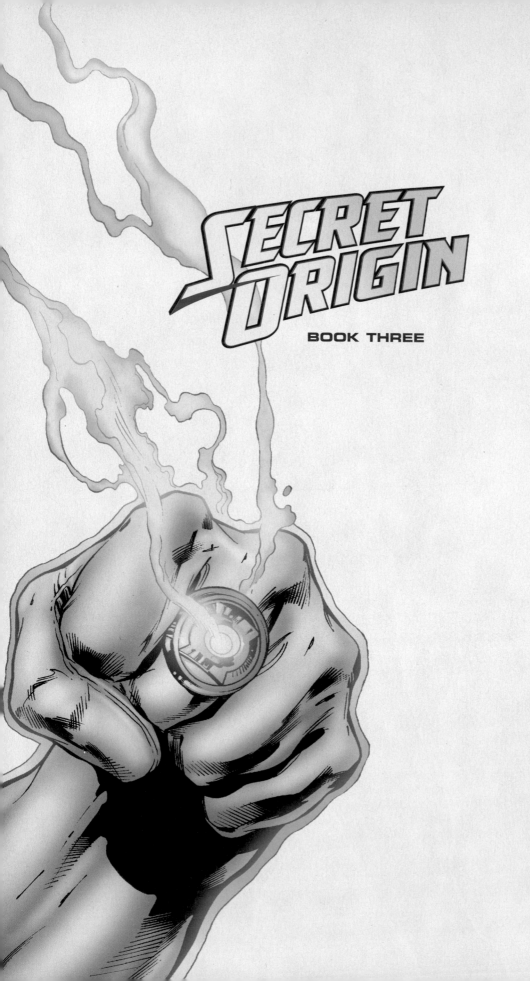

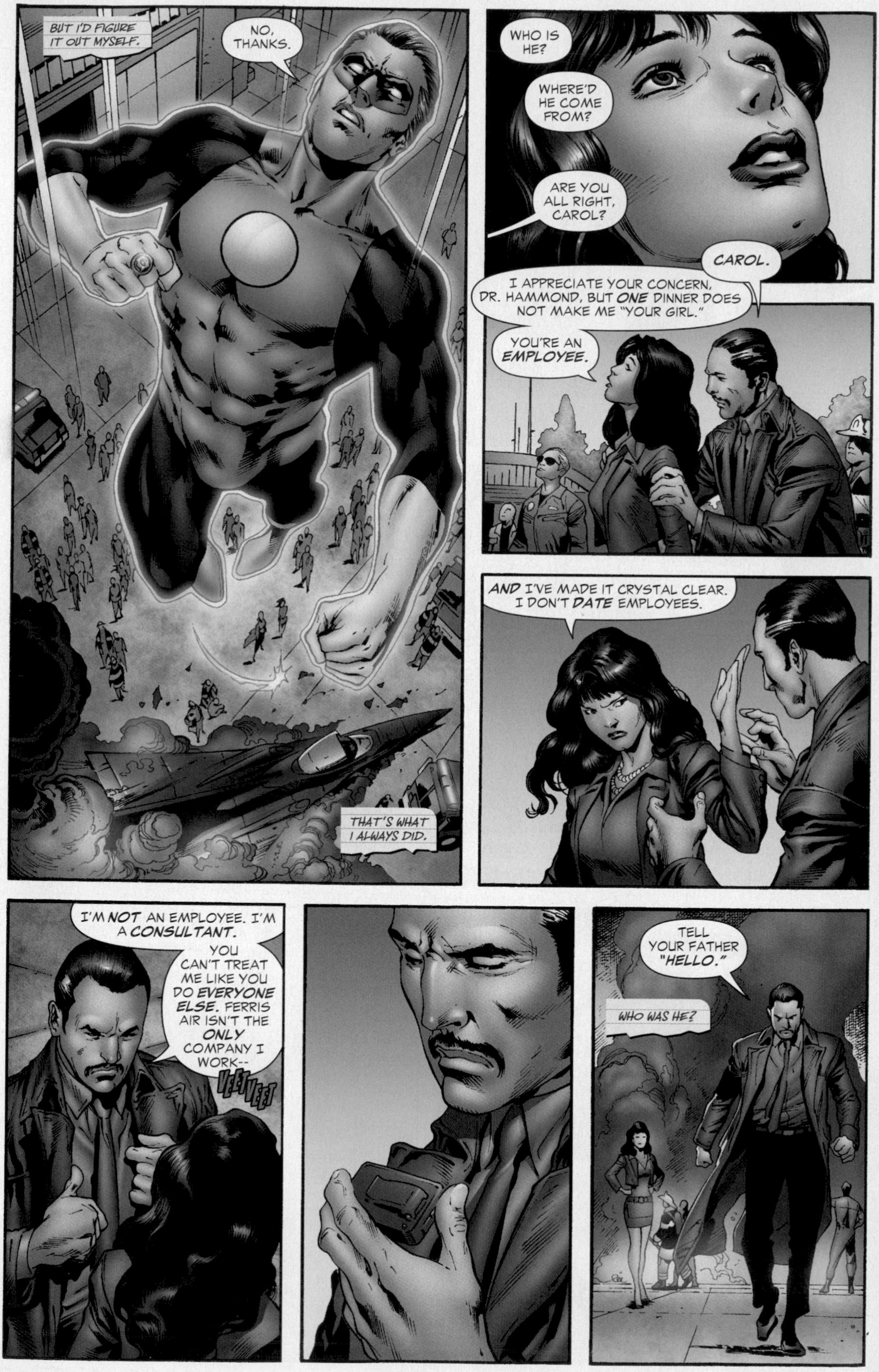
BUT I'D FIGURE IT OUT MYSELF.
NO, THANKS.
THAT'S WHAT I ALWAYS DID.
WHO IS HE?
WHERE'D HE COME FROM?
ARE YOU ALL RIGHT, CAROL?
CAROL.
I APPRECIATE YOUR CONCERN, DR. HAMMOND, BUT ONE DINNER DOES NOT MAKE ME "YOUR GIRL."
YOU'RE AN EMPLOYEE.
AND I'VE MADE IT CRYSTAL CLEAR. I DON'T DATE EMPLOYEES.
I'M NOT AN EMPLOYEE. I'M A CONSULTANT.
YOU CAN'T TREAT ME LIKE YOU DO EVERYONE ELSE. FERRIS AIR ISN'T THE ONLY COMPANY I WORK--
VEET VEET
TELL YOUR FATHER "HELLO."
WHO WAS HE?

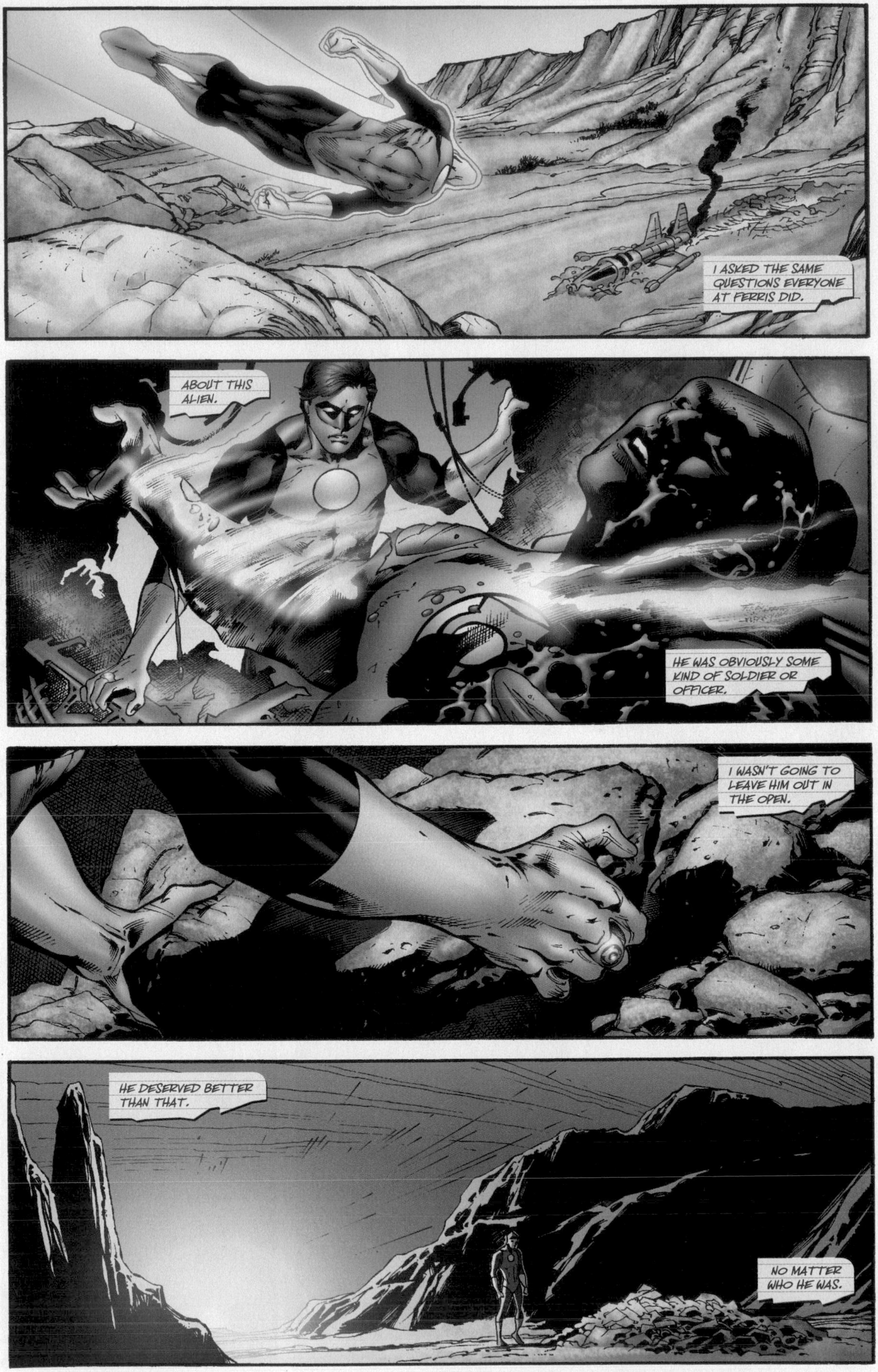
I ASKED THE SAME QUESTIONS EVERYONE AT FERRIS DID.
ABOUT THIS ALIEN.
HE WAS OBVIOUSLY SOME KIND OF SOLDIER OR OFFICER.
I WASN'T GOING TO LEAVE HIM OUT IN THE OPEN.
HE DESERVED BETTER THAN THAT.
NO MATTER WHO HE WAS.

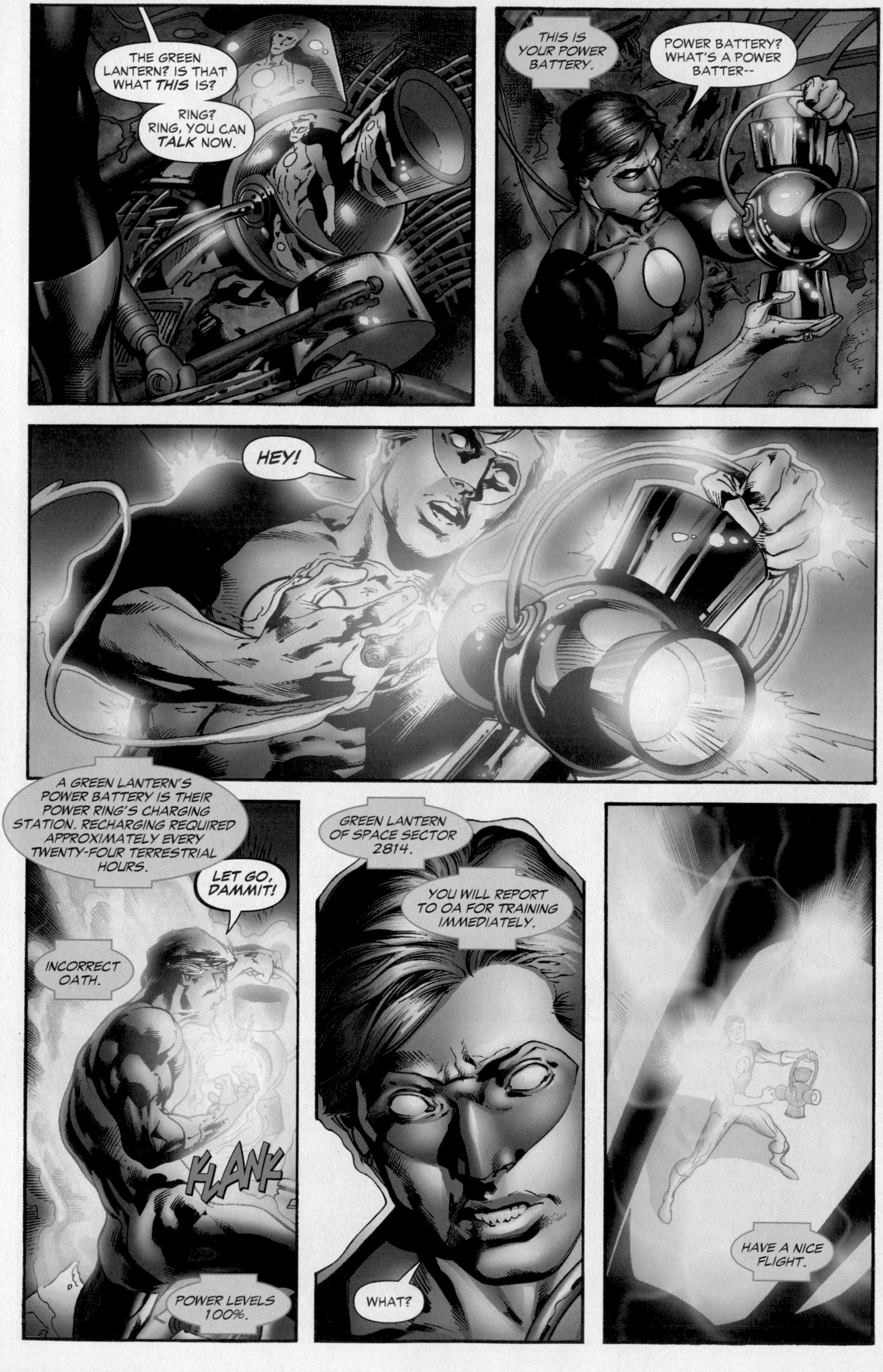
THE GREEN LANTERN? IS THAT WHAT THIS IS?
RING? RING, YOU CAN TALK NOW.
THIS IS YOUR POWER BATTERY.
POWER BATTERY? WHAT'S A POWER BATTER--
HEY!
A GREEN LANTERN'S POWER BATTERY IS THEIR POWER RING'S CHARGING STATION. RECHARGING REQUIRED APPROXIMATELY EVERY TWENTY-FOUR TERRESTRIAL HOURS.
LET GO, DAMMIT!
INCORRECT OATH.
KLANK
POWER LEVELS 100%.
GREEN LANTERN OF SPACE SECTOR 2814.
YOU WILL REPORT TO OA FOR TRAINING IMMEDIATELY.
WHAT?
HAVE A NICE FLIGHT.

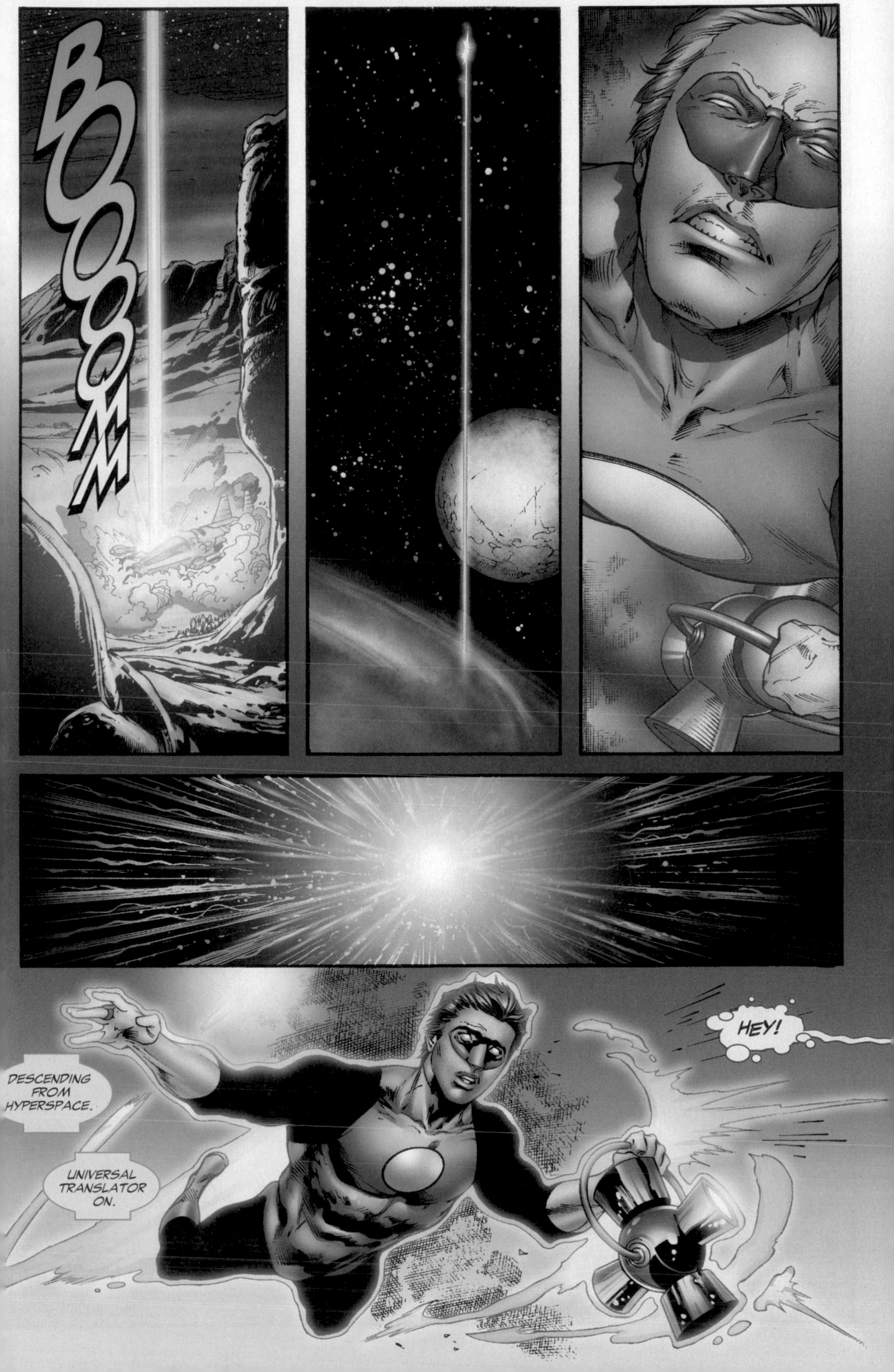
BOOOOOMM
HEY!
DESCENDING FROM HYPERSPACE.
UNIVERSAL TRANSLATOR ON.

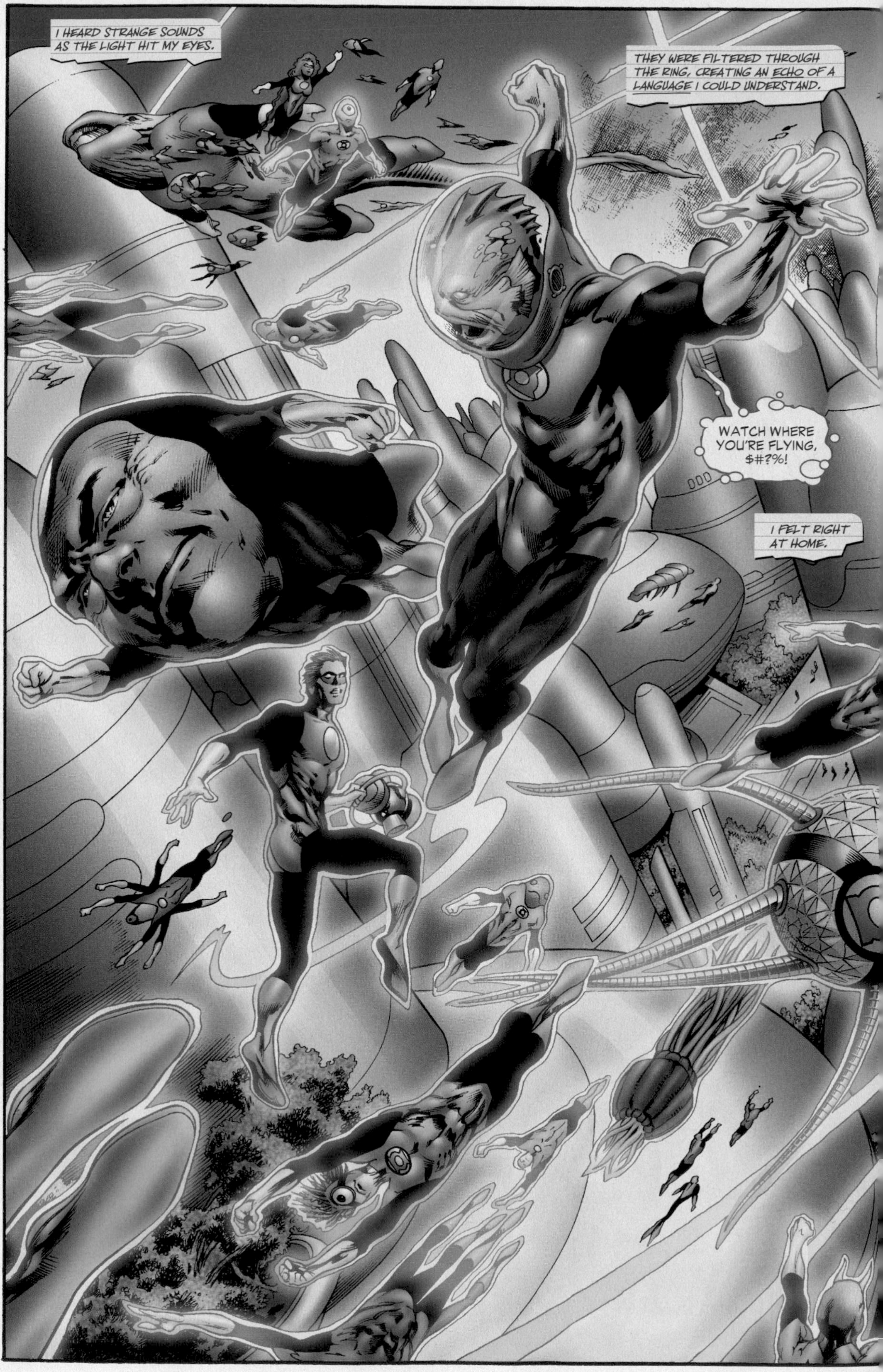
I HEARD STRANGE SOUNDS AS THE LIGHT HIT MY EYES.
THEY WERE FILTERED THROUGH THE RING, CREATING AN ECHO OF A LANGUAGE I COULD UNDERSTAND.
WATCH WHERE YOU'RE FLYING, $#?%!
I FELT RIGHT AT HOME.

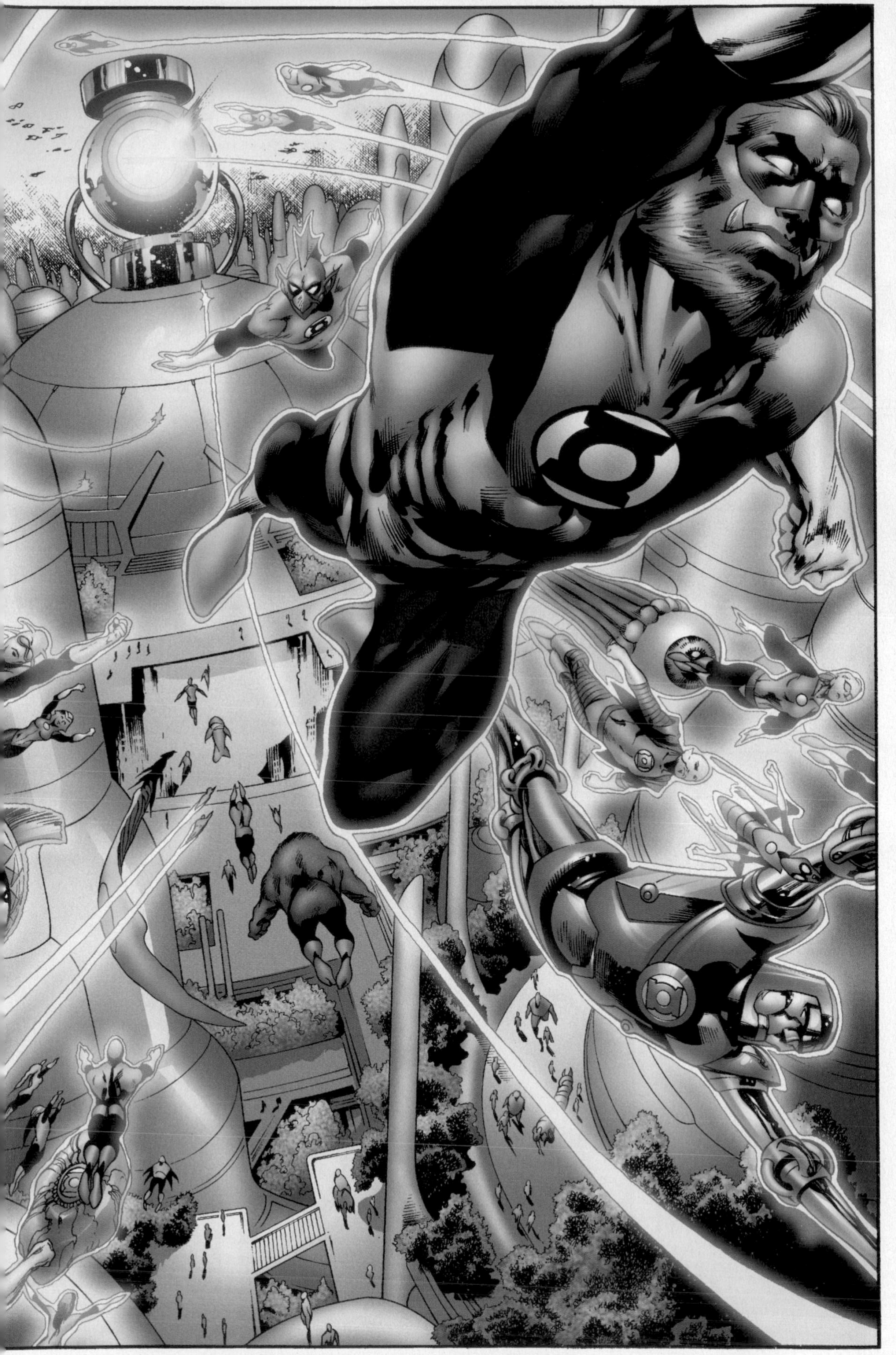

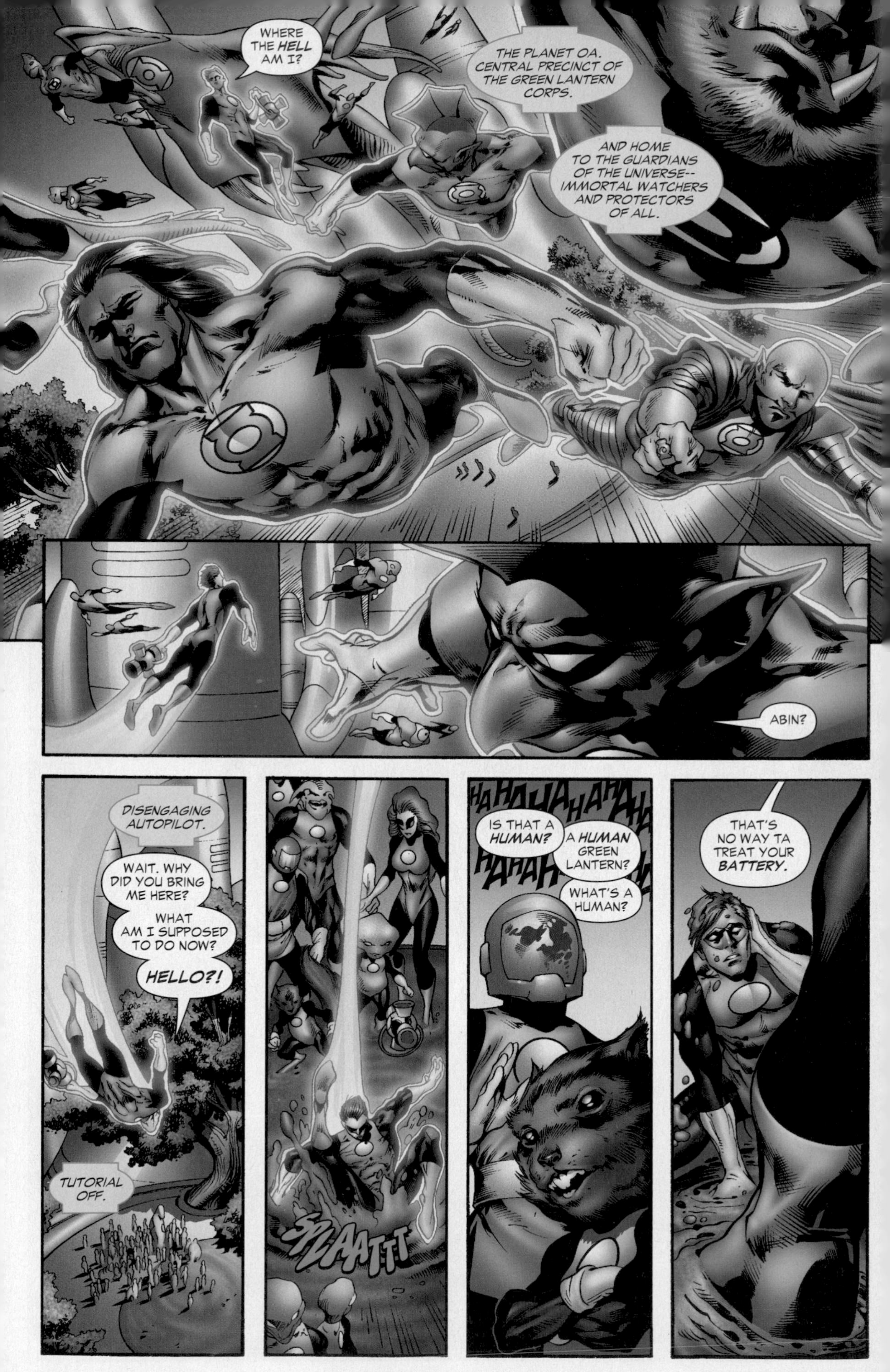
WHERE THE HELL AM I?
THE PLANET OA. CENTRAL PRECINCT OF THE GREEN LANTERN CORPS.
AND HOME TO THE GUARDIANS OF THE UNIVERSE-- IMMORTAL WATCHERS AND PROTECTORS OF ALL.
ABIN?
DISENGAGING AUTOPILOT.
WAIT. WHY DID YOU BRING ME HERE?
WHAT AM I SUPPOSED TO DO NOW?
HELLO?!
TUTORIAL OFF.
SPLAAATTT
HAHAHAHA
IS THAT A HUMAN?
A HUMAN GREEN LANTERN?
WHAT'S A HUMAN?
THAT'S NO WAY TA TREAT YOUR BATTERY.

NICE LANDIN', *POOZER.*

NAME'S *KILOWOG.*

WELCOME TA RINGSLINGIN' 101. OR AS KE'HAAN AND I LIKE TO CALL IT--

--THE *WORST* DAY A' YOUR *WORTHLESS LIFE!*

OH, I GET IT.

THIS IS *BOOT* CAMP.

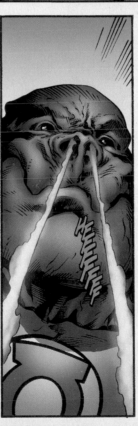

GET IN *LINE* WITH THE REST OF THE WHITE CIRCLES.

IT'S WHERE YOU PRIMORDIAL QUADRUPEDS *BELONG.*

YOU WANNA *BOX?*

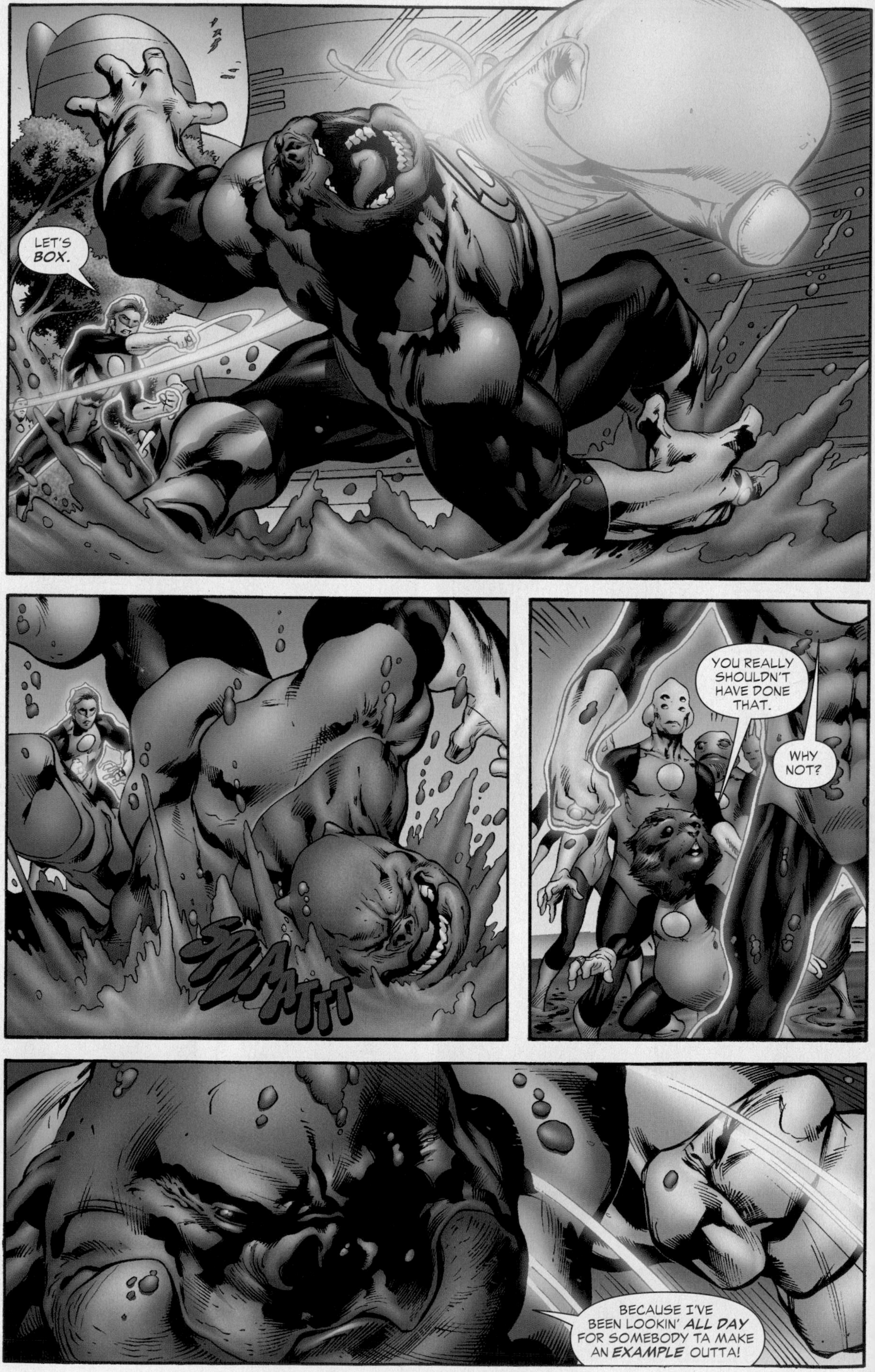
LET'S BOX.
SNAATTT
YOU REALLY SHOULDN'T HAVE DONE THAT.
WHY NOT?
BECAUSE I'VE BEEN LOOKIN' ALL DAY FOR SOMEBODY TA MAKE AN EXAMPLE OUTTA!

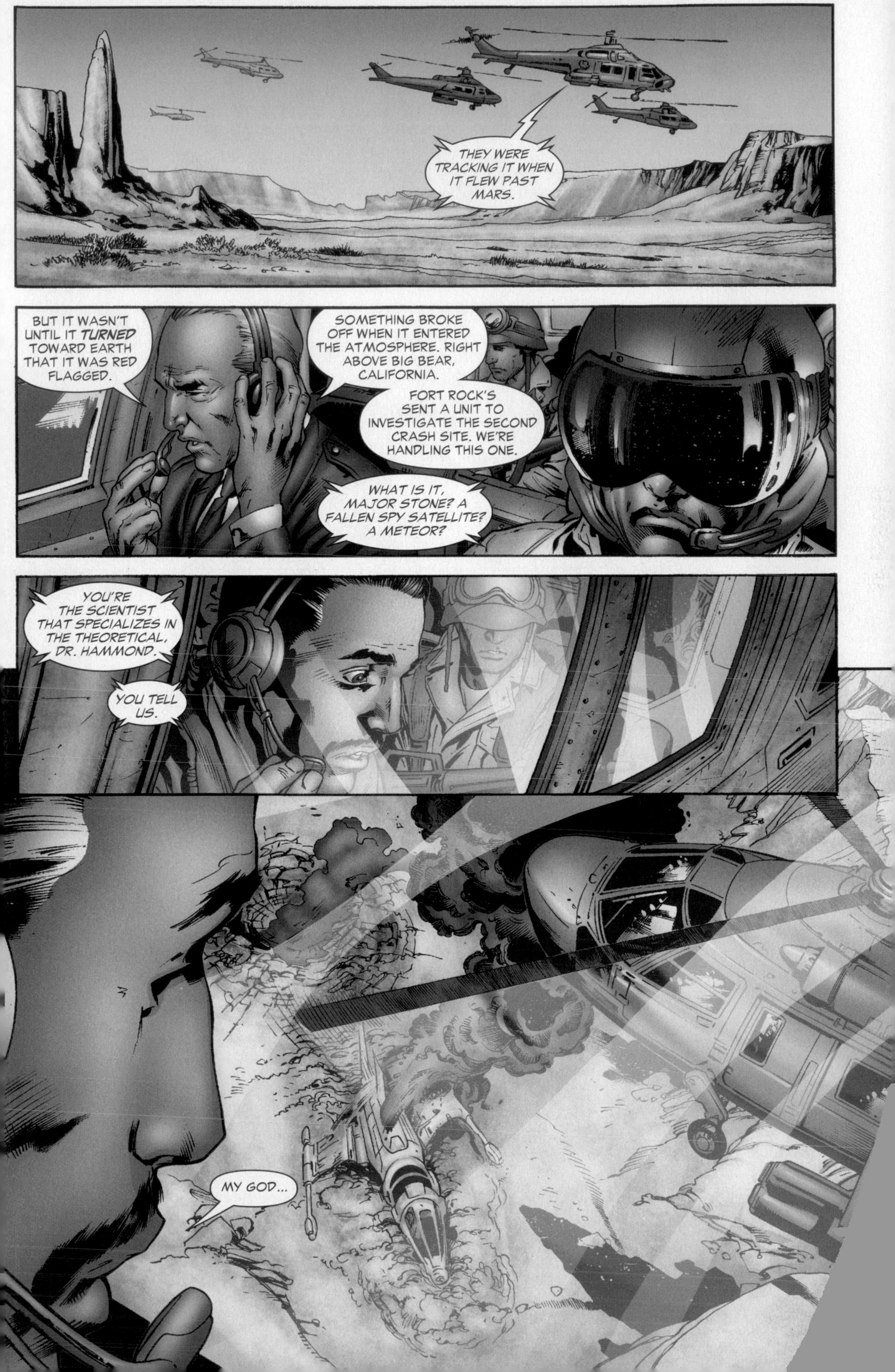
THEY WERE TRACKING IT WHEN IT FLEW PAST MARS.
BUT IT WASN'T UNTIL IT TURNED TOWARD EARTH THAT IT WAS RED FLAGGED.
SOMETHING BROKE OFF WHEN IT ENTERED THE ATMOSPHERE. RIGHT ABOVE BIG BEAR, CALIFORNIA.
FORT ROCK'S SENT A UNIT TO INVESTIGATE THE SECOND CRASH SITE. WE'RE HANDLING THIS ONE.
WHAT IS IT, MAJOR STONE? A FALLEN SPY SATELLITE? A METEOR?
YOU'RE THE SCIENTIST THAT SPECIALIZES IN THE THEORETICAL, DR. HAMMOND.
YOU TELL US.
MY GOD...

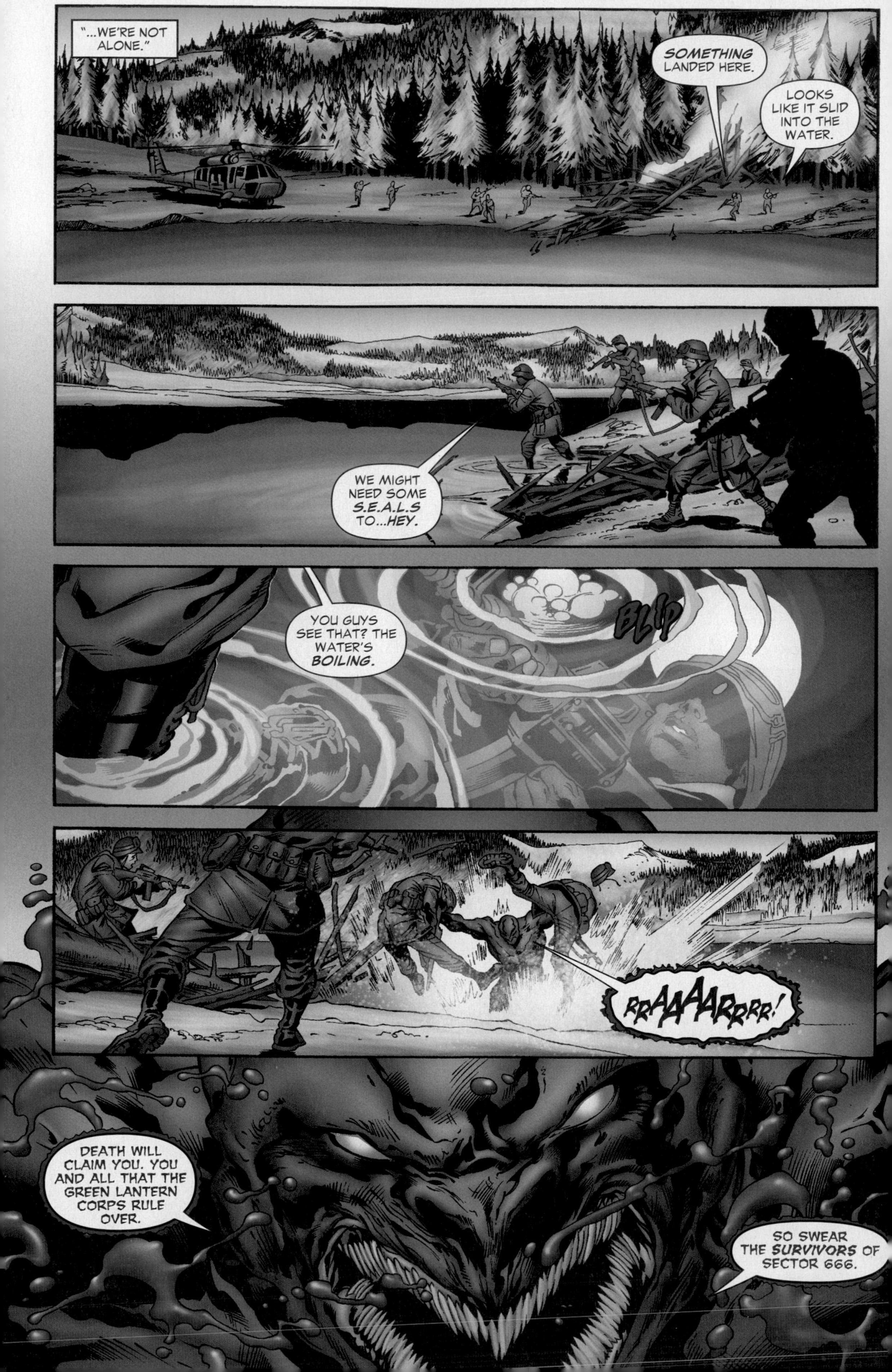
"...WE'RE NOT ALONE."
SOMETHING LANDED HERE.
LOOKS LIKE IT SLID INTO THE WATER.
WE MIGHT NEED SOME S.E.A.L.S TO...HEY.
YOU GUYS SEE THAT? THE WATER'S BOILING.
BLIP
RRAAAARRRR!
DEATH WILL CLAIM YOU. YOU AND ALL THAT THE GREEN LANTERN CORPS RULE OVER.
SO SWEAR THE SURVIVORS OF SECTOR 666.

THE RING CAN MAKE WHATEVER *TOOL* YA NEED. JUST GOTTA PICTURE IT IN YOUR MIND. *WILL* IT TO *LIFE*.

FORCE FIELDS. ENERGY BEAMS.

EVERYONE SEE THAT?

YES, *SIR*.

YOU PRACTICE *WELL*, AHTIER. WHY DO YOU SPEAK SO *LITTLE*?

BECAUSE I *FEAR* MY *DUTY*, KE'HAAN.

GREEN LANTERNS BURN *BRIGHT*, BUT THEY BURN OUT *QUICKLY*.

IF THAT *HUMAN* CAN MAKE IT, SO CAN *YOU*.

THANKS FOR THE RIDE, BUT I'LL GET OFF HERE.

KKRSHH

YOU *WILLED* YOURSELF FREE, EARTHMAN...

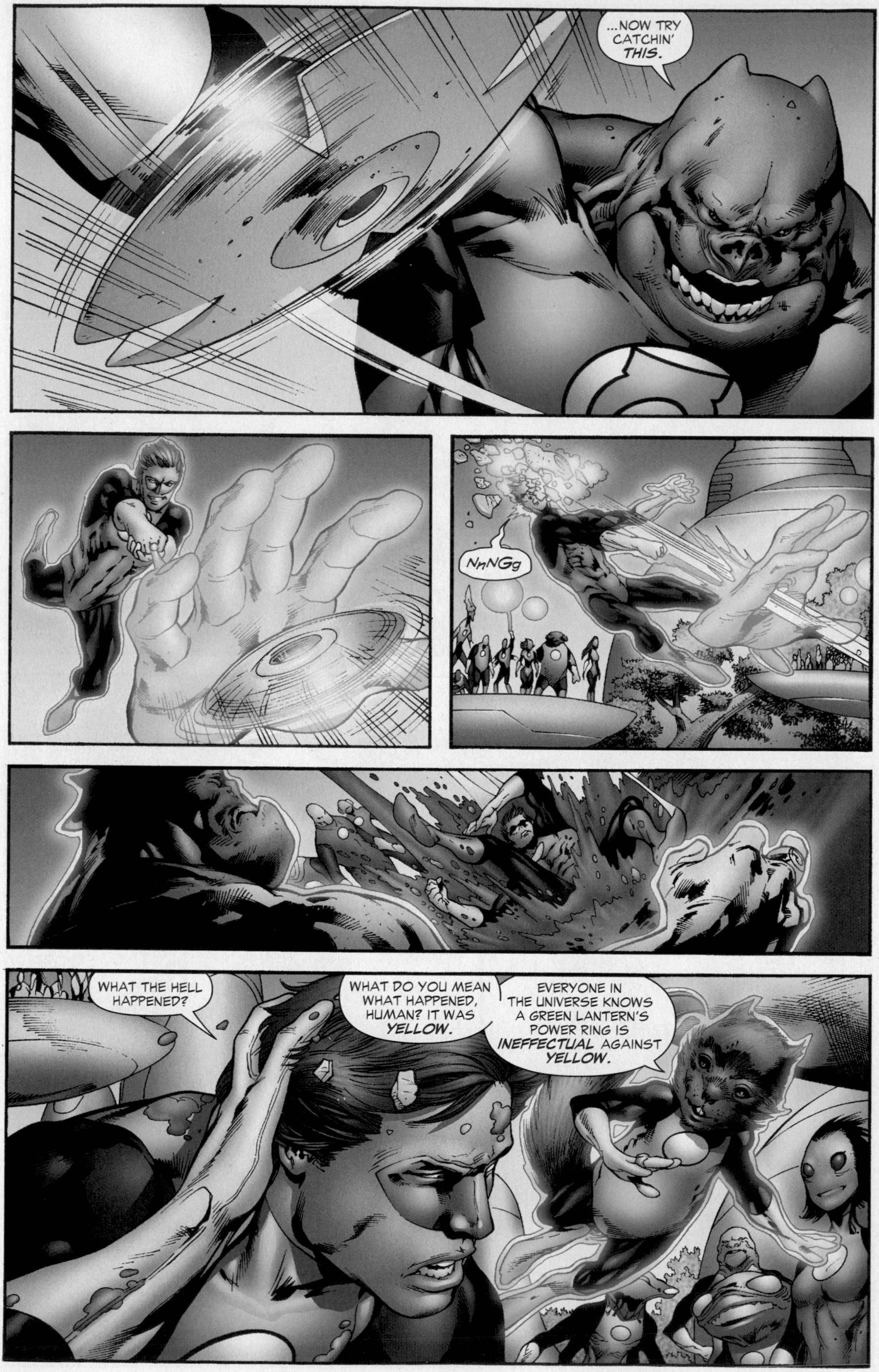
...NOW TRY CATCHIN' THIS.
NnNGg
WHAT THE HELL HAPPENED?
WHAT DO YOU MEAN WHAT HAPPENED, HUMAN? IT WAS YELLOW.
EVERYONE IN THE UNIVERSE KNOWS A GREEN LANTERN'S POWER RING IS INEFFECTUAL AGAINST YELLOW.

HE DON'T KNOW NOTHIN' 'BOUT THE CORPS, CH'P. HE'S FROM *EARTH*.

ASK ME, KILOWOG, EARTH'S A BACKWARD WORLD BEST LEFT TO THEIR *OWN*.

WHY *YELLOW*?

WHAT?

WHY WOULD THESE RINGS NOT BE ABLE TO AFFECT ANYTHING *YELLOW*?

YOU DON'T ASK QUESTIONS IN THE CORPS. YOU DO YOUR *DUTY*.

I DON'T EVEN KNOW WHAT THAT "DUTY" IS.

NOW DON'T GET ALL *PUFFY CHESTED* AGAIN. NEXT TIME, I WON'T BE SO NICE.

"TO SERVE AND PROTECT YOUR RESPECTIVE SECTORS AND ALL LIFE WITHIN THEM."

KILOWOG.

LET ME SPEAK WITH THE EARTHMAN.

WHAT BUSINESS IS HE OF YOURS, TOMAR?

HE'S WEARING *ABIN SUR'S* RING.

MY NAME IS *TOMAR-RE* OF *XUDAR*. GREEN LANTERN OF SPACE SECTOR 2815.

BY ALL ACCOUNTS, I AM YOUR *NEIGHBOR*.

I'M HAL JORDAN.

ABIN SUR'S REPLACEMENT IN THE CORPS. MY RING IS UNABLE TO *UNLOCK* HIS LOG...HOW DID HE DIE?

HE CRASHED HIS SHIP IN THE DESERT.

HIS *SHIP?*

HE DIDN'T *NEED* THAT SHIP.

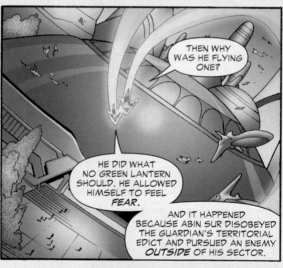

THEN WHY WAS HE FLYING ONE?

HE DID WHAT NO GREEN LANTERN SHOULD. HE ALLOWED HIMSELF TO FEEL *FEAR*.

AND IT HAPPENED BECAUSE ABIN SUR DISOBEYED THE GUARDIAN'S TERRITORIAL EDICT AND PURSUED AN ENEMY *OUTSIDE* OF HIS SECTOR.

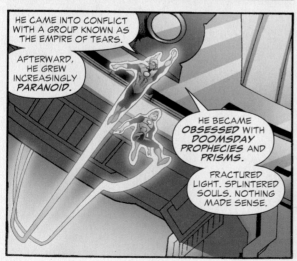

HE CAME INTO CONFLICT WITH A GROUP KNOWN AS THE EMPIRE OF TEARS.

AFTERWARD, HE GREW INCREASINGLY *PARANOID*.

HE BECAME *OBSESSED* WITH *DOOMSDAY PROPHECIES* AND PRISMS.

FRACTURED LIGHT. SPLINTERED SOULS. NOTHING MADE SENSE.

NOTHING MAKES SENSE TO ME RIGHT NOW.

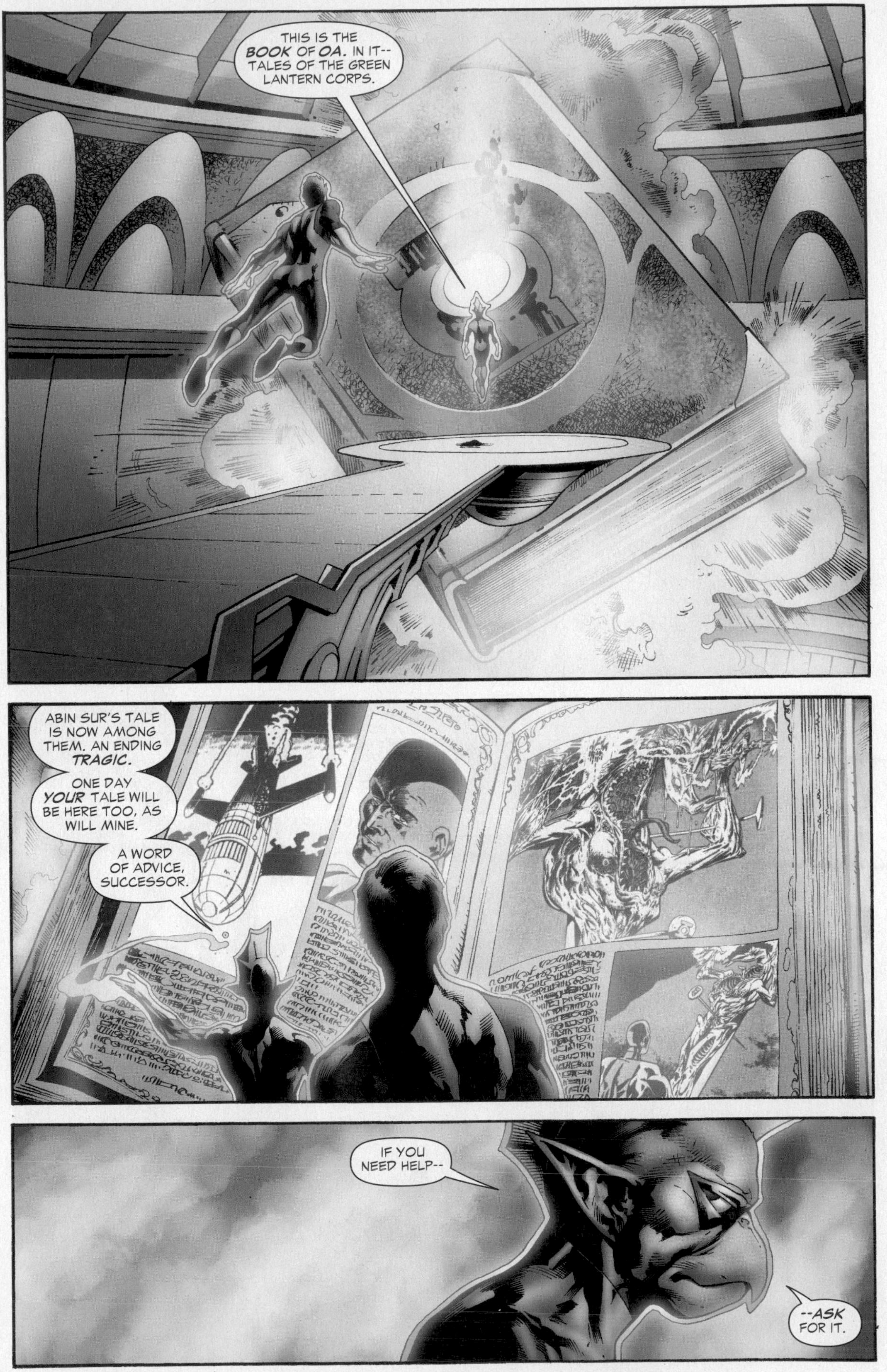
THIS IS THE BOOK OF OA. IN IT-- TALES OF THE GREEN LANTERN CORPS.
ABIN SUR'S TALE IS NOW AMONG THEM. AN ENDING TRAGIC.
ONE DAY YOUR TALE WILL BE HERE TOO, AS WILL MINE.
A WORD OF ADVICE, SUCCESSOR.
IF YOU NEED HELP--
--ASK FOR IT.

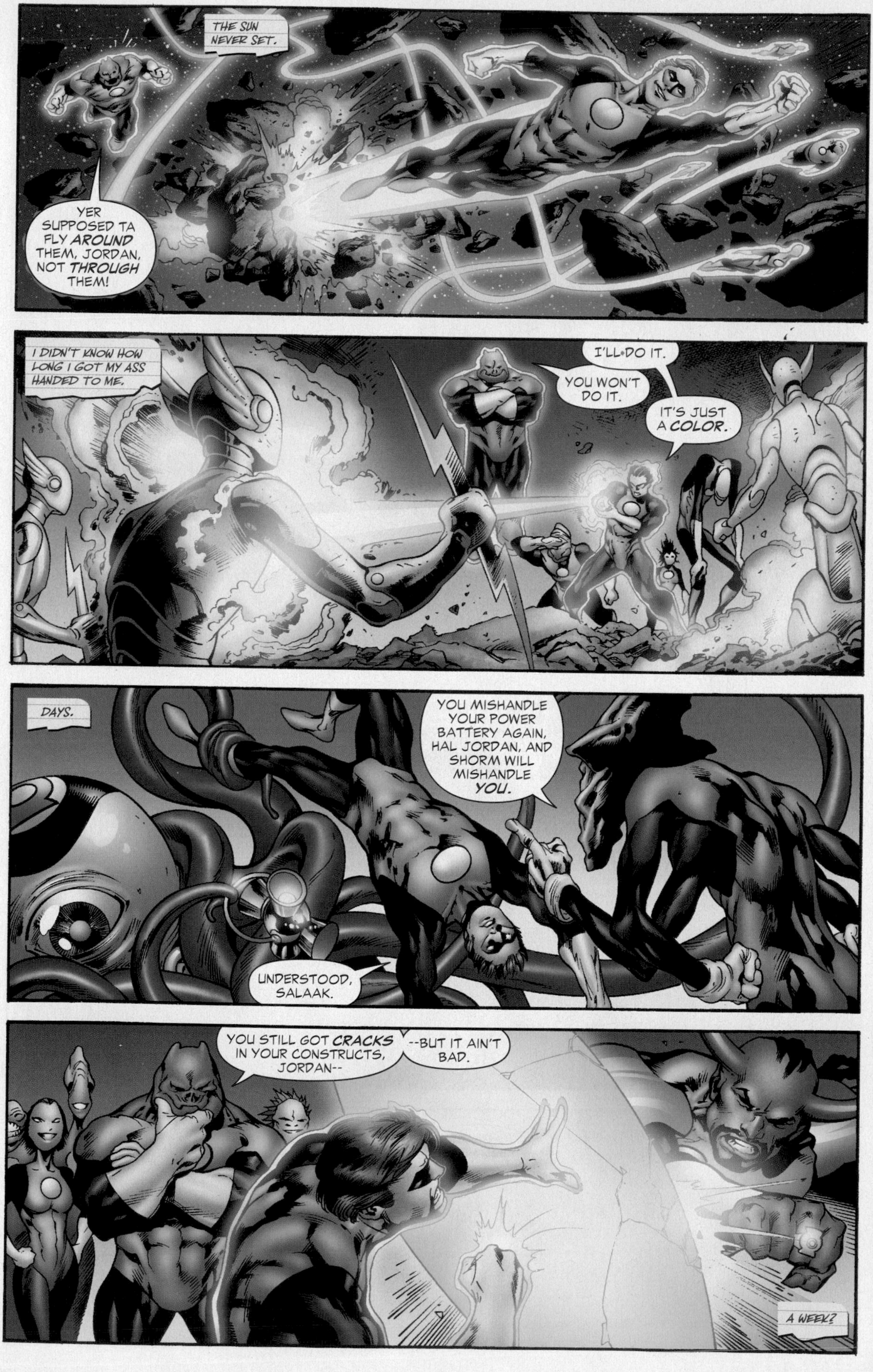
THE SUN NEVER SET.
YER SUPPOSED TA FLY AROUND THEM, JORDAN, NOT THROUGH THEM!
I DIDN'T KNOW HOW LONG I GOT MY ASS HANDED TO ME.
I'LL DO IT.
YOU WON'T DO IT.
IT'S JUST A COLOR.
DAYS.
YOU MISHANDLE YOUR POWER BATTERY AGAIN, HAL JORDAN, AND SHORM WILL MISHANDLE YOU.
UNDERSTOOD, SALAAK.
YOU STILL GOT CRACKS IN YOUR CONSTRUCTS, JORDAN--
--BUT IT AIN'T BAD.
A WEEK?

In brightest day... in blackest night

No evil shall escape my sight

Let those who worship evil's might

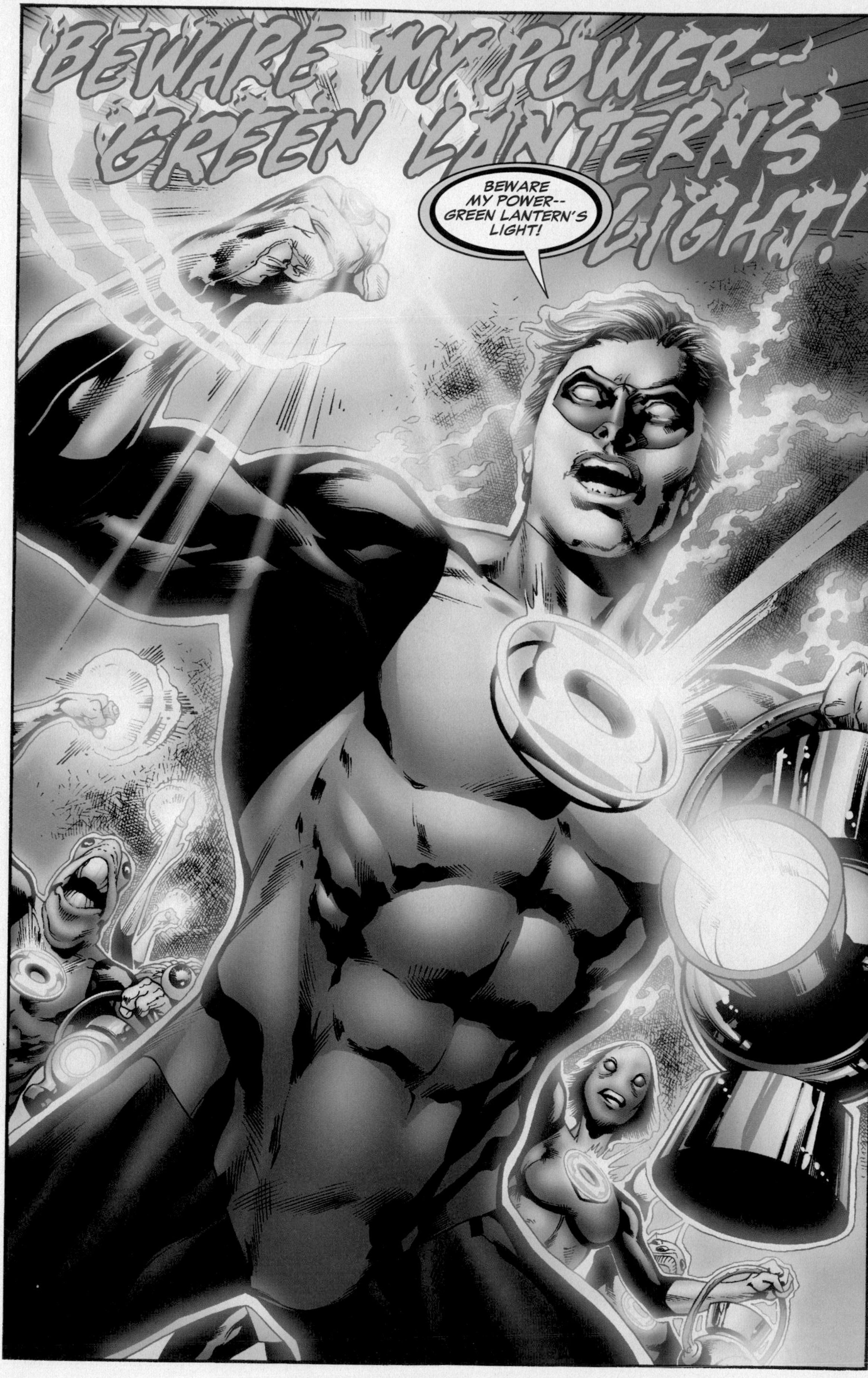
BEWARE MY POWER--GREEN LANTERN'S LIGHT!
BEWARE MY POWER--GREEN LANTERN'S LIGHT!

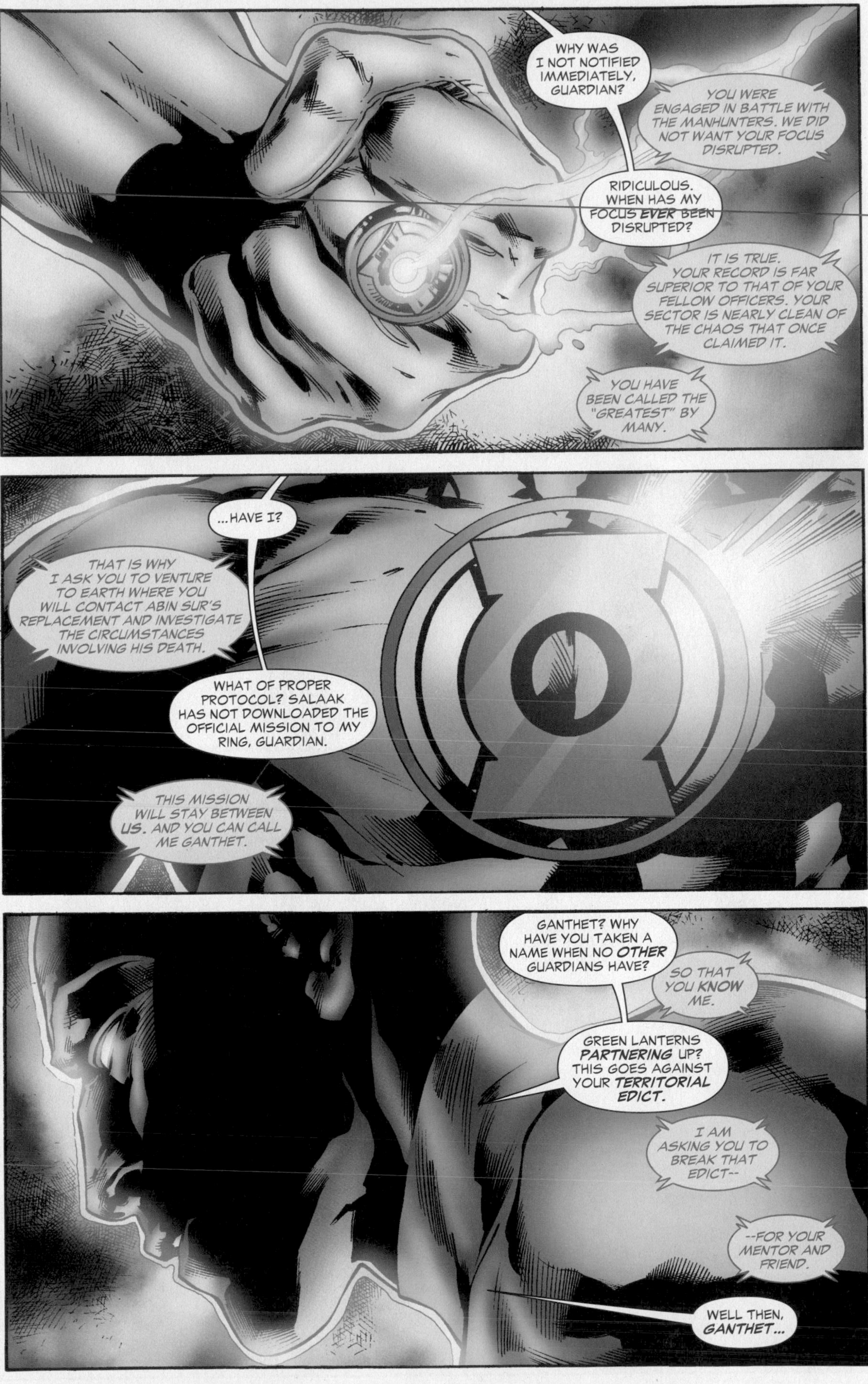

WHY WAS I NOT NOTIFIED IMMEDIATELY, GUARDIAN?
YOU WERE ENGAGED IN BATTLE WITH THE MANHUNTERS. WE DID NOT WANT YOUR FOCUS DISRUPTED.
RIDICULOUS. WHEN HAS MY FOCUS EVER BEEN DISRUPTED?
IT IS TRUE. YOUR RECORD IS FAR SUPERIOR TO THAT OF YOUR FELLOW OFFICERS. YOUR SECTOR IS NEARLY CLEAN OF THE CHAOS THAT ONCE CLAIMED IT.
YOU HAVE BEEN CALLED THE "GREATEST" BY MANY.
...HAVE I?
THAT IS WHY I ASK YOU TO VENTURE TO EARTH WHERE YOU WILL CONTACT ABIN SUR'S REPLACEMENT AND INVESTIGATE THE CIRCUMSTANCES INVOLVING HIS DEATH.
WHAT OF PROPER PROTOCOL? SALAAK HAS NOT DOWNLOADED THE OFFICIAL MISSION TO MY RING, GUARDIAN.
THIS MISSION WILL STAY BETWEEN US. AND YOU CAN CALL ME GANTHET.
GANTHET? WHY HAVE YOU TAKEN A NAME WHEN NO OTHER GUARDIANS HAVE?
SO THAT YOU KNOW ME.
GREEN LANTERNS PARTNERING UP? THIS GOES AGAINST YOUR TERRITORIAL EDICT.
I AM ASKING YOU TO BREAK THAT EDICT--
--FOR YOUR MENTOR AND FRIEND.
WELL THEN, GANTHET...

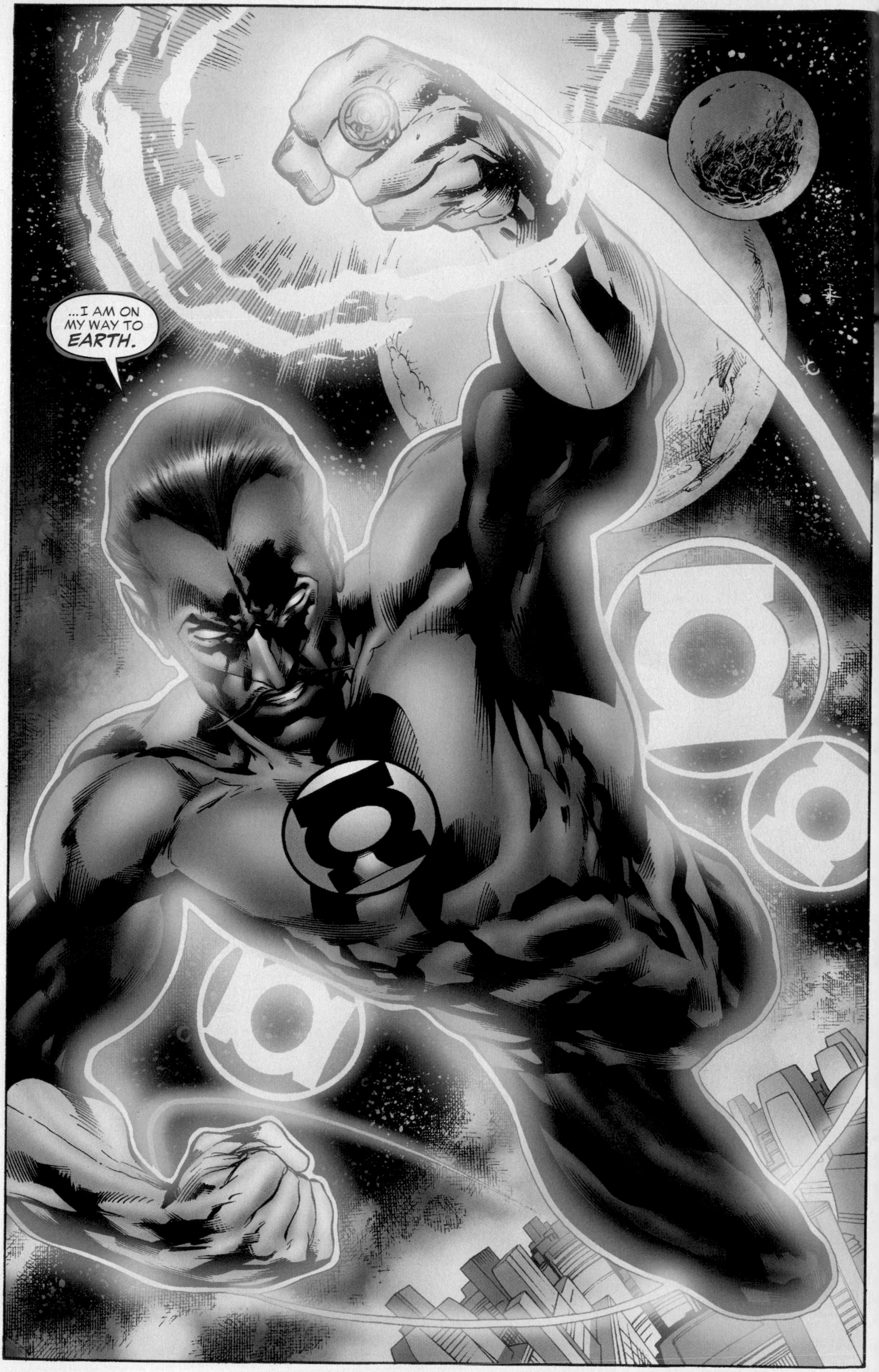
...I AM ON MY WAY TO EARTH.

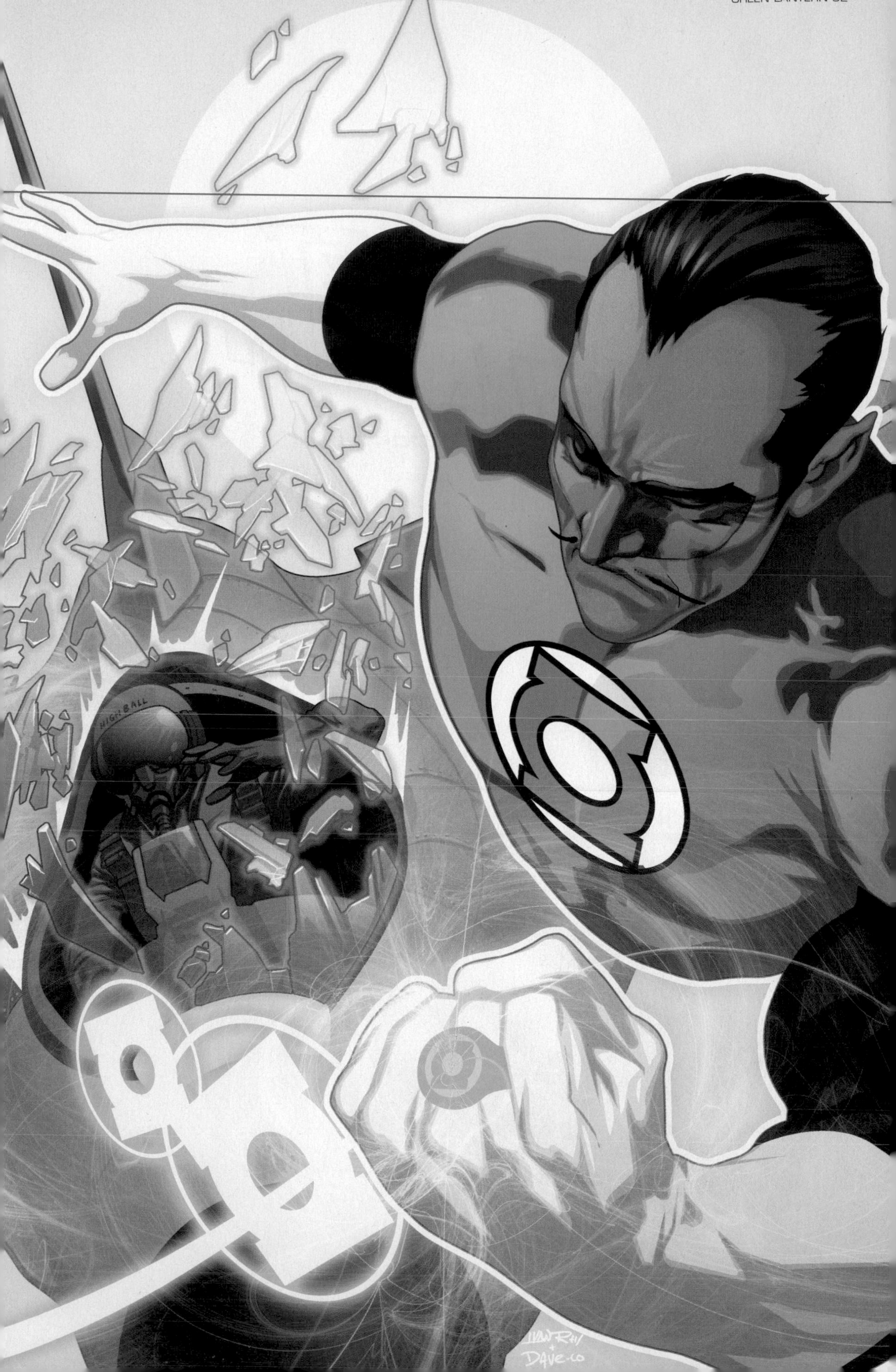
HIGH BALL

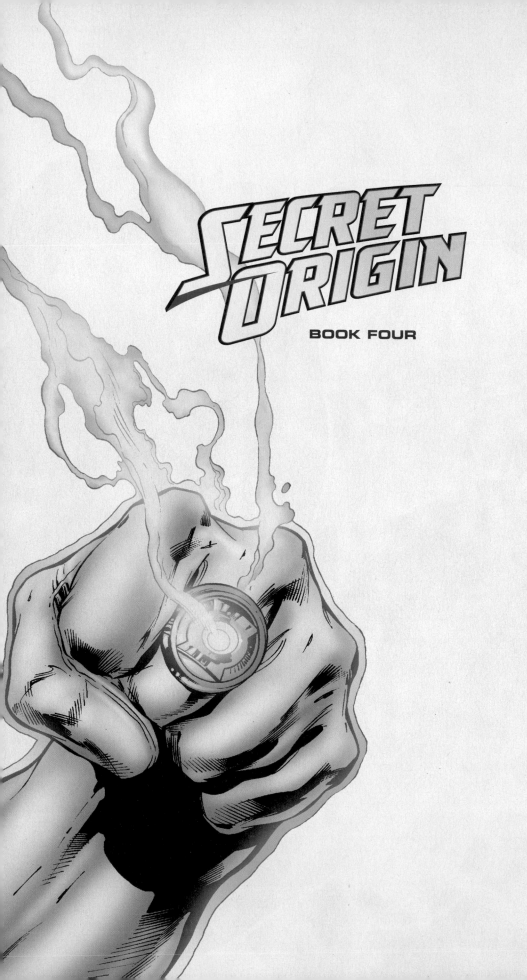

SECRET ORIGIN

BOOK FOUR

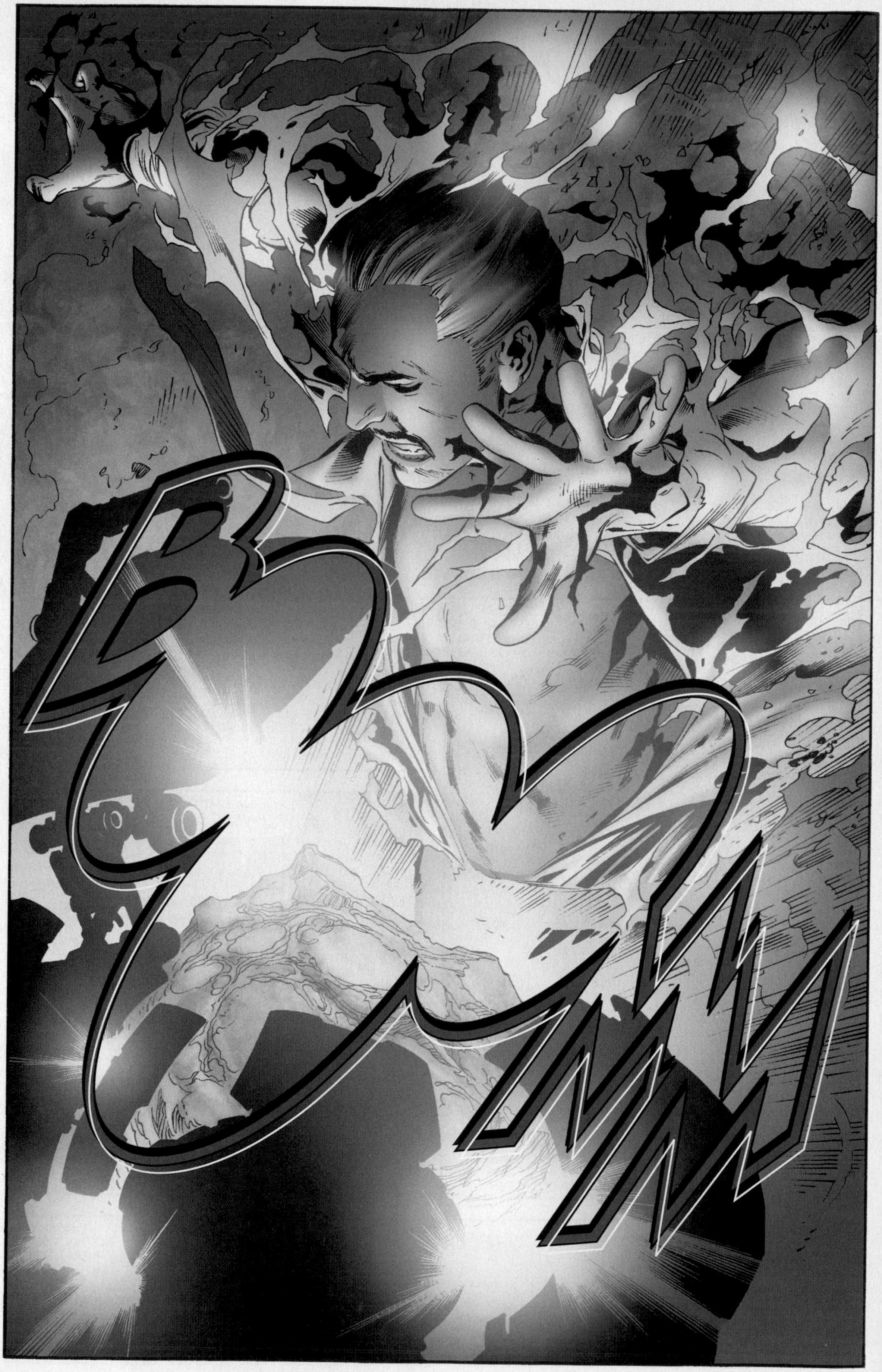
BOOM

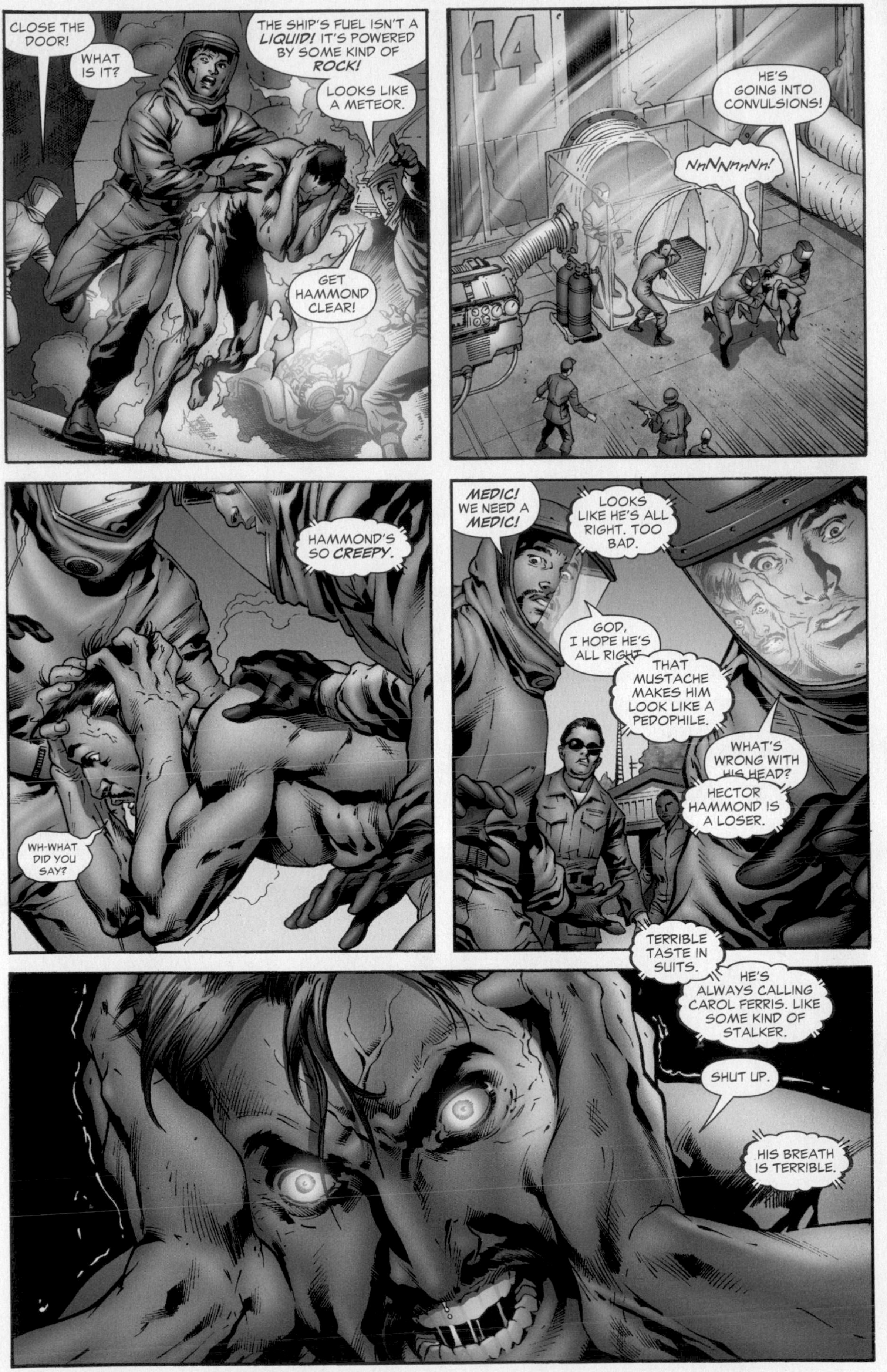
CLOSE THE DOOR!
WHAT IS IT?
THE SHIP'S FUEL ISN'T A LIQUID! IT'S POWERED BY SOME KIND OF ROCK!
LOOKS LIKE A METEOR.
GET HAMMOND CLEAR!
44
HE'S GOING INTO CONVULSIONS!
NnNNnnNn!
HAMMOND'S SO CREEPY.
WH-WHAT DID YOU SAY?
MEDIC! WE NEED A MEDIC!
LOOKS LIKE HE'S ALL RIGHT. TOO BAD.
GOD, I HOPE HE'S ALL RIGHT.
THAT MUSTACHE MAKES HIM LOOK LIKE A PEDOPHILE.
WHAT'S WRONG WITH HIS HEAD?
HECTOR HAMMOND IS A LOSER.
TERRIBLE TASTE IN SUITS.
HE'S ALWAYS CALLING CAROL FERRIS. LIKE SOME KIND OF STALKER.
SHUT UP.
HIS BREATH IS TERRIBLE.

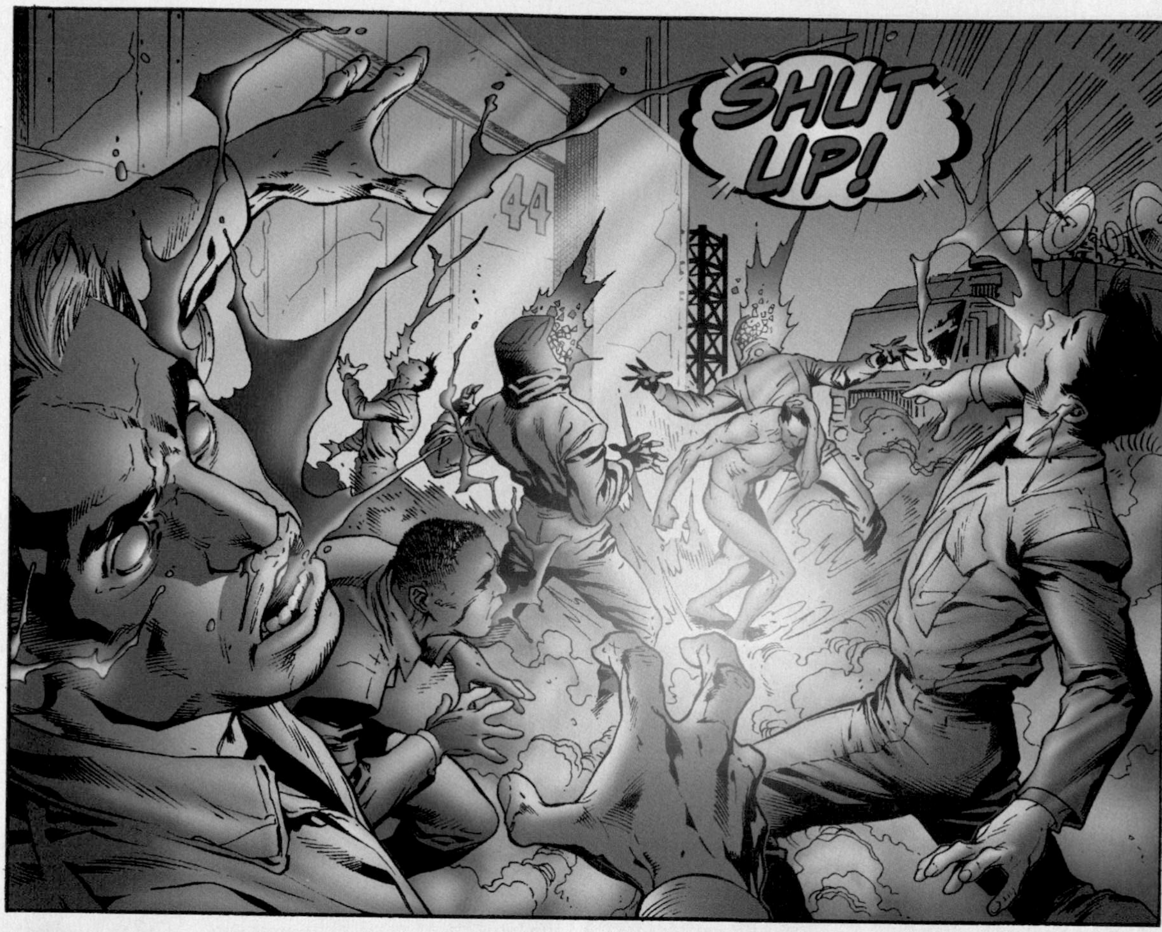
SHUT UP!
44

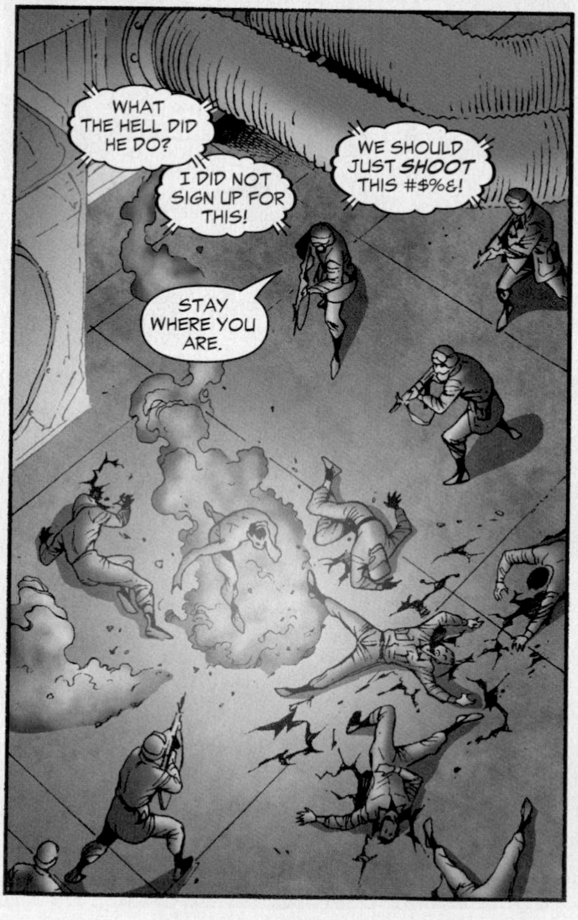
WHAT THE HELL DID HE DO?
I DID NOT SIGN UP FOR THIS!
WE SHOULD JUST SHOOT THIS #$%&!
STAY WHERE YOU ARE.

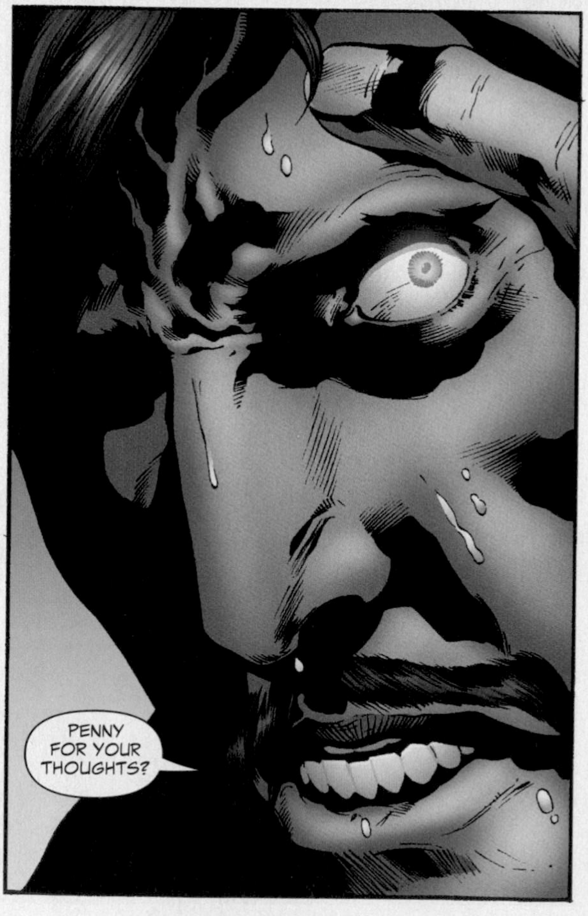
PENNY FOR YOUR THOUGHTS?

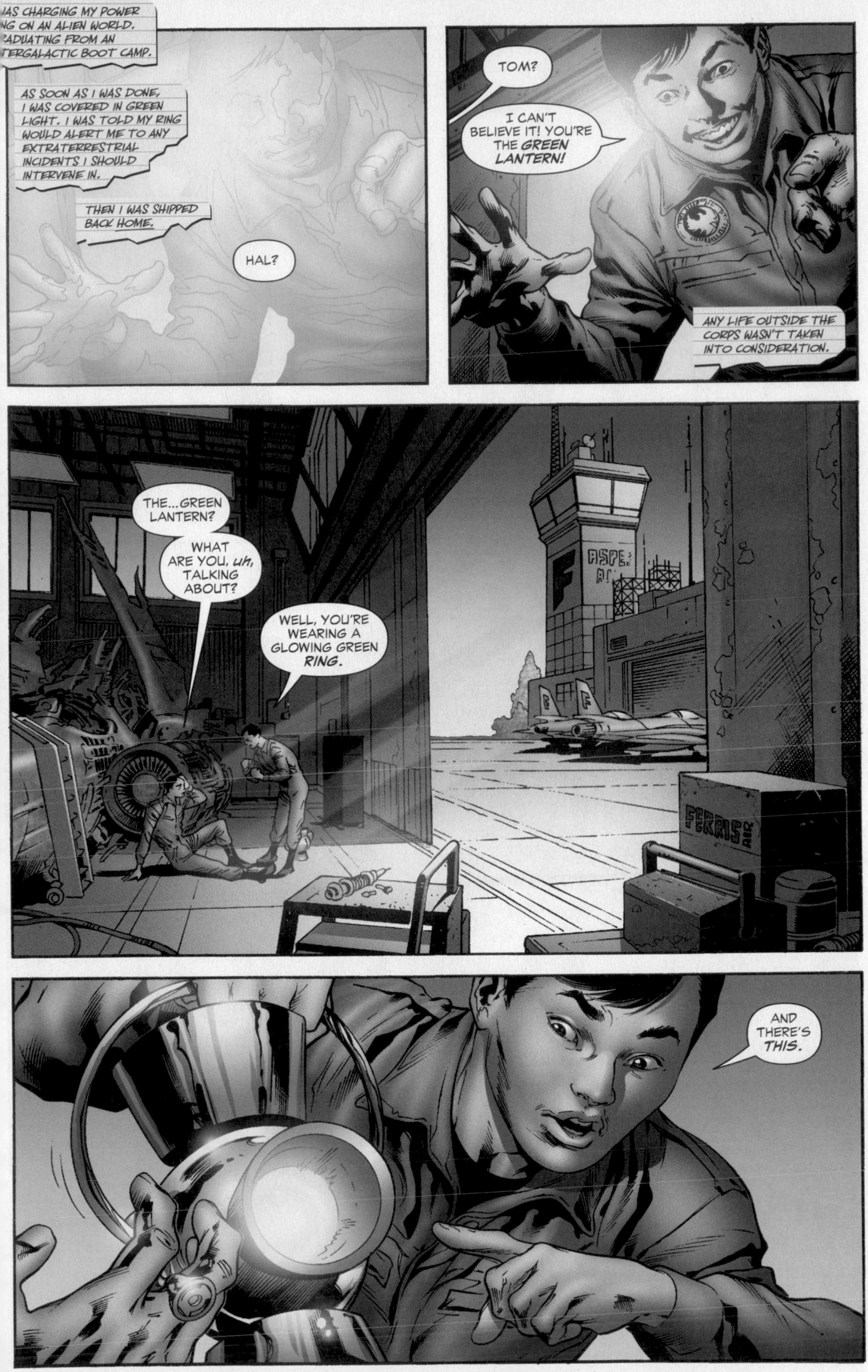
WAS CHARGING MY POWER RING ON AN ALIEN WORLD. GRADUATING FROM AN INTERGALACTIC BOOT CAMP.
AS SOON AS I WAS DONE, I WAS COVERED IN GREEN LIGHT. I WAS TOLD MY RING WOULD ALERT ME TO ANY EXTRATERRESTRIAL INCIDENTS I SHOULD INTERVENE IN.
THEN I WAS SHIPPED BACK HOME.
HAL?
TOM?
I CAN'T BELIEVE IT! YOU'RE THE GREEN LANTERN!
ANY LIFE OUTSIDE THE CORPS WASN'T TAKEN INTO CONSIDERATION.
THE...GREEN LANTERN?
WHAT ARE YOU, uh, TALKING ABOUT?
WELL, YOU'RE WEARING A GLOWING GREEN RING.
FERRIS AIR
AND THERE'S THIS.

WHAT DO YOU MEAN YOU'RE NOT A SUPER-HERO?

YOU *CAUGHT* LAMINSKI'S PLANE LAST WEEK!

ANYONE ELSE WOULD'VE DONE THE SAME IF THEY *COULD*.

EVEN IF HE *IS* A JERK.

WELL, YOU'RE NOT GONNA HAVE TO WORRY ABOUT *HIM* ANYMORE.

I'M NOT SUPPOSED TO USE THE RING TO SORT OUT *PERSONAL PROBLEMS*, TOM.

NO, I MEAN THE *WALKOUT*.

WHAT WALKOUT?

KLANG

SEE ALL THE *EMPTY* LOCKERS?

ONCE WORD SPREAD THAT CAROL "LADY" FERRIS WAS TAKING THE REINS FROM MR. ARDEN, NO ONE WAS PARTICULARLY *EXCITED*.

AND AFTER HER FATHER DIDN'T SHOW FOR THE BIG *COMPANY SPEECH*, SHE HAD TO GIVE IT HERSELF--

--AFTERWARDS JUST ABOUT EVERYONE *QUIT*.

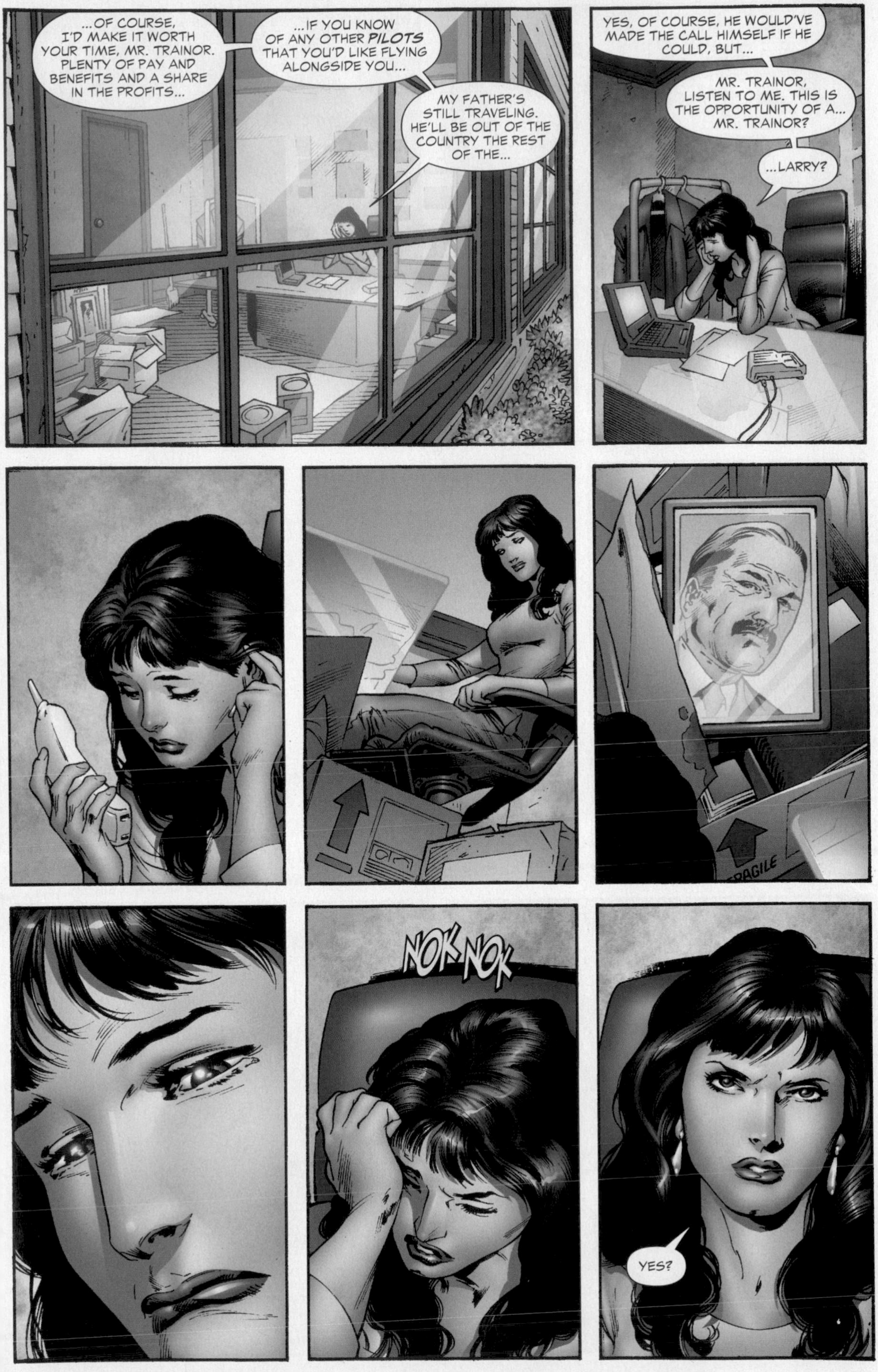
...OF COURSE, I'D MAKE IT WORTH YOUR TIME, MR. TRAINOR. PLENTY OF PAY AND BENEFITS AND A SHARE IN THE PROFITS...
...IF YOU KNOW OF ANY OTHER PILOTS THAT YOU'D LIKE FLYING ALONGSIDE YOU...
MY FATHER'S STILL TRAVELING. HE'LL BE OUT OF THE COUNTRY THE REST OF THE...
YES, OF COURSE, HE WOULD'VE MADE THE CALL HIMSELF IF HE COULD, BUT...
MR. TRAINOR, LISTEN TO ME. THIS IS THE OPPORTUNITY OF A... MR. TRAINOR?
...LARRY?
NOK NOK
YES?

MISS FERRIS.

MR. JORDAN? WHAT ARE YOU DOING HERE?

I JUST WANTED TO THROW IN MY RESIGNATION ALONG WITH THE REST.

YOU HAVEN'T SHOWN YOUR FACE HERE ALL *WEEK*. I ASSUMED YOU ALREADY HAD.

YOU ASSUMED RIGHT. I GUESS I WANTED TO MAKE IT *OFFICIAL*.

AND IF YOUR *FATHER* WAS HERE--

WHAT?

WHAT WOULD YOU *DO* IF MY FATHER *WAS* HERE?

I'D TELL HIM WHAT I'VE BEEN WANTING TO FOR *YEARS*.

I'D TELL HIM EVERYTHING MY MOTHER *BEGGED* ME *NOT* TO.

YOU KNOW WHAT, JORDAN? LET'S MAKE THIS DAY EVEN *BETTER* THAN IT *HAS* BEEN.

TELL *ME*.

YOUR FATHER PUT *MINE* IN A *DEATH TRAP!*

HE SAVED A FEW *BUCKS* AND HE SENT HIM OFF IN A PLANE THAT NEVER HAD A *CHANCE* AT *LANDING*.

AND NOW, WHILE *MY DAD* IS *ROTTING* IN THE *GROUND*, YOURS IS PLAYING *PUTT-PUTT* ON THE GULF OF THE MEXICO, DRINKING A MARGARITA AND PROBABLY SMOKING A CIGAR THAT COSTS MORE THAN WHAT I MAKE IN A DAY!

YOU DON'T MAKE *ANYTHING,* JORDAN. YOU JUST *QUIT,* REMEMBER?

NOW IS THAT *ALL* YOU'VE GOT TO *BARK* ABOUT?

FORGET IT, "LADY" FERRIS. I'LL SAVE THE REST FOR *HIM* WHEN HE'S *BACK* FROM HIS EXTENDED *HOLIDAY.*

DO YOU WANT TO FLY AGAIN?

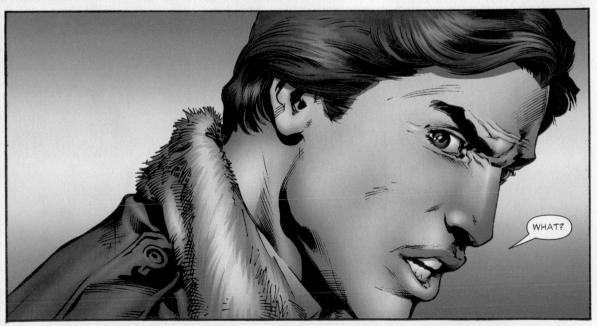

WHAT?

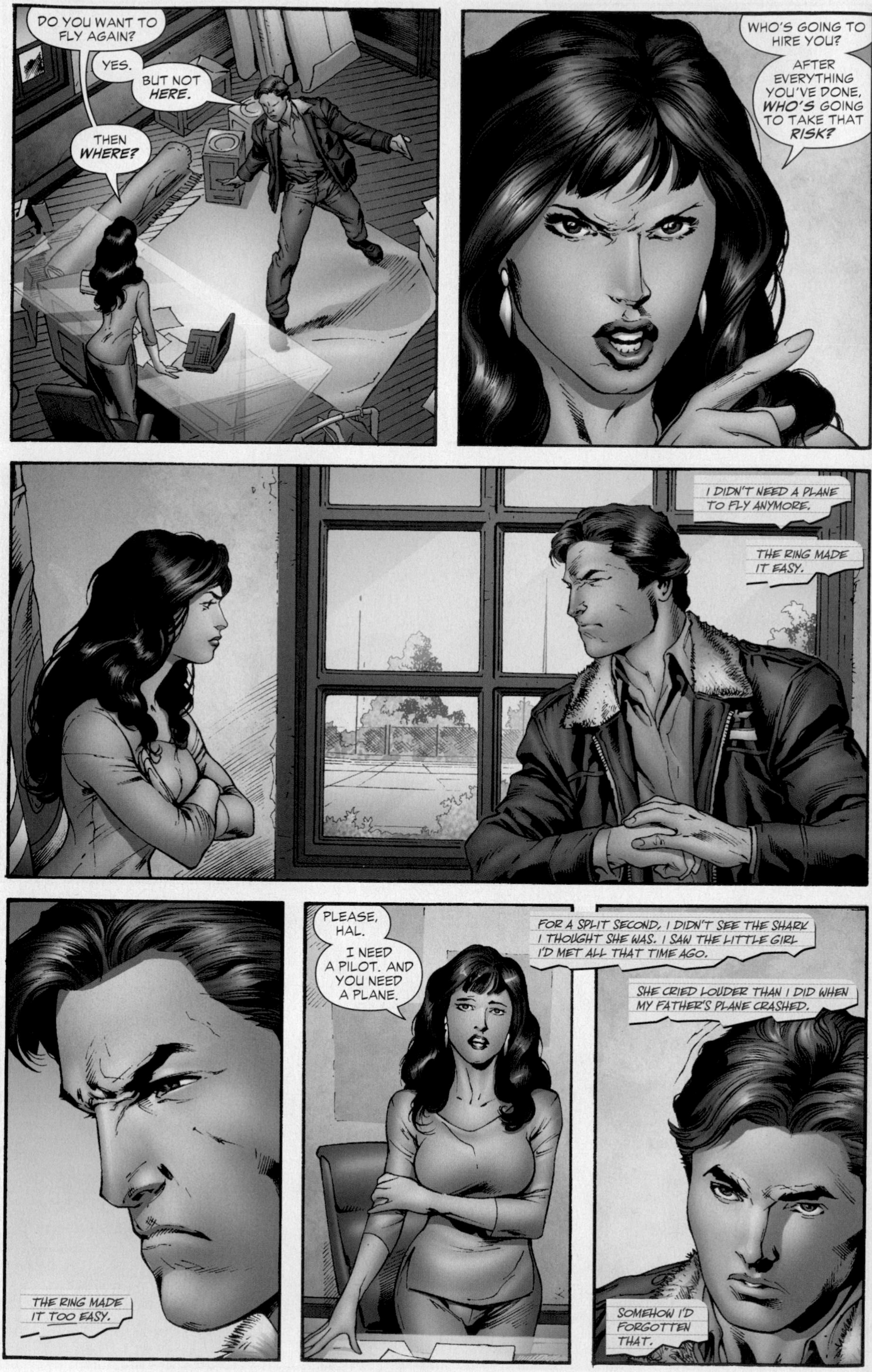
DO YOU WANT TO FLY AGAIN?
YES.
BUT NOT HERE.
THEN WHERE?
WHO'S GOING TO HIRE YOU?
AFTER EVERYTHING YOU'VE DONE, WHO'S GOING TO TAKE THAT RISK?
I DIDN'T NEED A PLANE TO FLY ANYMORE.
THE RING MADE IT EASY.
THE RING MADE IT TOO EASY.
PLEASE, HAL.
I NEED A PILOT. AND YOU NEED A PLANE.
FOR A SPLIT SECOND, I DIDN'T SEE THE SHARK I THOUGHT SHE WAS. I SAW THE LITTLE GIRL I'D MET ALL THAT TIME AGO.
SHE CRIED LOUDER THAN I DID WHEN MY FATHER'S PLANE CRASHED.
SOMEHOW I'D FORGOTTEN THAT.

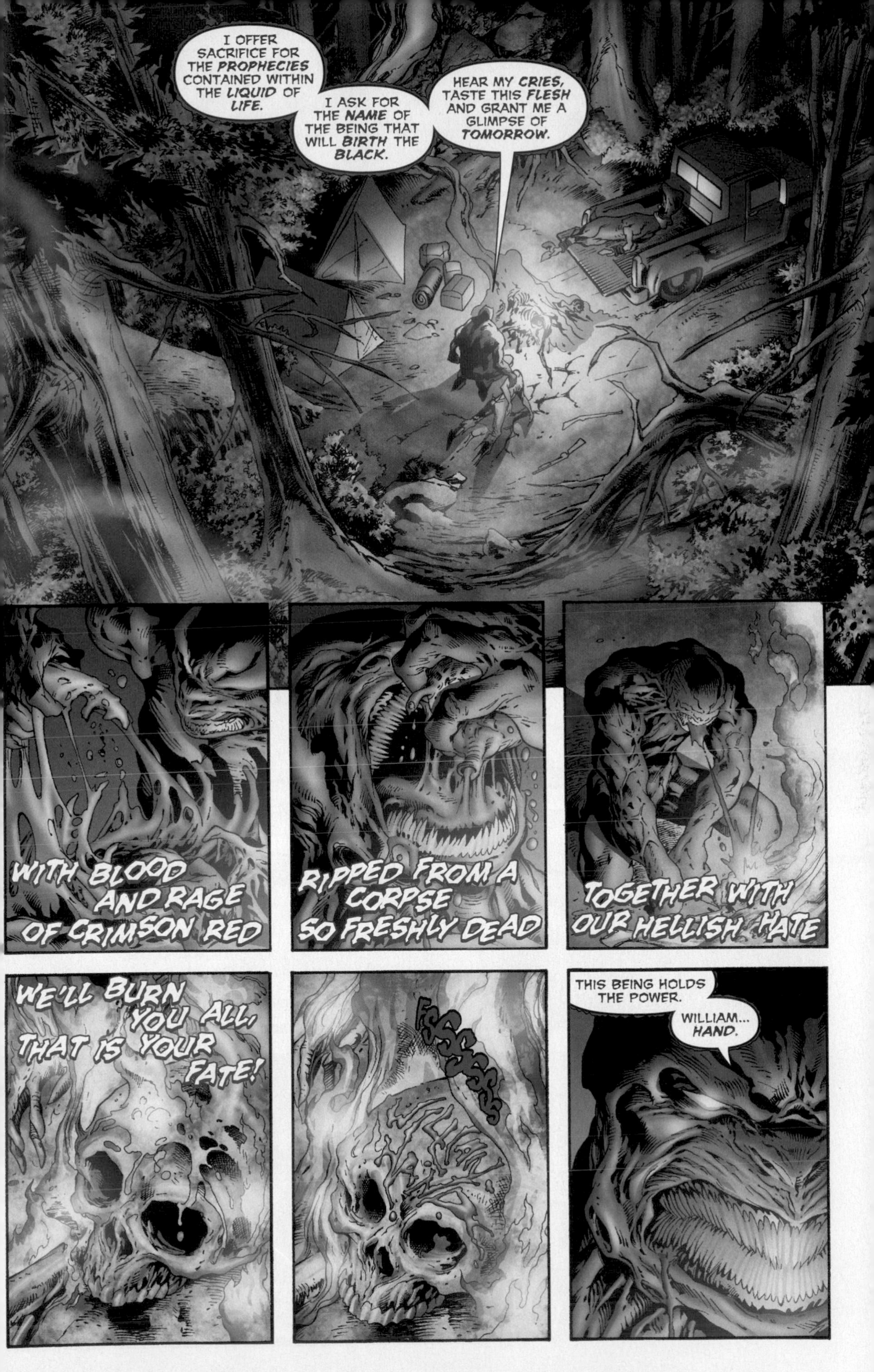

I OFFER SACRIFICE FOR THE PROPHECIES CONTAINED WITHIN THE LIQUID OF LIFE.
I ASK FOR THE NAME OF THE BEING THAT WILL BIRTH THE BLACK.
HEAR MY CRIES, TASTE THIS FLESH AND GRANT ME A GLIMPSE OF TOMORROW.
WITH BLOOD AND RAGE OF CRIMSON RED
RIPPED FROM A CORPSE SO FRESHLY DEAD
TOGETHER WITH OUR HELLISH HATE
WE'LL BURN YOU ALL, THAT IS YOUR FATE!
FSSSSSSS
THIS BEING HOLDS THE POWER.
WILLIAM... HAND.

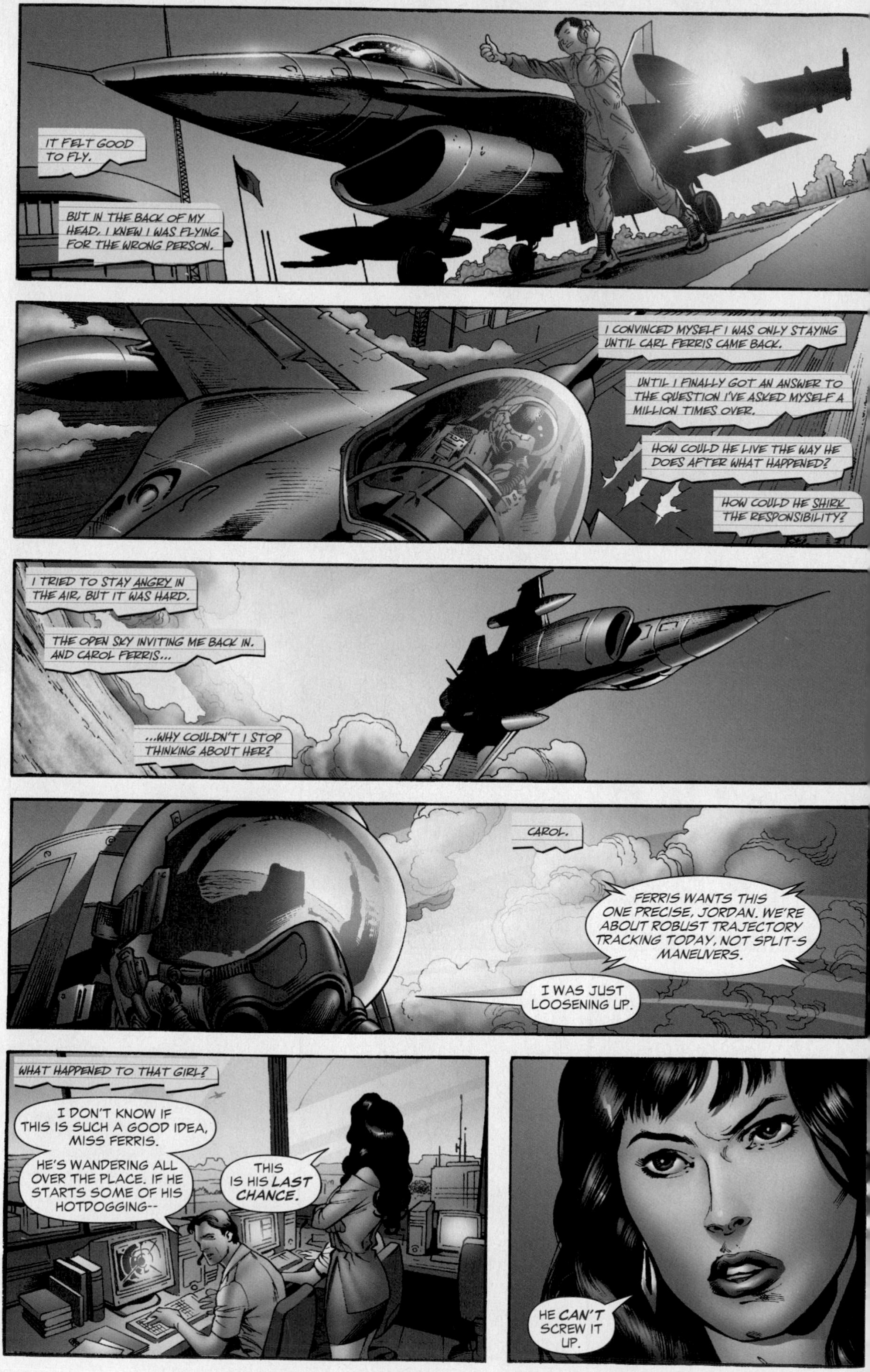
IT FELT GOOD TO FLY.
BUT IN THE BACK OF MY HEAD, I KNEW I WAS FLYING FOR THE WRONG PERSON.
I CONVINCED MYSELF I WAS ONLY STAYING UNTIL CARL FERRIS CAME BACK.
UNTIL I FINALLY GOT AN ANSWER TO THE QUESTION I'VE ASKED MYSELF A MILLION TIMES OVER.
HOW COULD HE LIVE THE WAY HE DOES AFTER WHAT HAPPENED?
HOW COULD HE SHIRK THE RESPONSIBILITY?
I TRIED TO STAY ANGRY IN THE AIR, BUT IT WAS HARD.
THE OPEN SKY INVITING ME BACK IN. AND CAROL FERRIS...
...WHY COULDN'T I STOP THINKING ABOUT HER?
CAROL.
FERRIS WANTS THIS ONE PRECISE, JORDAN. WE'RE ABOUT ROBUST TRAJECTORY TRACKING TODAY, NOT SPLIT-S MANEUVERS.
I WAS JUST LOOSENING UP.
WHAT HAPPENED TO THAT GIRL?
I DON'T KNOW IF THIS IS SUCH A GOOD IDEA, MISS FERRIS.
HE'S WANDERING ALL OVER THE PLACE. IF HE STARTS SOME OF HIS HOTDOGGING--
THIS IS HIS LAST CHANCE.
HE CAN'T SCREW IT UP.

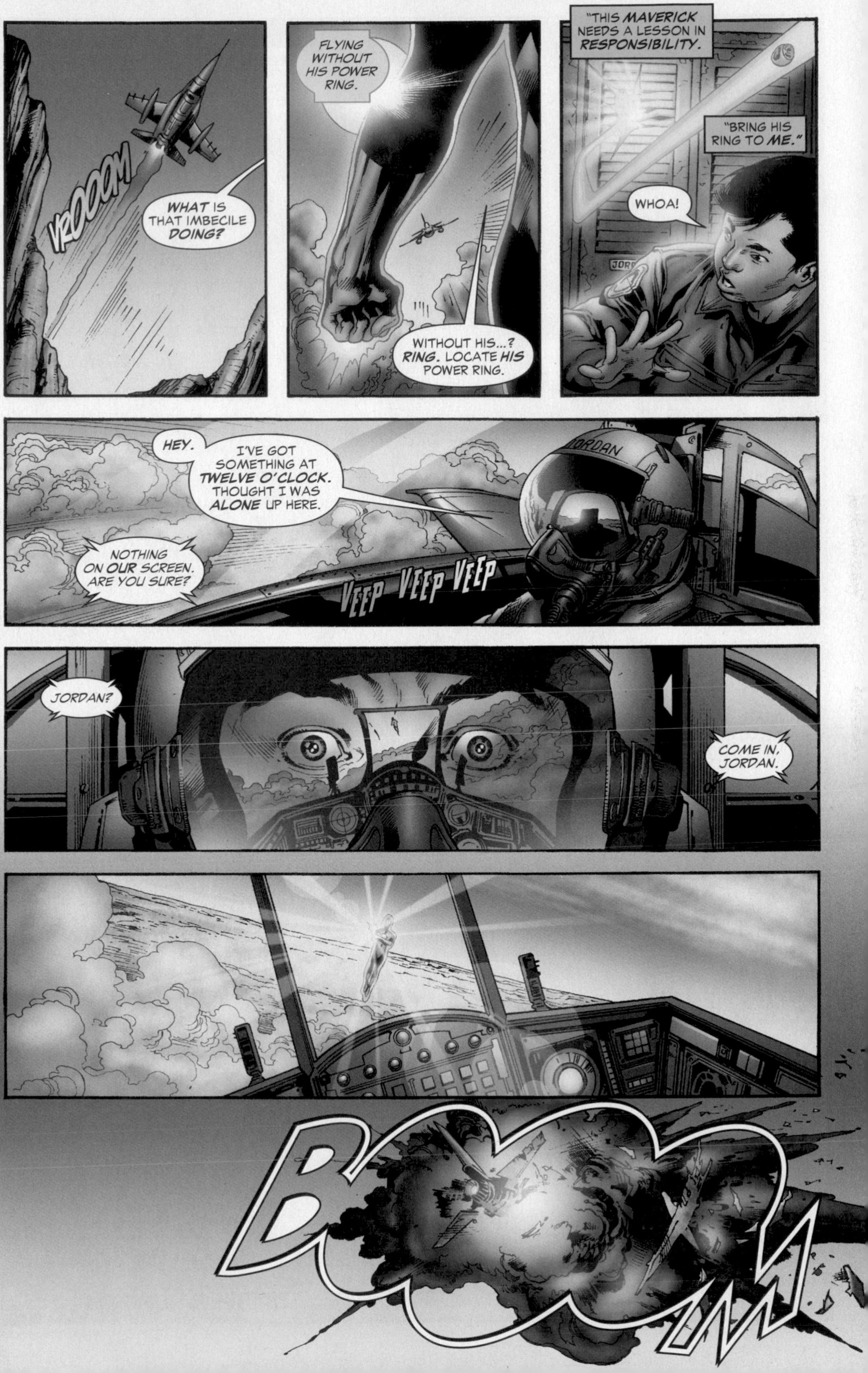
VROOOM
WHAT IS THAT IMBECILE DOING?
FLYING WITHOUT HIS POWER RING.
WITHOUT HIS...? RING. LOCATE HIS POWER RING.
"THIS MAVERICK NEEDS A LESSON IN RESPONSIBILITY.
"BRING HIS RING TO ME."
WHOA!
HEY.
I'VE GOT SOMETHING AT TWELVE O'CLOCK. THOUGHT I WAS ALONE UP HERE.
NOTHING ON OUR SCREEN. ARE YOU SURE?
VEEP VEEP VEEP
JORDAN?
COME IN, JORDAN.
BOOM

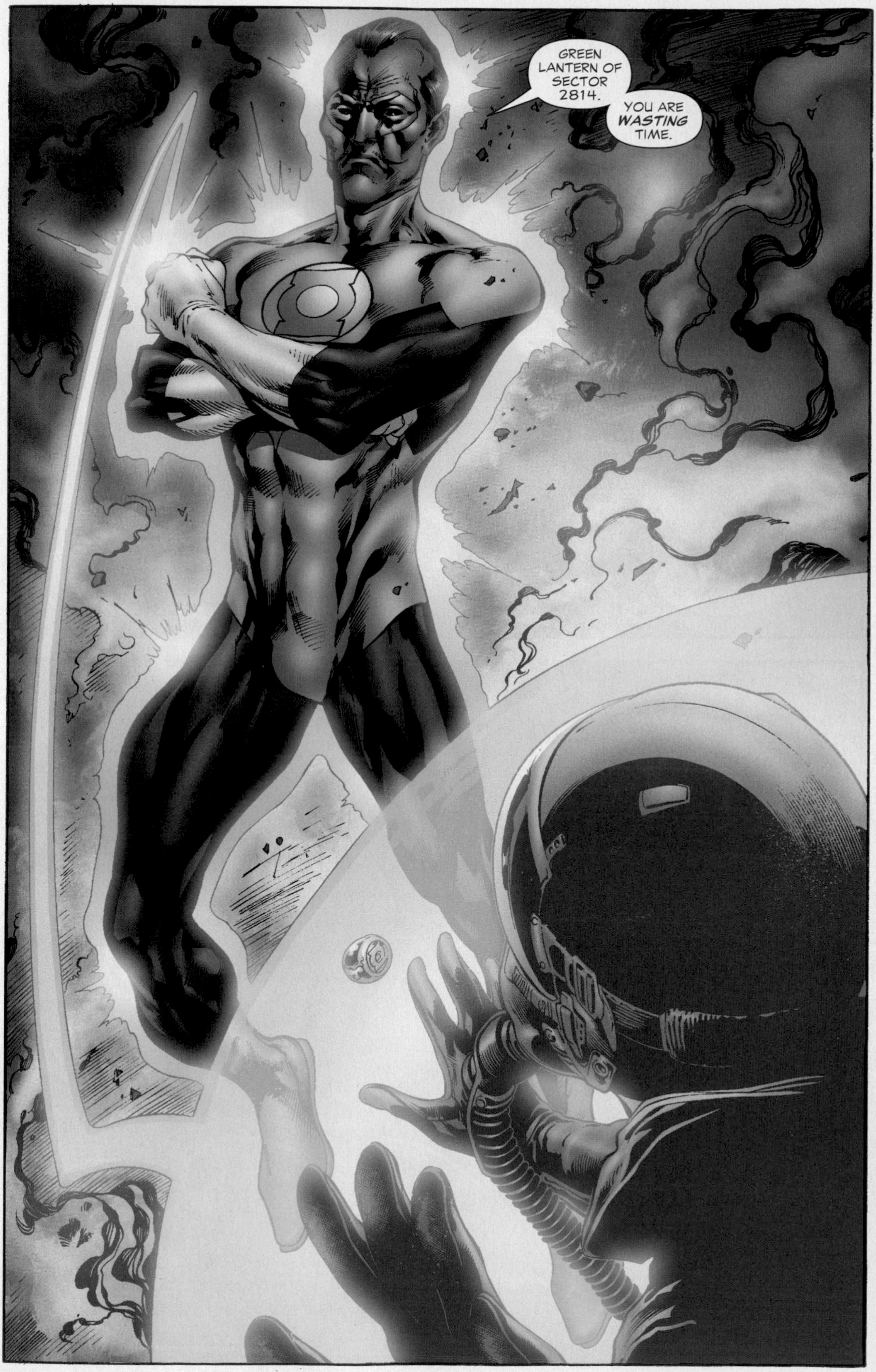
GREEN LANTERN OF SECTOR 2814.
YOU ARE WASTING TIME.

WHAT ARE YOU DOING?! *WHO* THE HELL *ARE* YOU?

I AM *SINESTRO.*

GREEN LANTERN OF *SECTOR 1417.*

IS THAT SUPPOSED TO *IMPRESS* ME?

I WOULDN'T REMEMBER UNTIL LATER. "SINESTRO" WAS ABIN SUR'S LAST WORD.

I NEVER THOUGHT IT WAS A NAME.

Hr. RING?

SECTOR 1417. THE MOST ORDERLY SECTOR IN ALL THE UNIVERSE.

AND I AM THE *GREATEST* GREEN LANTERN.

WHAT THE HELL HAPPENED UP THERE?

WE DON'T KNOW, MISS FERRIS.

HE JUST *DISAPPEARED.* AND WE CAN'T MAKE CONTACT.

...WHO'S GOING TO SHELL OUT THE *TWENTY MILLION* DOLLARS FOR THAT JET?

I DON'T *SEE* ANY POCKETS.

YOUR *TERRESTRIAL AFFAIRS* SHOULD BE OF *LITTLE* CONCERN, EARTHMAN. YOU ARE IN THE PRESENCE OF A *VETERAN*.

NEVER QUESTION A *SUPERIOR* OFFICER.

NEVER CHALLENGE THOSE MORE *POWERFUL* THAN *YOU*.

Um... *YEAH*.

THAT'S *NOT* GONNA WORK FOR *ME*.

DO YOU HAVE *ANY* IDEA WHAT YOU JUST *DID?* WHAT YOU JUST *COST* ME?

RING. CAN YOU *REBUILD* THE PLANE?

THE QUESTION SHOULDN'T BE POSED TO YOUR *RING*, IT SHOULD BE POSED TO *YOU*.

WHAT DOES *KILOWOG* TEACH YOU WHITE CIRCLES THESE DAYS?

HE TAUGHT ME THAT MY *DUTY* WAS TO LOCATE ANY *ALIENS* CAUSING *TROUBLE* AND KICK THEM *OFF* PLANET.

YOUR CONSTRUCTS ARE *WEAK.*

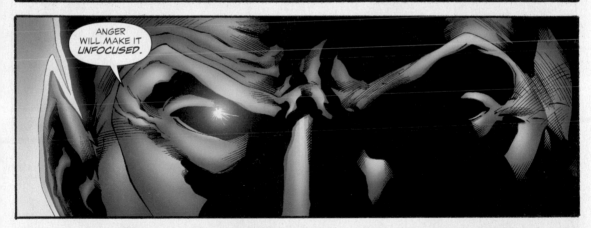

THEY'RE LACED WITH *ANGER.*

AND ALTHOUGH THE GUARDIANS BELIEVE *FEAR* CREATES *CRACKS* IN OUR *WILLPOWER*--

--ANGER WILL *DISTORT* IT.

ANGER WILL MAKE IT *UNFOCUSED.*

A GREEN LANTERN *NEEDS* TO BE *FOCUSED.*

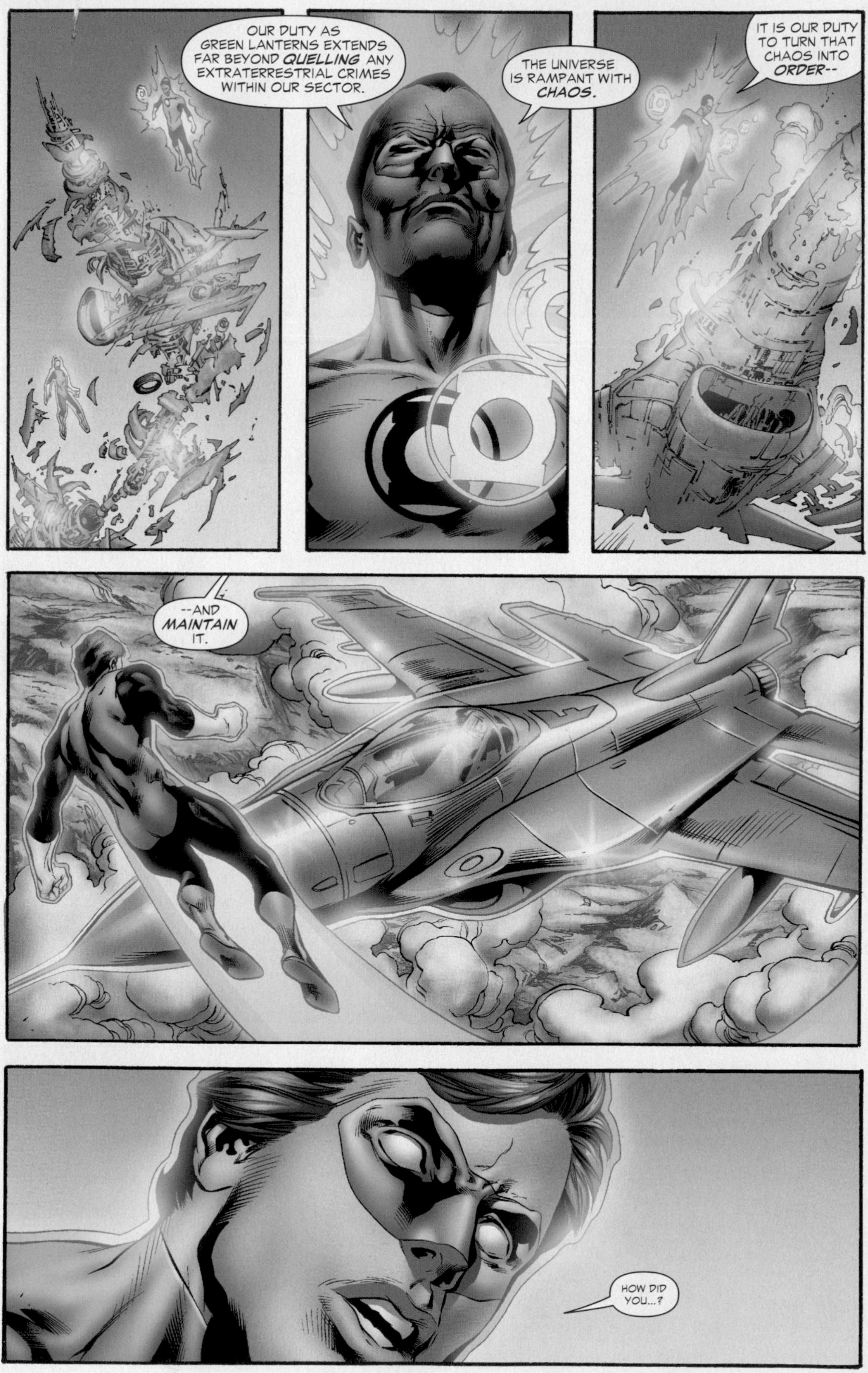
OUR DUTY AS GREEN LANTERNS EXTENDS FAR BEYOND QUELLING ANY EXTRATERRESTRIAL CRIMES WITHIN OUR SECTOR.
THE UNIVERSE IS RAMPANT WITH CHAOS.
IT IS OUR DUTY TO TURN THAT CHAOS INTO ORDER--
--AND MAINTAIN IT.
HOW DID YOU...?

I NEED TO GO.

GO? GO WHERE?

BACK TO MY *REAL* JOB.

YOU NEED MORE *TRAINING,* ROOKIE.

WHAT THE HELL ARE YOU DOING HERE *ANYWAY?* TOMAR-RE TOLD ME ALL OF US ARE SUPPOSED TO STAY IN OUR *OWN* SECTOR.

YES, THE GUARDIANS' TERRITORIAL EDICT DISSUADES FRATERNIZING AMONG THE CORPS.

BUT I HAVE MY ORDERS. AND THEY ARE FROM A MUCH *HIGHER* AUTHORITY THAN TOMAR-RE.

I'VE BEEN DISPATCHED TO THIS PRIMITIVE PLANET PLAGUED WITH POLITICAL BORDERS AND TERRESTRIAL WAR TO INVESTIGATE THE DEATH OF YOUR PREDECESSOR.

ABIN SUR CRASHED HIS SHIP IN THE CALIFORNIA DESERT.

WHY?

I DON'T KNOW. HE DIDN'T TELL--

GREEN LANTERN OF SPACE SECTOR 1417--MESSAGE FROM GREEN LANTERN 2814 WAITING.

WHAT? WHAT DID YOUR RING SAY?

I DON'T KNOW. MAYBE YOURS IS SCREWING WITH IT.

MESSAGE WAITING.

STAY OUT OF MY FLIGHT PATH, SINESTRO.

I DON'T BELIEVE IT.

WHAT?

LOOK.

EEERRRTT

OH, BOY.

WHAT THE HELL WAS *THAT?*

IT'S NOT WHAT IT LOOKS LIKE.

IT LOOKS LIKE YOU'RE PLAYING *GAMES,* MR. JORDAN.

PURPOSELY FLYING BELOW RADAR, REFUSING TO COMMUNICATE.

CAROL--

I MUST'VE BEEN *CRAZY* TO THINK THIS WAS A GOOD IDEA.

YOU'RE NOT *INSANE,* CAROL.

...OH, THIS IS WONDERFUL.

WHAT *UNIQUE* EXPERIENCES *THIS* ONE HAS.

HAL JORDAN. I SEE YOUR LIFE.

WHAT A *LIFE*--

--GREEN LANTERN!

...*REVENGE* WILL BE *MINE.*

COAST CITY
66 miles

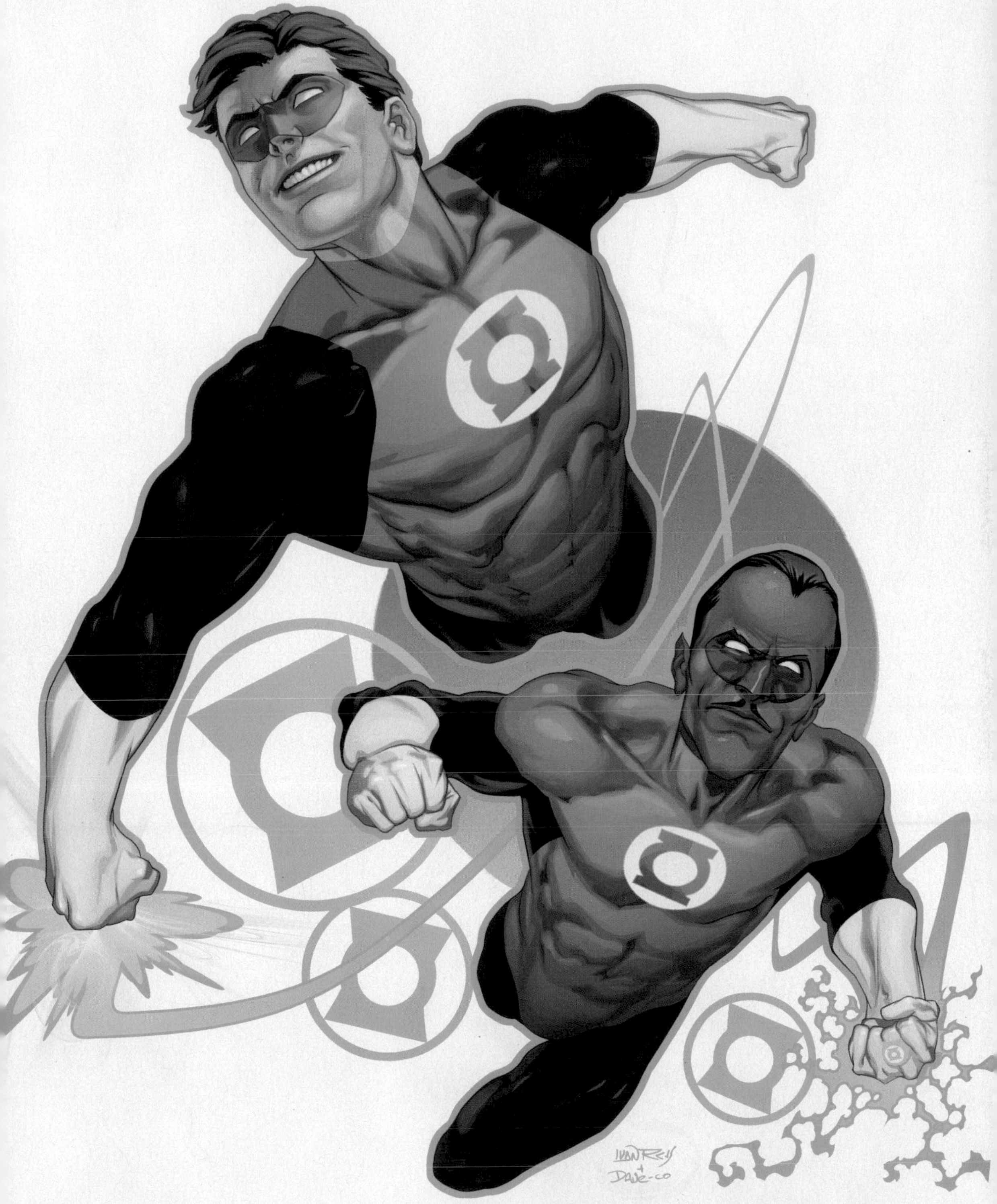
IVAN REIS
+
DAVE-CO

SECRET ORIGIN

BOOK FIVE

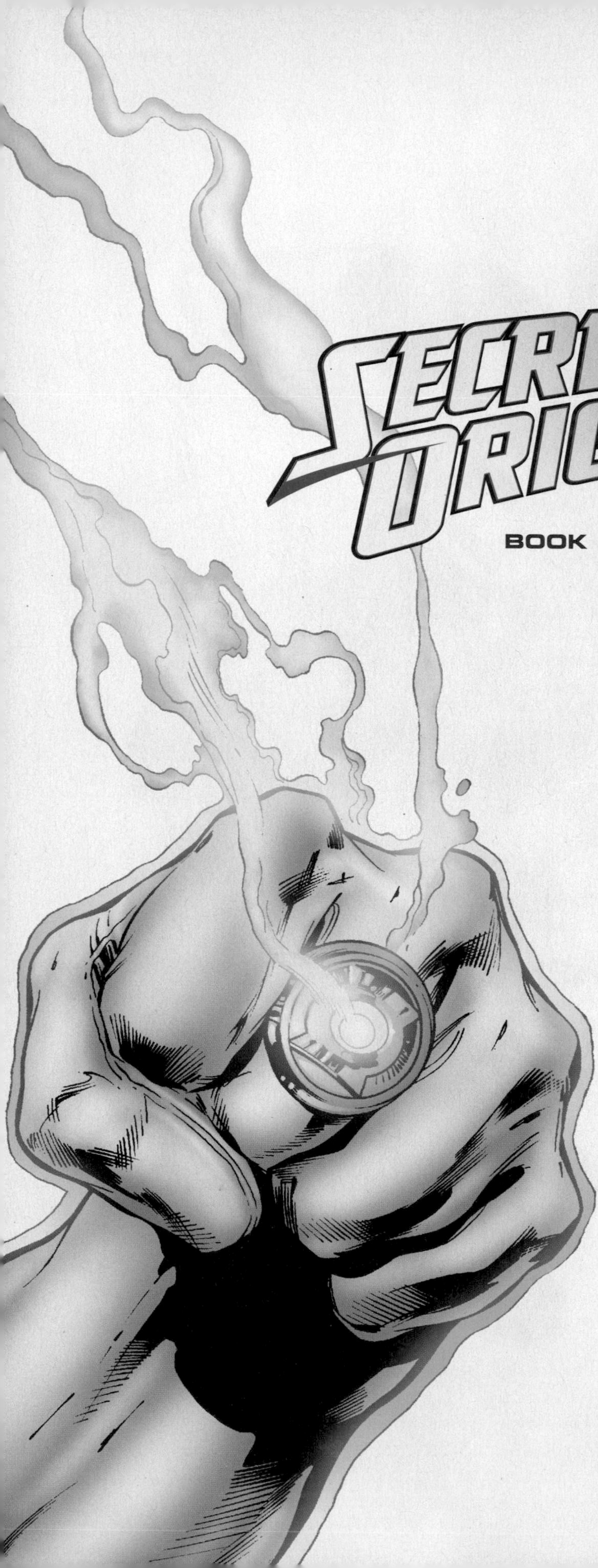

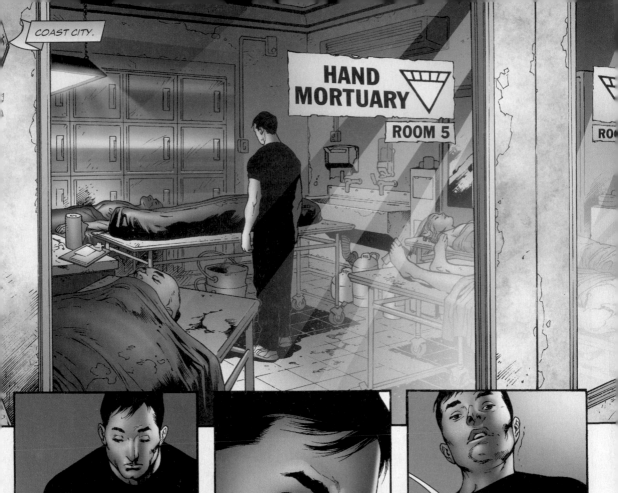

COAST CITY.

HAND MORTUARY

ROOM 5

RO

WILLIAM.

YOUR FATHER JUST FINISHED CLEANING THIS ONE UP!

I WASN'T D-D-DOING ANYTHING, MOM! I SWEAR!

HOW MANY TIMES HAVE WE TOLD YOU TO STAY *OUT* OF THE BASEMENT?

I KNOW, BUT...I JUST WANTED TO L-L-LOOK.

WHY? WHY CAN'T YOU BE A *GOOD CHRISTIAN* LIKE YOUR *BROTHERS?*

I DON'T KNOW.

YOU HAVE MET EXTRA-TERRESTRIALS.

LIFE FAR *BEYOND* OURS.

THEY GAVE YOU A *POWER RING.* A BAND OF *ENERGY* AND *WILL.*

THEY CALLED IT THE GREATEST *WEAPON* IN THE UNIVERSE.

THE GREATEST *TECHNOLOGY.*

HA HA HA HA HA!

GIVE ME THIS *EMERALD MIRACLE,* HAL JORDAN. GIVE...

...NO.

NO, YOU CAN'T HAVE *HER.*

NO, CAROL FERRIS IS MINE.

CHRISTINE FERRIS
Loving Wife and Mother

SHE'S *MINE!*

I DON'T... *WANT* HER, HAMMOND.

A RUDIMENTARY TELEPATH LIKE THAT ACTUALLY *DISRUPTED* YOUR CONCENTRATION?

GREEN... LANTERN?

COME, ROOKIE.

WOOOSHH

...HAL?

YOU WILL CONTAIN THIS POWER OF THE BLACK FOR MY JOURNEY *HOME.*

NOW TAKE ME TO ITS HOST.

KRIK

TAKE ME TO *WILLIAM* HAND.

KRIK
KRIK
KRIK
KRIK

...REMOVING THE AIR FROM HIS LUNGS WAS A SIMPLE SOLUTION. WITHOUT IT, HIS TELEKINETIC BRAIN HAD NO CHOICE BUT TO SHUT DOWN.

I WOULD'VE THOUGHT OF THAT.

I DON'T THINK YOU THINK OF ANYTHING, JORDAN. DO YOU EVER PLAN AHEAD?

FOR EXAMPLE: FLYING TODAY.

IF I HAD NOT BROUGHT YOU YOUR RING, YOU WOULD HAVE DIED.

AND YOU WOULD'VE BEEN A MURDERER. YOU WERE THE ONE IN MY FLIGHT PATH.

WHY WOULD YOU EVEN FLY WITHOUT YOUR RING?

SOMEHOW, I DOUBT THAT.

I FORGOT IT.

FINE. LESSON LEARNED. CAN YOU GO NOW? I'VE HAD ALL THE TRAINING I NEED.

KILOWOG TAUGHT ME HOW TO RING SLING.

POORLY.

SALAAK HAD ME TEST THE CHARGING LIMITATIONS.

SALAAK'S "TESTS" ARE WORTHLESS WHEN FACED WITH THE REALITY OF A "DEAD" RING.

AND EVERYONE WARNED ME ABOUT THE YELLOW IMPURITY.

OF COURSE, NO ONE CAN ACTUALLY TELL ME WHAT THAT IS OR WHY IT'S THERE.

IT DOESN'T EVEN MAKE ANY SENSE.

YELLOW.

Hh.

WHAT?

I HAVE BEEN ATTEMPTING TO SEEK THE TRUTH ABOUT THE YELLOW IMPURITY FOR YEARS. I WAS SUSPENDED AFTER ACCUSING THE GUARDIANS OF PUTTING IT THERE THEMSELVES WHEN I WAS A ROOKIE.

DID YOU KNOW HIM?

ABIN SUR WAS *MY* MENTOR.

I SUPPOSE I QUESTIONED HIM AND DISRESPECTED HIM AS MUCH AS YOU DO ME.

HE SHOWED ME HOW TO TEMPER THAT. AND WHY IT WAS NECESSARY FOR A MEMBER OF THE GREEN LANTERN CORPS.

SO HE TOLD YOU TO SHUT UP AND PLAY GOOD SOLDIER?

OF COURSE NOT. I AM AN INDIVIDUALISTIC THINKER, AS YOU ARE. I'D NEVER BELONGED TO A GROUP LIKE THE CORPS BEFORE.

SO I HAD NEVER LEARNED HOW TO *TRUST* THE BEINGS AROUND ME.

IN PART, THAT'S WHERE MY QUESTIONING CAME FROM.

HE HELPED ME LEARN TO TRUST MY FELLOW CORPSMAN. THANKFULLY, IT DIDN'T CHANGE MY DRIVE TO SEEK THE TRUTH OR MY DETERMINATION TO ARGUE AGAINST THE THEOLOGIES I DISAGREE WITH.

THEN WHAT *DID* IT HELP YOU DO, SINESTRO?

SINESTRO. GREEN LANTERN 1417 REGISTERED IN DIRECT VICINITY. MESSAGE 22 UNLOCKED.

I REALIZE I HAVE NOT BEEN AS RIGHTEOUS AND EFFECTIVE AN OFFICER LIKE YOU OF LATE.

BUT THIS TEACHER FEARS **NOT** BEING SURPASSED BY HIS STUDENT.

YOUR SUCCESS IS ALL I HOPE FOR, SINESTRO.

I HAVE LEARNED THE **SECRETS** OF LIFE.

AND TO UNDERSTAND THE SEVERITY OF MY MISSION IS TO UNDERSTAND THE GREATEST **TRAGEDY** THAT HAS EVER BEFALLEN THE UNIVERSE.

A CRIME SO HORRENDOUS AND UNFATHOMABLE, IT IS MYTH.

LONG BEFORE THE GUARDIANS OF THE UNIVERSE RECRUITED SENTIENT LIFE FORMS INTO THE GREEN LANTERN CORPS, THEY CREATED A DIFFERENT POLICE FORCE.

ONE THEY BELIEVED WOULD NEVER BE MANIPULATED BY EMOTION. THE GUARDIANS SAW EMOTION AS A WEAKNESS IN INTELLIGENT LIFE.

THEY CONSTRUCTED THOUSANDS OF ARTIFICIAL SOLDIERS. MANHUNTERS. THEY DISPATCHED THEM ACROSS THE UNIVERSE TO MAINTAIN ORDER.

FOR EONS, THEY DID JUST THAT.

UNTIL THE MASSACRE.

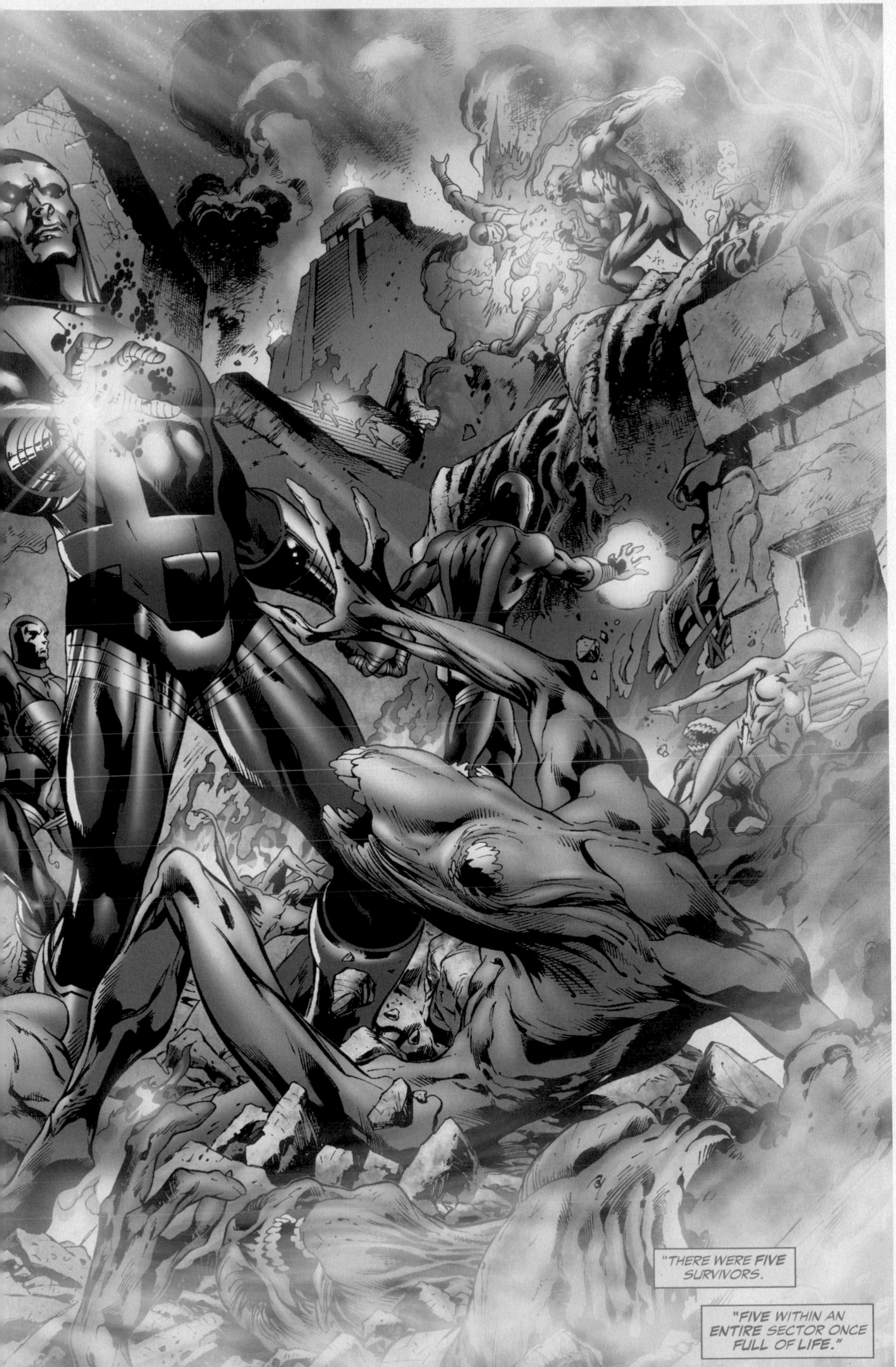
"THERE WERE FIVE SURVIVORS.
"FIVE WITHIN AN ENTIRE SECTOR ONCE FULL OF LIFE."

THOSE FIVE BECAME KNOWN AS THE FIVE INVERSIONS. A TERRORIST CELL BENT ON THE DESTRUCTION OF THE GUARDIANS OF THE UNIVERSE.

CHIEF AMONG THEM, ATROCITUS.

IT WAS FORETOLD, THAT POWER WOULD BE FOUND ON EARTH. I KNOW YOU DO NOT BELIEVE THESE PROPHECIES, SINESTRO, NOR DO THE GUARDIANS. BUT I ASK, IN THE NAME OF OUR FRIENDSHIP, TRUST ME.

ALONG WITH QULL, THEY SOUGHT THE INNER POWERS OF THE UNIVERSE. WITH THEIR RITUALS AND SACRIFICES, THEY PEERED INTO THE DEEPEST DEPTHS OF THE FUTURE.

AND THEY SAW DARKNESS.

A BLACK SO DEVOID OF LIFE, EVEN THE GUARDIANS' LIGHT COULD NOT PENETRATE IT.

THEY SEEK TO TAKE THIS DARKNESS FOR THEMSELVES AND TURN IT AGAINST US.

YOU MUST STOP THEM FROM UNLEASHING THIS DARKNESS.

IT WILL DESTROY THE UNIVERSE.

HE LOOKED... SCARED--

WHAT?

WHEN YOU SPOKE TO ABIN SUR, DID YOU SEE ANOTHER BODY?

ANOTHER BODY, JORDAN?

ABIN SUR WAS THE ONLY ONE I SAW IN THE SHIP. BUT HE WAS TORE UP PRETTY BAD. I THOUGHT IT WAS FROM THE CRASH. I DIDN'T THINK IT WAS BY SOMEBODY.

IT WAS.

ATROCITUS SURVIVED.

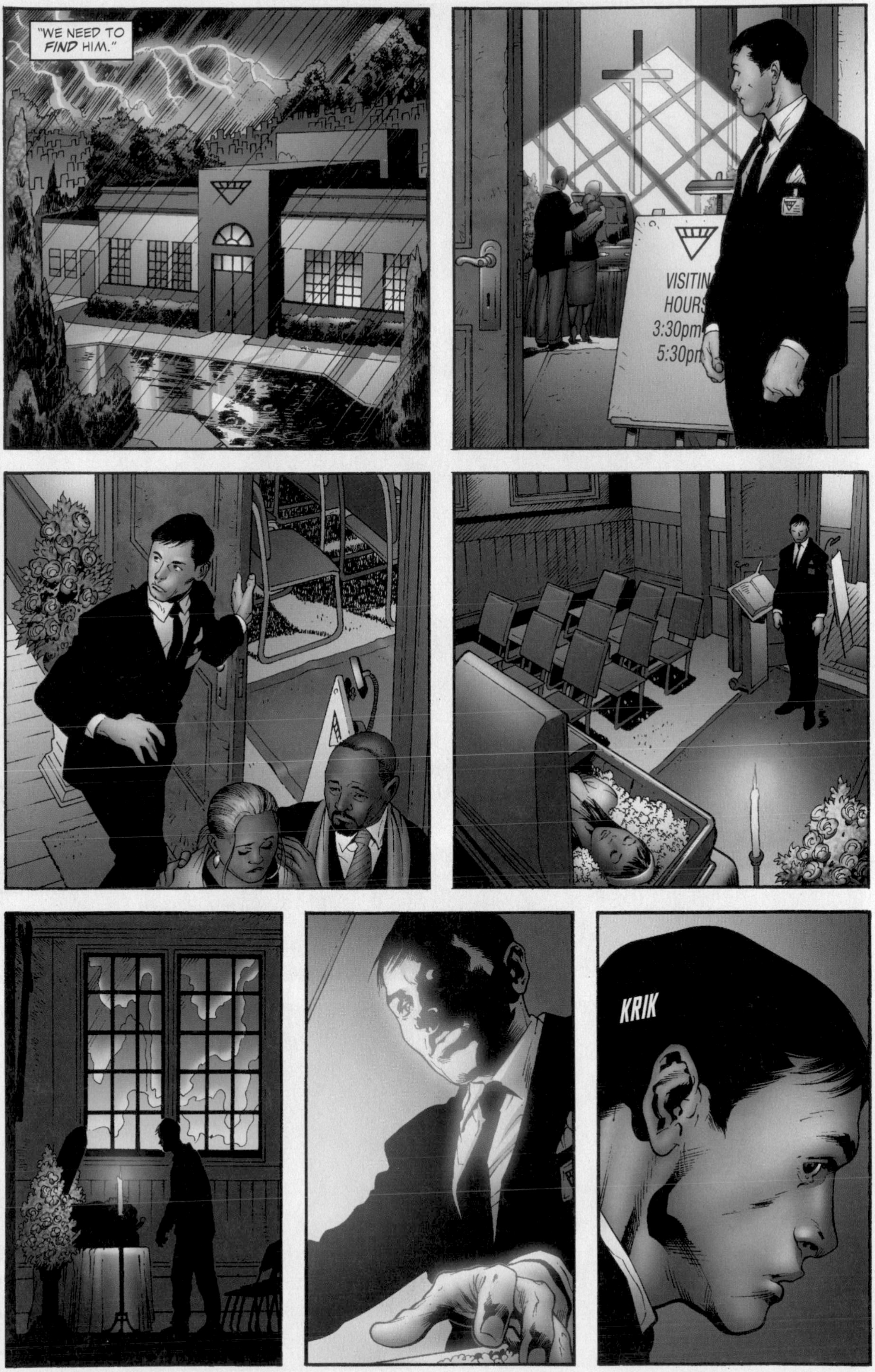
"WE NEED TO FIND HIM."
VISITING HOURS 3:30pm 5:30pm
KRIK

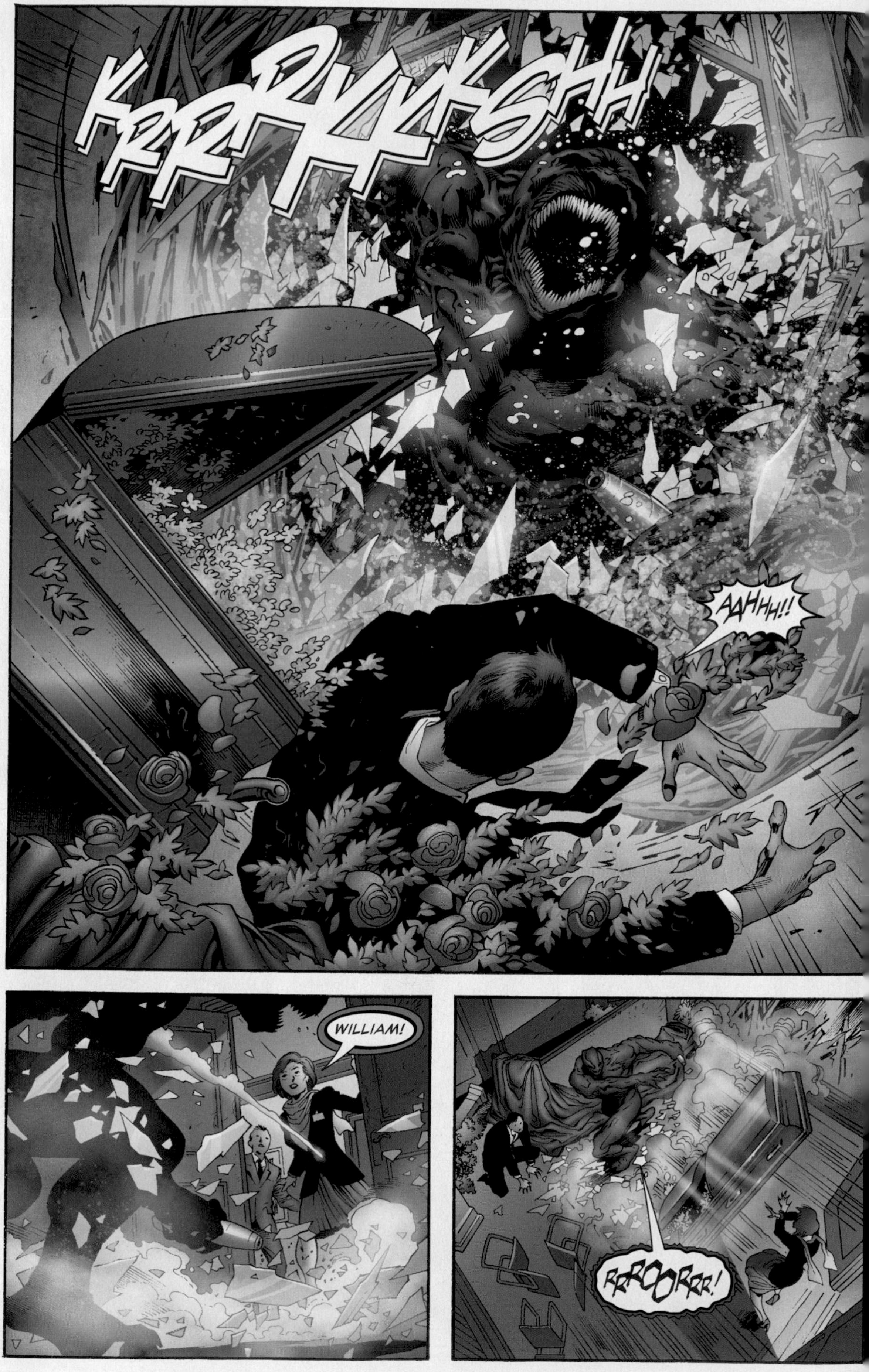
KRRRUKSHH
AAHHH!!
WILLIAM!
RRRROORRR!

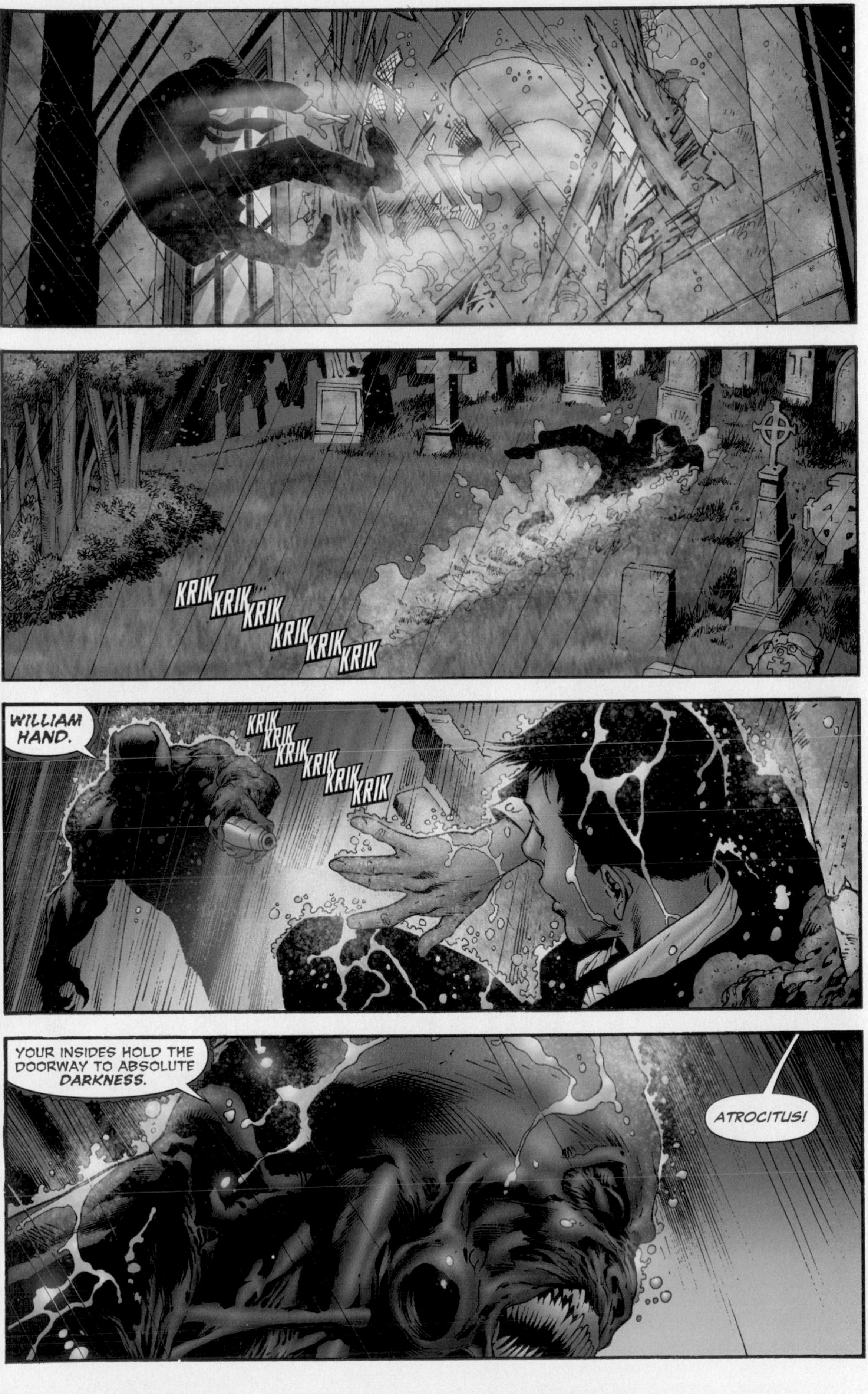
KRIK KRIK KRIK KRIK KRIK KRIK
WILLIAM HAND.
KRIK KRIK KRIK KRIK KRIK KRIK
YOUR INSIDES HOLD THE DOORWAY TO ABSOLUTE DARKNESS.
ATROCITUS!

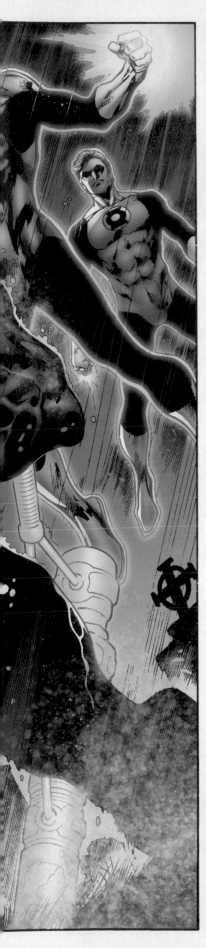

FEEL MY **RAGE.**

KID! GET OUT OF HERE!

RUN, **DAMMIT!**

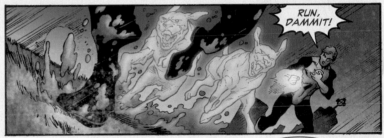

NNGGFF!

WARNING. POWER LEVELS DEPLETING.

POWER LEVELS AT 38.7%

SINESTRO? WHAT'S... HAPPENING?

HE'S BUILT A COSMIC **DIVINING ROD.**

IT CAN **LOCATE** POWER--

--AND IT CAN **TAKE** IT.

WARNING. POWER LEVELS APPROACHING 0.0%

GET ON YOUR **FEET,** JORDAN.

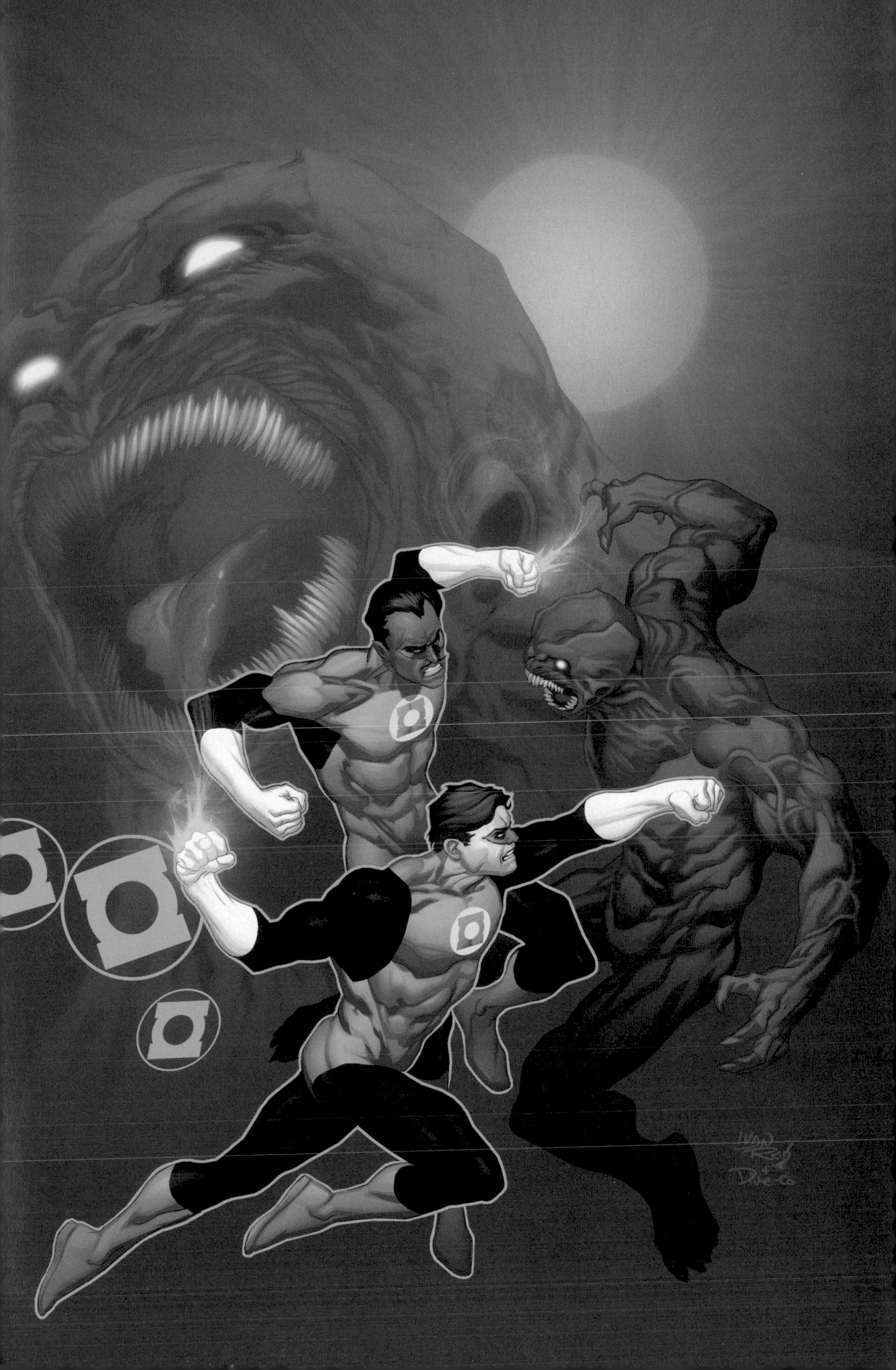

SECRET ORIGIN

BOOK SIX

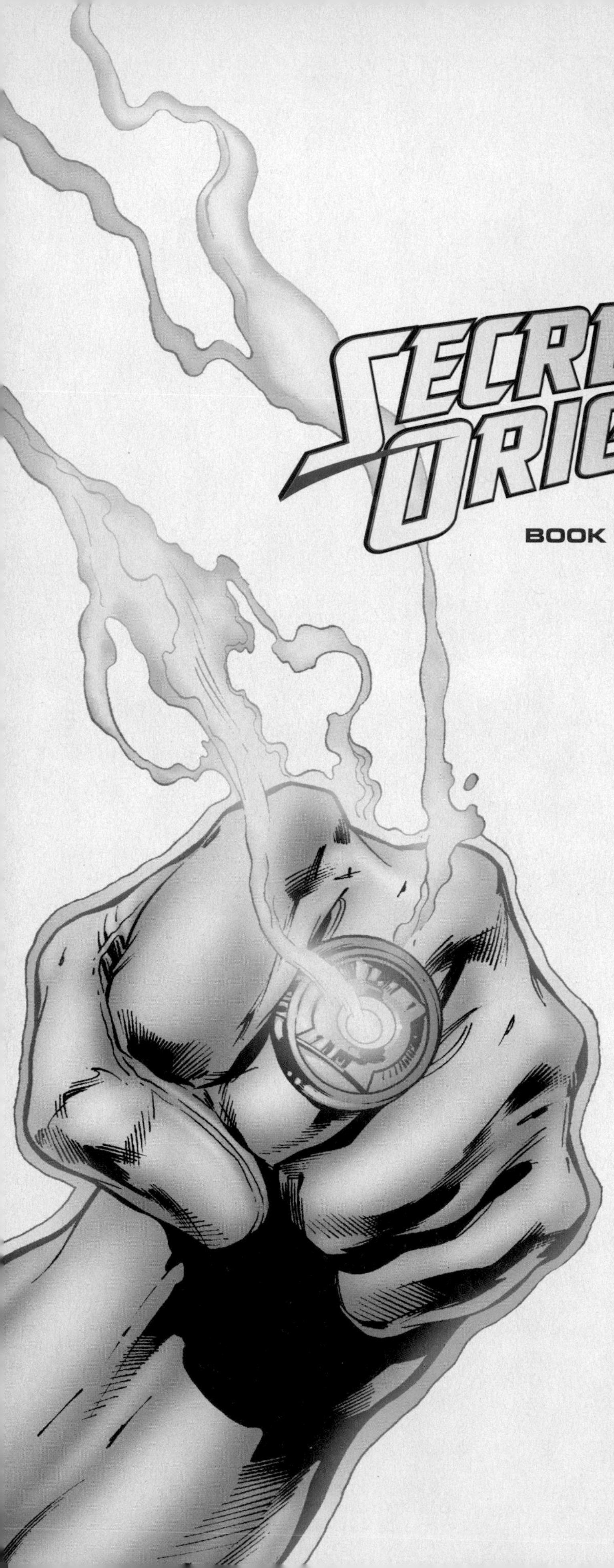

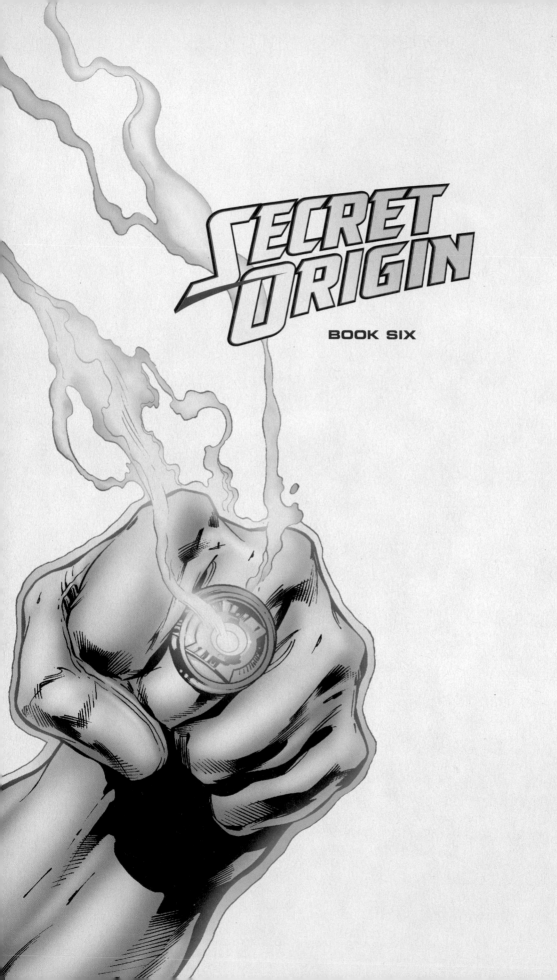

...O ONE ELSE HAD TO WATCH ...HEIR FATHER DIE IN FRONT ...F THEIR EYES.

THAT'S WHAT I THOUGHT MOST OF MY LIFE.

I THOUGHT I WAS ALONE.

GROWING UP, THE PILOTS WHO KNEW DAD WOULD LOOK AT ME WITH PITY WHEN I'D BEG TO GO ON A FLIGHT.

THEY ALWAYS REFUSED.

WHEN I FLEW MYSELF, THEY WOULD LOOK AT ME WITH ANNOYANCE, THINKING I WAS BREAKING THE RULES AND PUSHING THE BOUNDARIES UNTIL THE RIVETS POPPED OFF MY WINGS OUT OF ARROGANCE.

MARTIN JORDAN

JESSICA JORDAN

NO ONE EVER LOOKED AT ME WITH ANY KIND OF UNDERSTANDING.

NO ONE KNEW WHY I WAS THE WAY I WAS.

NOT UNTIL I MET SINESTRO.

JORDAN, FALL BACK.

I'VE NEVER RUN FROM A FIGHT BEFORE, SINESTRO. NOT GONNA START NOW.

YOUR RING IS EMPTY, LANTERN.

YOU ARE NOTHING TO ME.

SLLAASSHH

GIVE ME YOUR BEST--

GET DOWN

BOOM

IDIOT!

SLAM!!!

KRIK KRIK KRIK KRIK

YOU ARE STILL HERE, BOY.

DOORWAY TO THE BLACK.

WILLIAM HAND...

...YOUR INSIDES HOLD THE POWER THAT WILL DESTROY THE GUARDIANS OF THE UNIVERSE.

YOU ARE THE INCUBATOR OF DEATH TO ALL!

"FALLING BACK" IS A *MILITARY TACTIC*, JORDAN.

IT IS *NOT* A SIGN OF *FEAR*.

STANDING IN THE *LINE OF FIRE* WITH A *DRAINED* POWER RING, HOWEVER, IS A SIGN OF *STUPIDITY*.

YOU SHOULD BE *DEAD*.

YOU'RE NOT THE *FIRST* ONE TO TELL ME THAT.

I'M *SHOCKED*. THAT DEVICE ATROCITUS IS HOLDING IS CAPABLE OF *REMOVING* AND *CONTAINING* THE ENERGY WITHIN OUR RINGS.

WE NEED TO KEEP *CLEAR* OF IT AND WE NEED TO *RECHARGE*.

WHAT ARE YOU DOING?

RECALLING MY *POWER BATTERY*.

DON'T TELL ME SALAAK DIDN'T *EDUCATE* YOU ON CONFINED POCKET DIMENSIONS AND THE STORAGE OF PERSONAL CHARGING UNITS.

I KEEP MINE IN MY LOCKER.

YOU'VE REDEFINED THE WORD *CARELESS* FOR ME, JORDAN.

SO *I* TAUGHT *YOU* SOMETHING?

JUST *LIGHT UP*, ROOKIE.

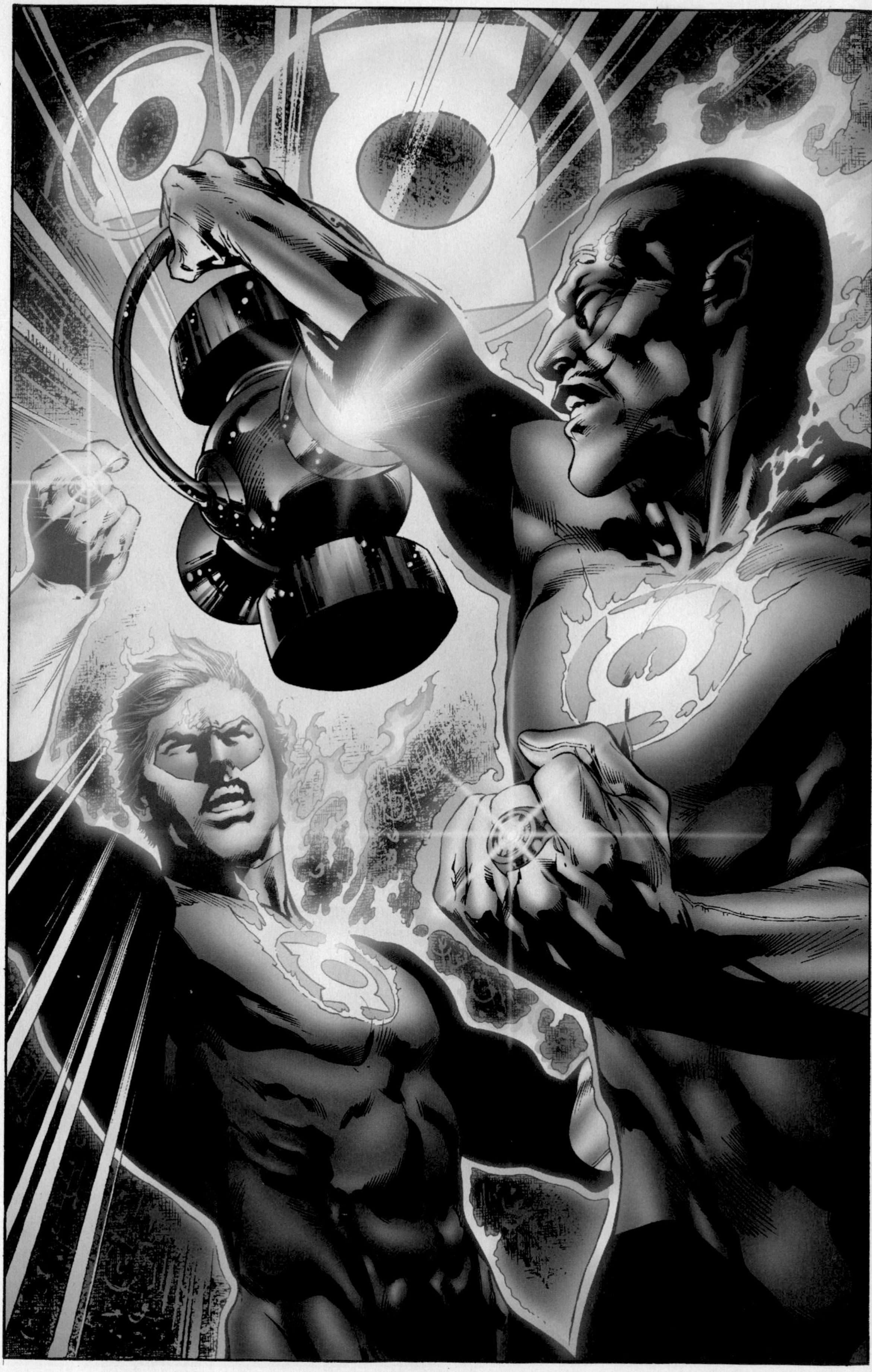

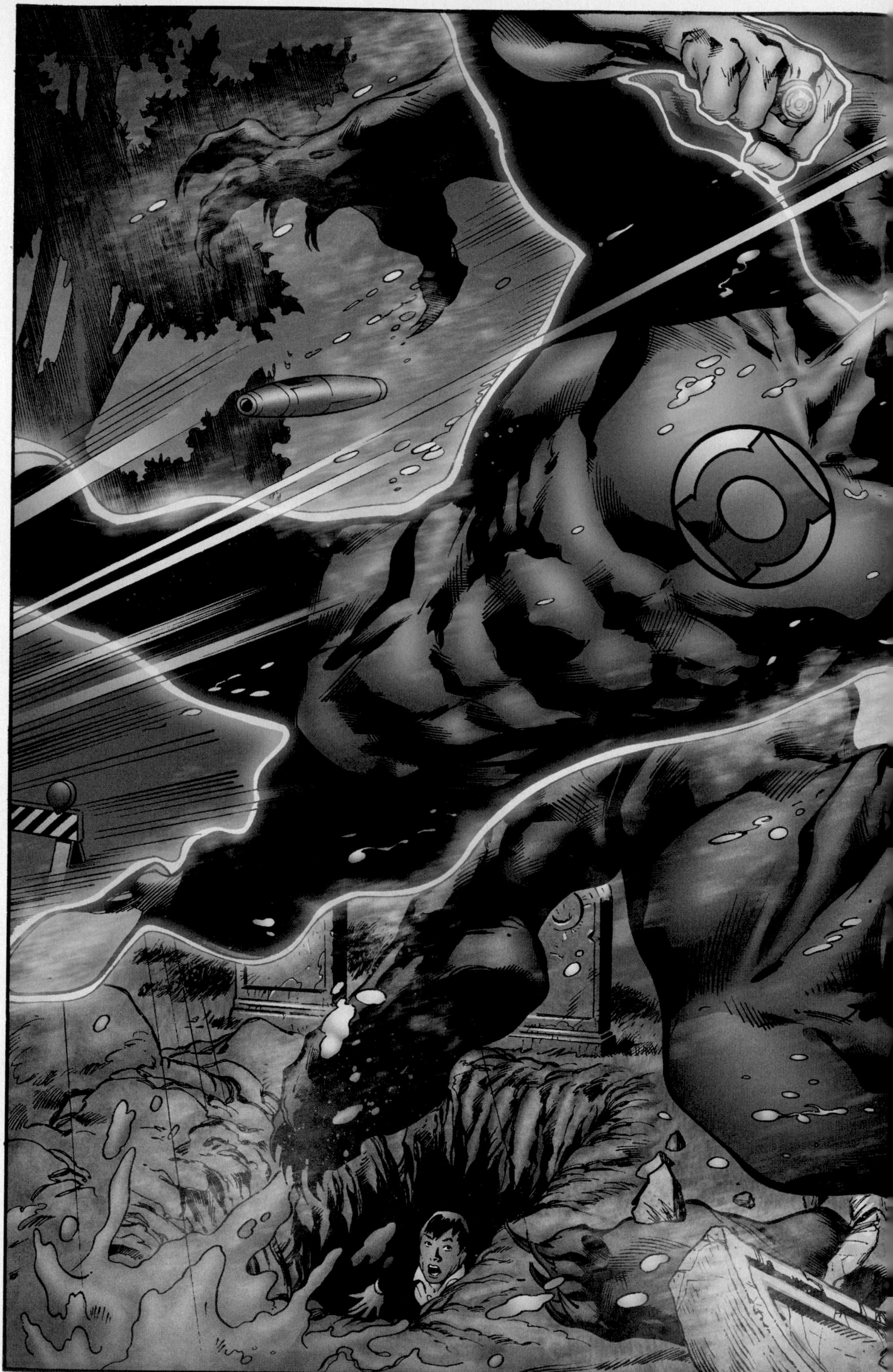

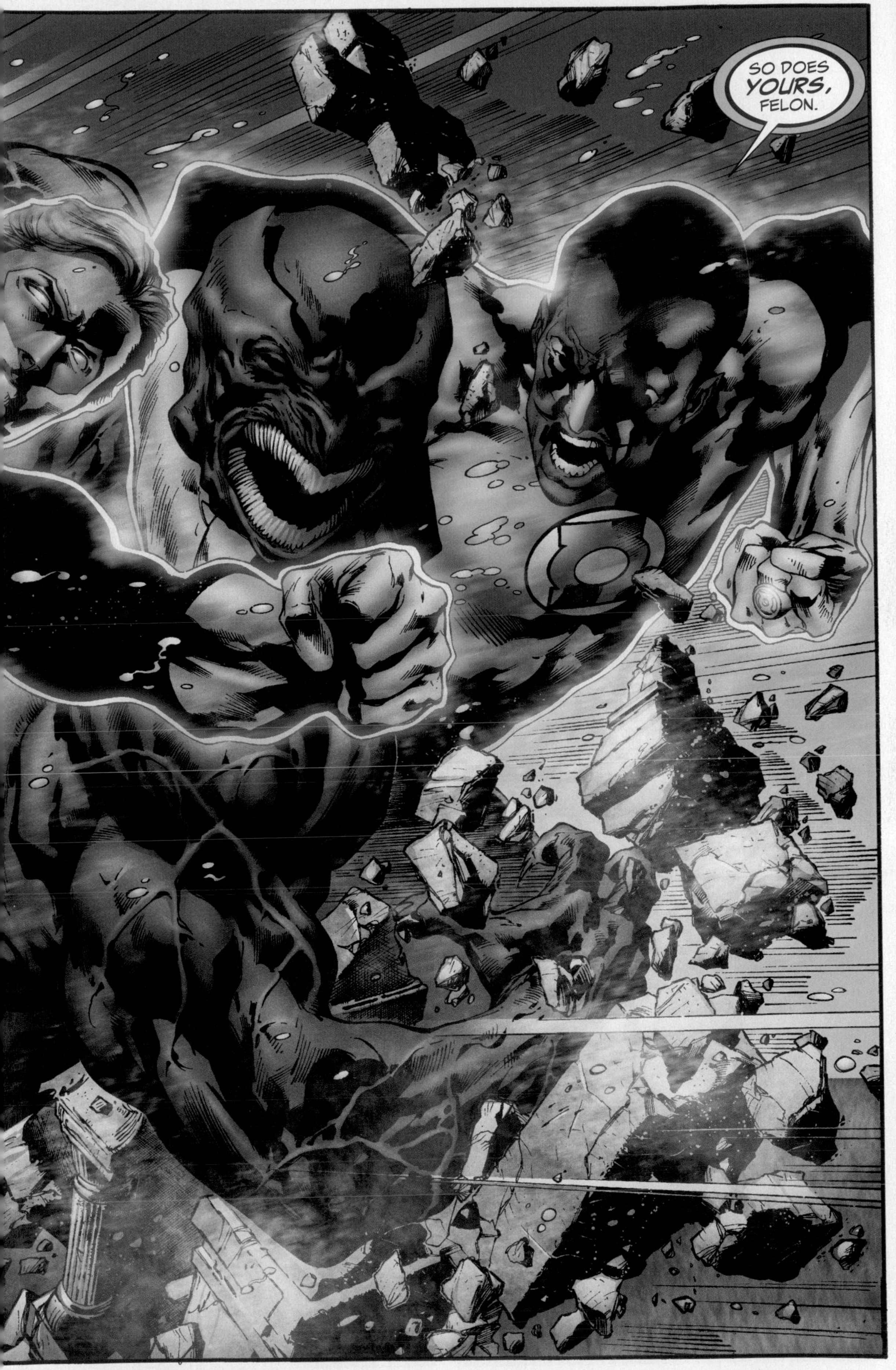
SO DOES YOURS, FELON.

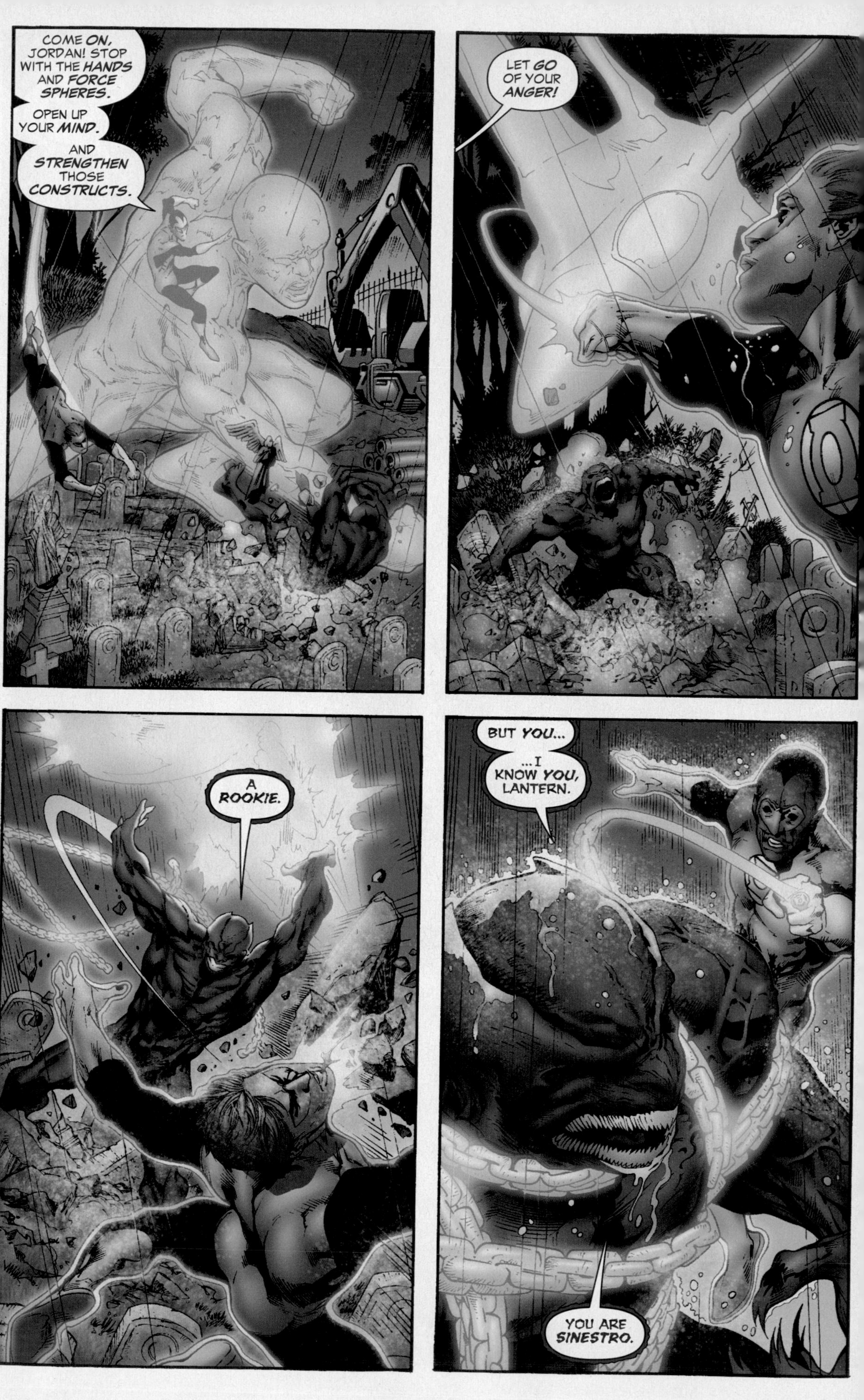
COME ON, JORDAN! STOP WITH THE HANDS AND FORCE SPHERES.
OPEN UP YOUR MIND.
AND STRENGTHEN THOSE CONSTRUCTS.
LET GO OF YOUR ANGER!
A ROOKIE.
BUT YOU...
...I KNOW YOU, LANTERN.
YOU ARE SINESTRO.

OUR PROPHECIES SAY YOU ARE THE *GREATEST* OF THEM ALL.

THEY SAY IF *ANYONE* IS TO OPPOSE OUR *REVENGE*, IT IS *YOU.*

Nn...

BUT THEY ALSO SAY YOU HAVE A *WEAKNESS.*

LIKE *ALL* OF THE GUARDIANS' TERRORISTS.

I WILL BATHE IN YOUR BLOOD, *"GREAT ONE."*

NO!

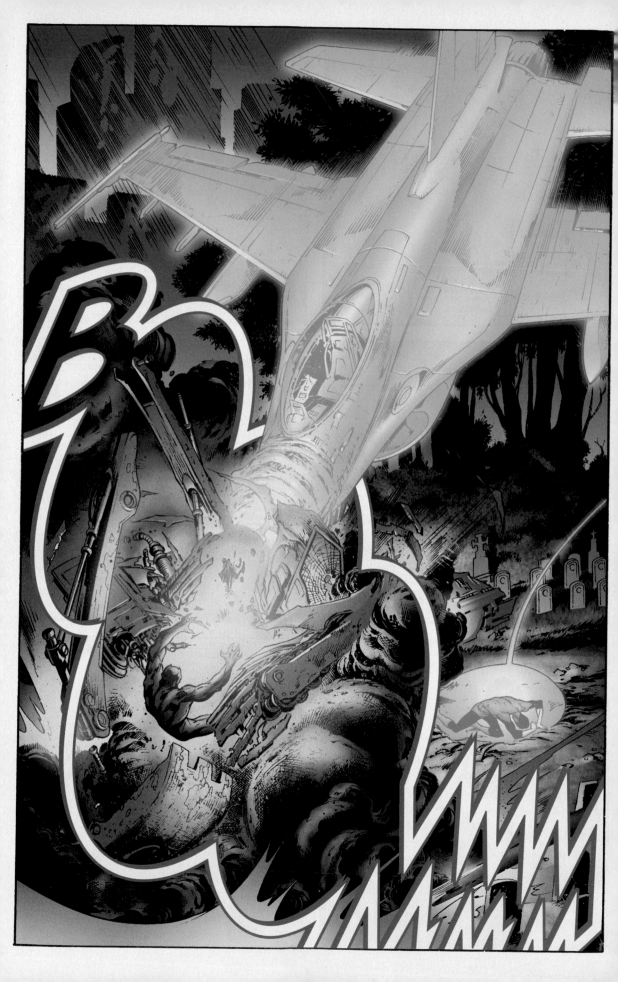

YELLOW...?

...THAT WAS...NOT POSSIBLE...

YOU KNOW MY NAME, ATROCITUS?

GOOD.

TELL THE OTHER *FOUR* OF THE *INVERSIONS* WHO THEY HAVE TO *FEAR*.

GHOOOMMM

SINESTRO. THE *GREATEST* GREEN LANTERN OF THEM *ALL*.

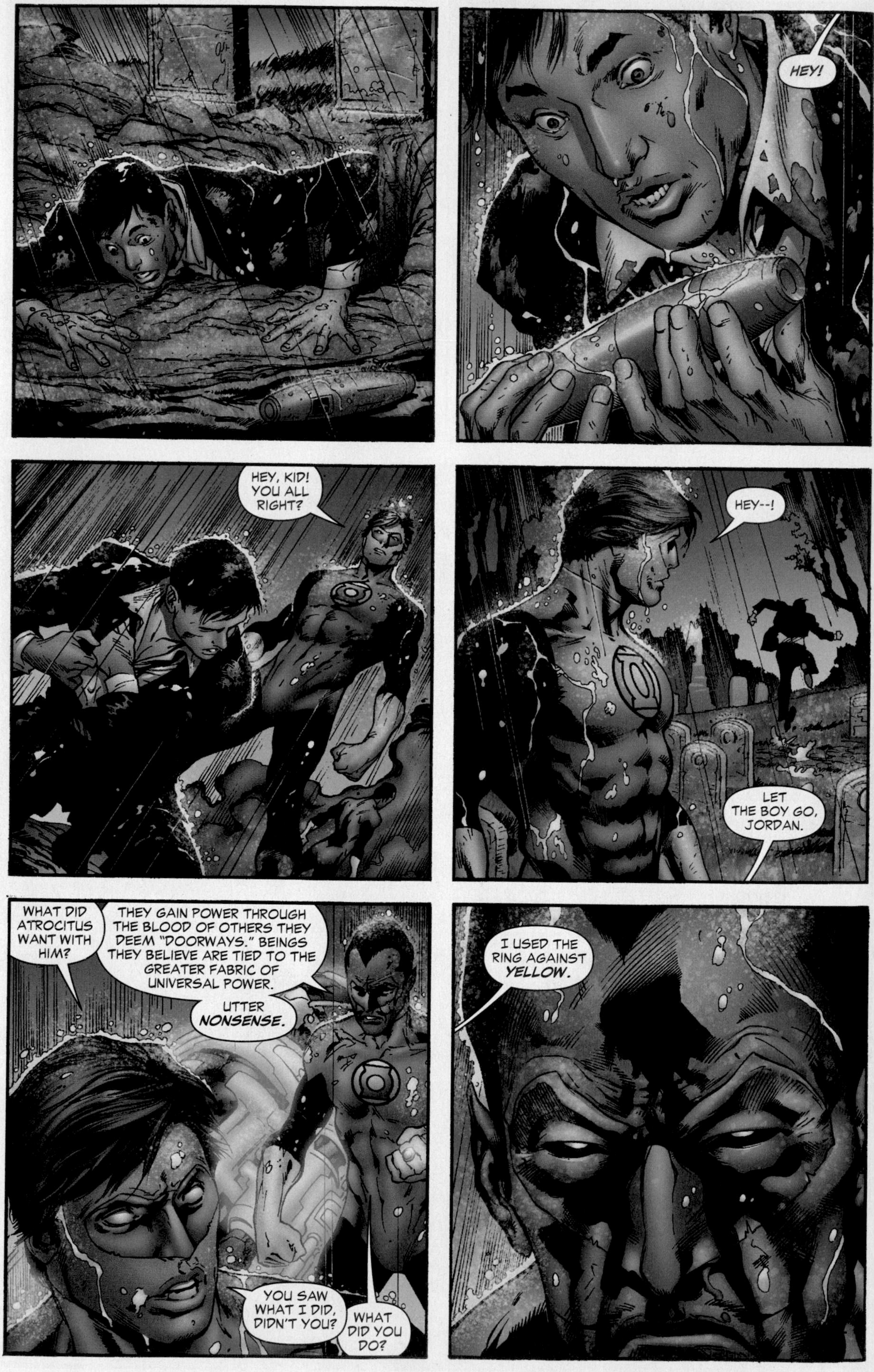
HEY!
HEY, KID! YOU ALL RIGHT?
HEY--!
LET THE BOY GO, JORDAN.
WHAT DID ATROCITUS WANT WITH HIM?
THEY GAIN POWER THROUGH THE BLOOD OF OTHERS THEY DEEM "DOORWAYS." BEINGS THEY BELIEVE ARE TIED TO THE GREATER FABRIC OF UNIVERSAL POWER.
UTTER NONSENSE.
YOU SAW WHAT I DID, DIDN'T YOU?
WHAT DID YOU DO?
I USED THE RING AGAINST YELLOW.

YOU ASSISTED IN THIS TAKEDOWN AND ARREST, JORDAN, WITHOUT YOUR RING SEEKING A REPLACEMENT.

YOU SURVIVED. THAT'S ENOUGH.

YOU DON'T BELIEVE ME?

YOU DON'T THINK I'VE TRIED TO PIERCE THE SPECTRUM BARRIER? IT IS *FUTILE*. EVEN FOR *ME*.

I *DID*.

ENOUGH.

#$%& YOU.

UNABLE TO TRANSLATE.

HFFF. YOU HAVE TO STAND OUT, DON'T YOU?

YOU CAN'T STAND TO BE UPSTAGED?

BEING A MEMBER OF THE CORPS, YOU'LL NEED TO GET *USED* TO IT.

WHAT MAKES ANYONE THINK I *WANT* TO BE AFTER ALL THIS?

YOU NEED TO GET HOLD OF YOUR *ANGER*, JORDAN. THAT'S WHAT ALMOST GOT YOU *KILLED* TODAY.

I DON'T KNOW *WHAT* OR *WHO* YOU'RE SO *ANGRY* WITH, BUT YOU CONTINUE TO DIRECT IT AT *ME*.

YOU NEED TO *GROW UP*, *DEAL* WITH IT AND GET *ON* WITH YOUR *LIFE*.

YOU KNOW WHAT? I WILL.

RING. TAKE ME TO *CARL FERRIS*.

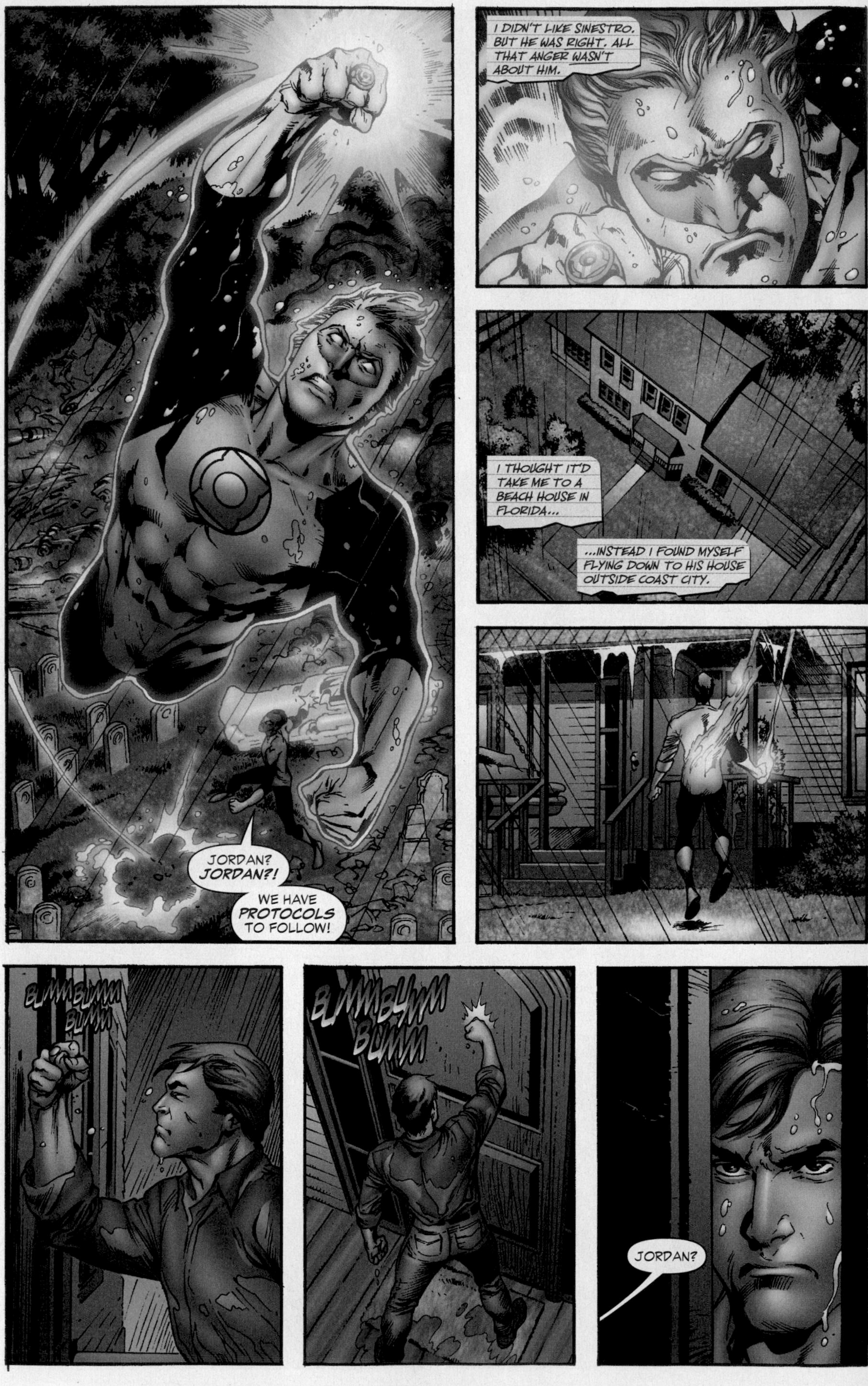
I DIDN'T LIKE SINESTRO. BUT HE WAS RIGHT. ALL THAT ANGER WASN'T ABOUT HIM.
JORDAN? JORDAN?!
WE HAVE PROTOCOLS TO FOLLOW!
I THOUGHT IT'D TAKE ME TO A BEACH HOUSE IN FLORIDA...
...INSTEAD I FOUND MYSELF FLYING DOWN TO HIS HOUSE OUTSIDE COAST CITY.
BLMM BLMM BLMM
BLMM BLMM BLMM
JORDAN?

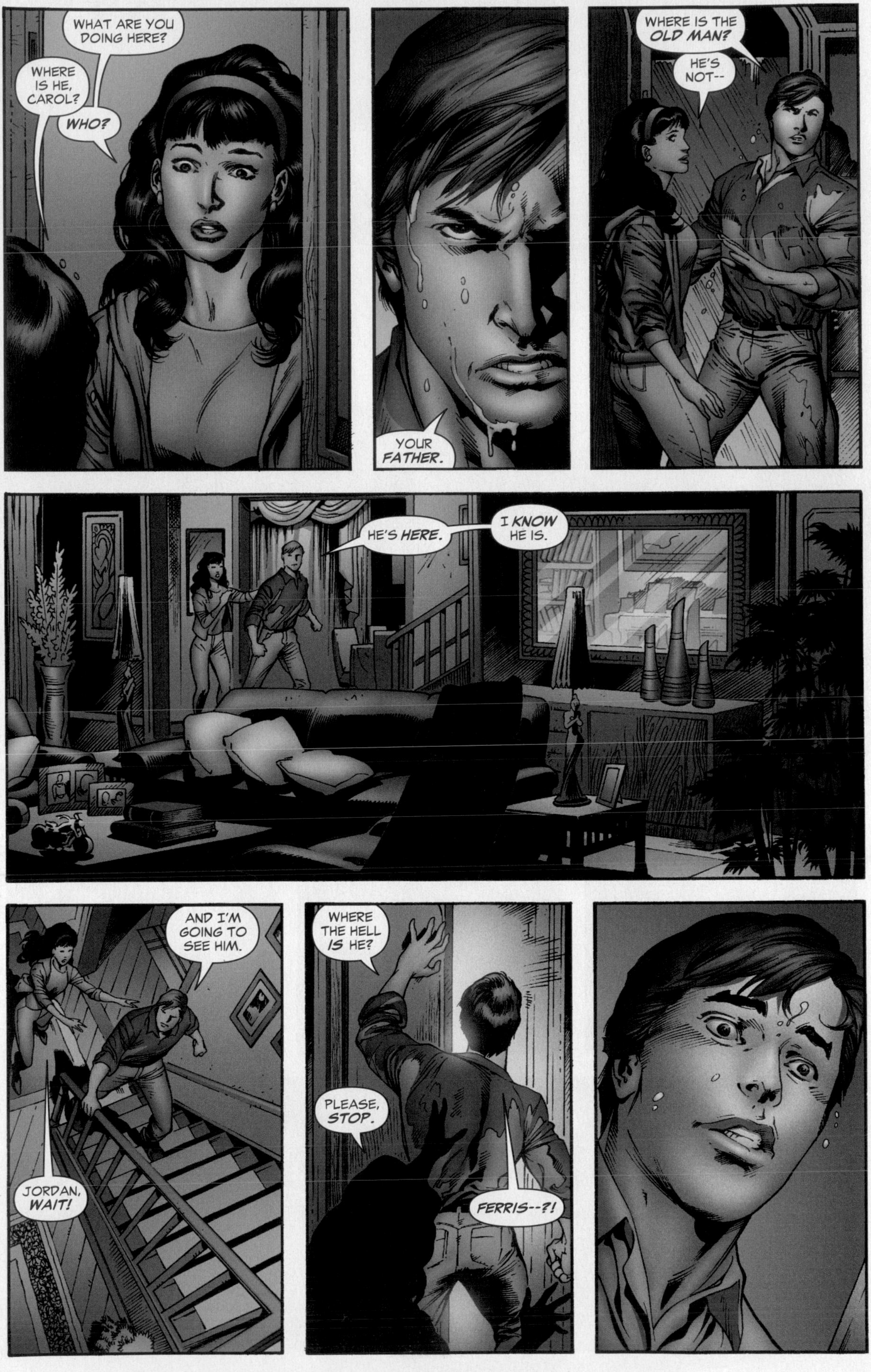
WHAT ARE YOU DOING HERE?
WHERE IS HE, CAROL?
WHO?
YOUR FATHER.
WHERE IS THE OLD MAN?
HE'S NOT--
HE'S HERE.
I KNOW HE IS.
AND I'M GOING TO SEE HIM.
JORDAN, WAIT!
WHERE THE HELL IS HE?
PLEASE, STOP.
FERRIS--?!

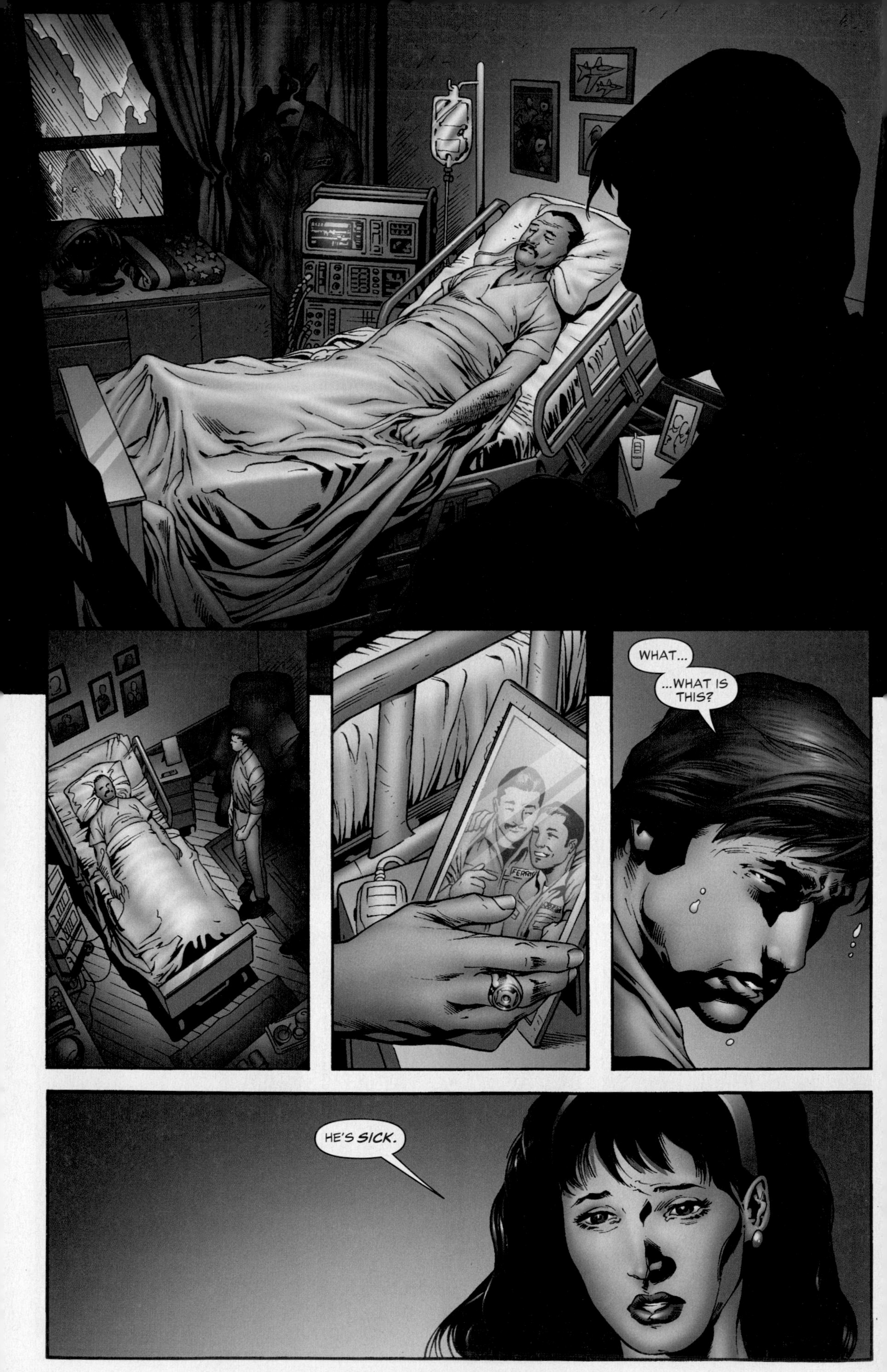
WHAT...
...WHAT IS THIS?
HE'S SICK.

YOUR FATHER WAS HIS *BEST FRIEND.*

AND AFTER THE CRASH...

...IT *TORE* HIM UP INSIDE. AND OVER THE YEARS, THE *GUILT* TOOK ITS TOLL.

HE WAS NEVER GOLFING ON PEBBLE BEACH?

HE'S NEVER PLAYED GOLF IN HIS LIFE.

LAST YEAR, WHEN HE GOT TOO SICK TO GET OUT OF BED, FERRIS AIR WAS ALREADY IN TROUBLE.

SO YOU STOPPED FLYING? YOU STARTED RUNNING FERRIS?

AND YOU LET EVERYONE THINK YOUR FATHER WAS DOING IT ALL THROUGH *YOU?*

I DIDN'T KNOW WHAT ELSE TO DO.

THAT COMPANY. AFTER MOM AND YOUR FATHER, IT'S ALL *HE* HAD *LEFT.*

HE STILL HAS *YOU.*

I WAS A *SPOILED BRAT.*

WHEN MOM DIED, HE'D GIVE ME ANYTHING I WANTED AS LONG AS I SCREAMED *LOUD* ENOUGH.

ONE DAY, HE *REFUSED.* I DON'T EVEN KNOW WHAT I WAS AFTER, BUT I REMEMBER I SAID...

...I SAID I WISHED *MOM* WAS THERE INSTEAD OF *HIM.*

HE SAW YOU BRING YOUR DAD A BROWN BAG LUNCH AND HE TOLD ME...

...HE WISHED HE HAD A SON LIKE *YOU.*

HE WOULDN'T IF HE *KNEW* ME.

YOU'RE *HERE* FOR HIM. *ME?*

I'VE *NEVER* BEEN THERE FOR *ANYONE* IN MY FAMILY.

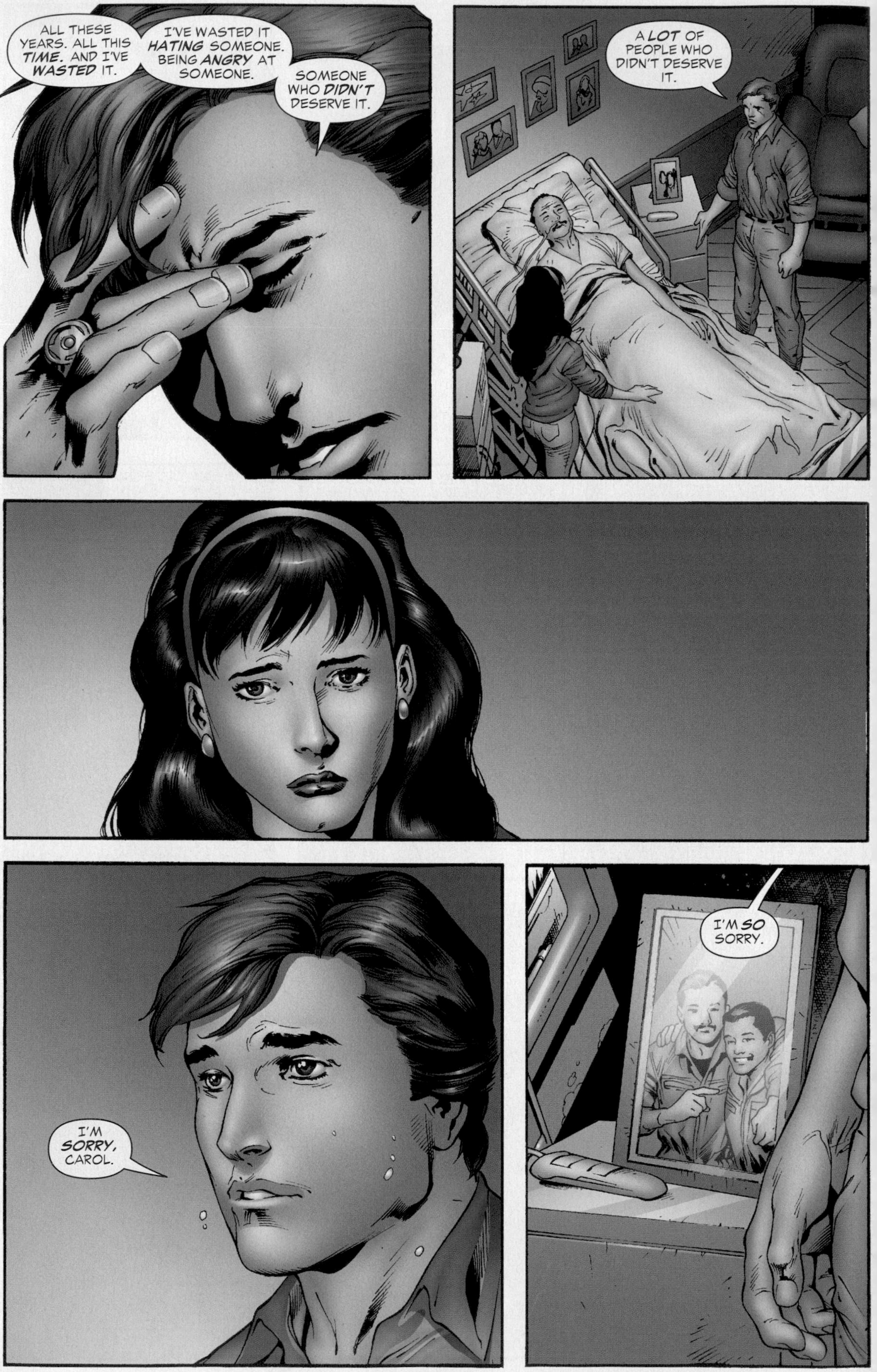
ALL THESE YEARS. ALL THIS TIME. AND I'VE WASTED IT.
I'VE WASTED IT HATING SOMEONE. BEING ANGRY AT SOMEONE.
SOMEONE WHO DIDN'T DESERVE IT.
A LOT OF PEOPLE WHO DIDN'T DESERVE IT.
I'M SORRY, CAROL.
I'M SO SORRY.

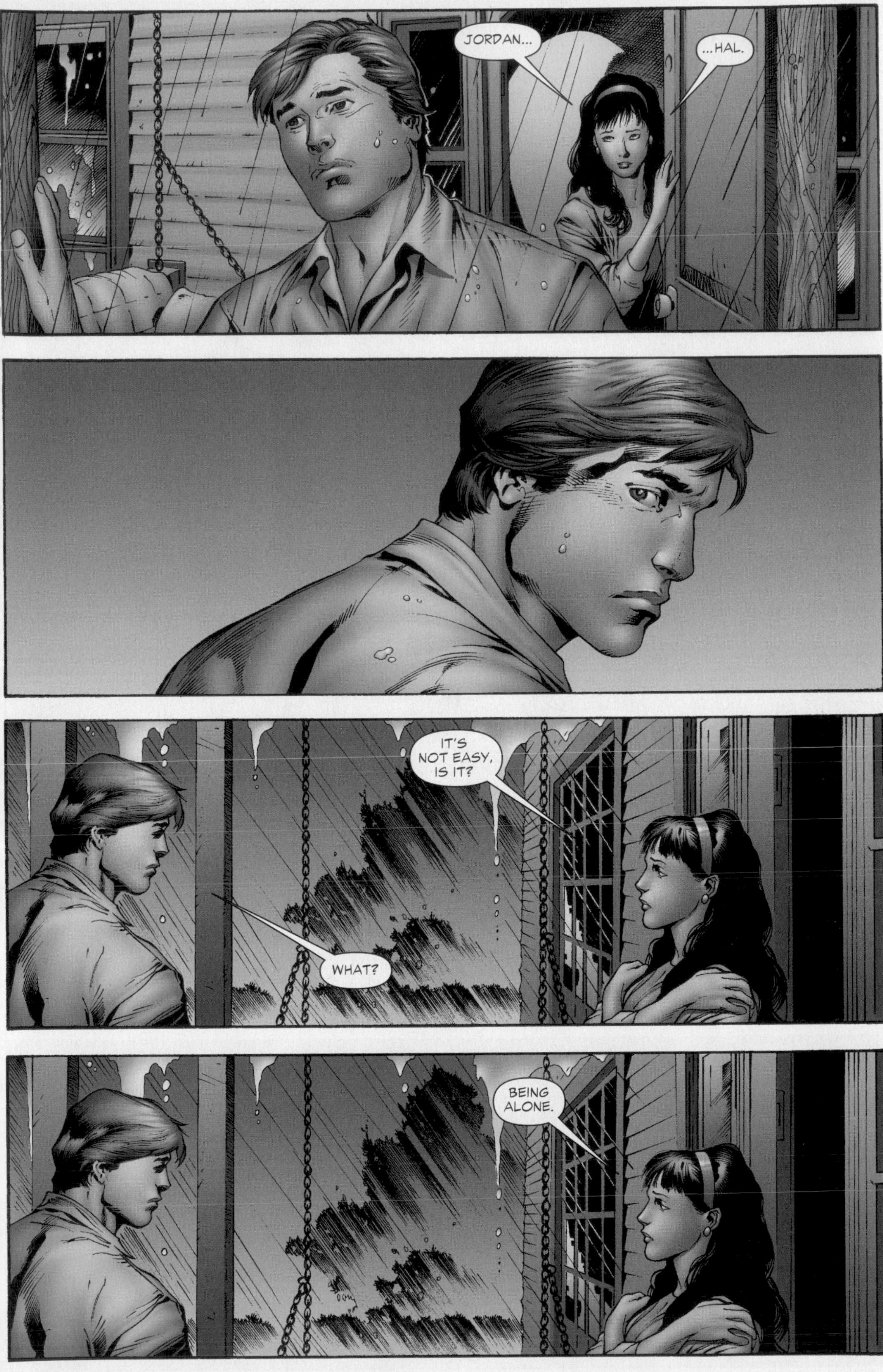
JORDAN...
...HAL.
IT'S NOT EASY, IS IT?
WHAT?
BEING ALONE.

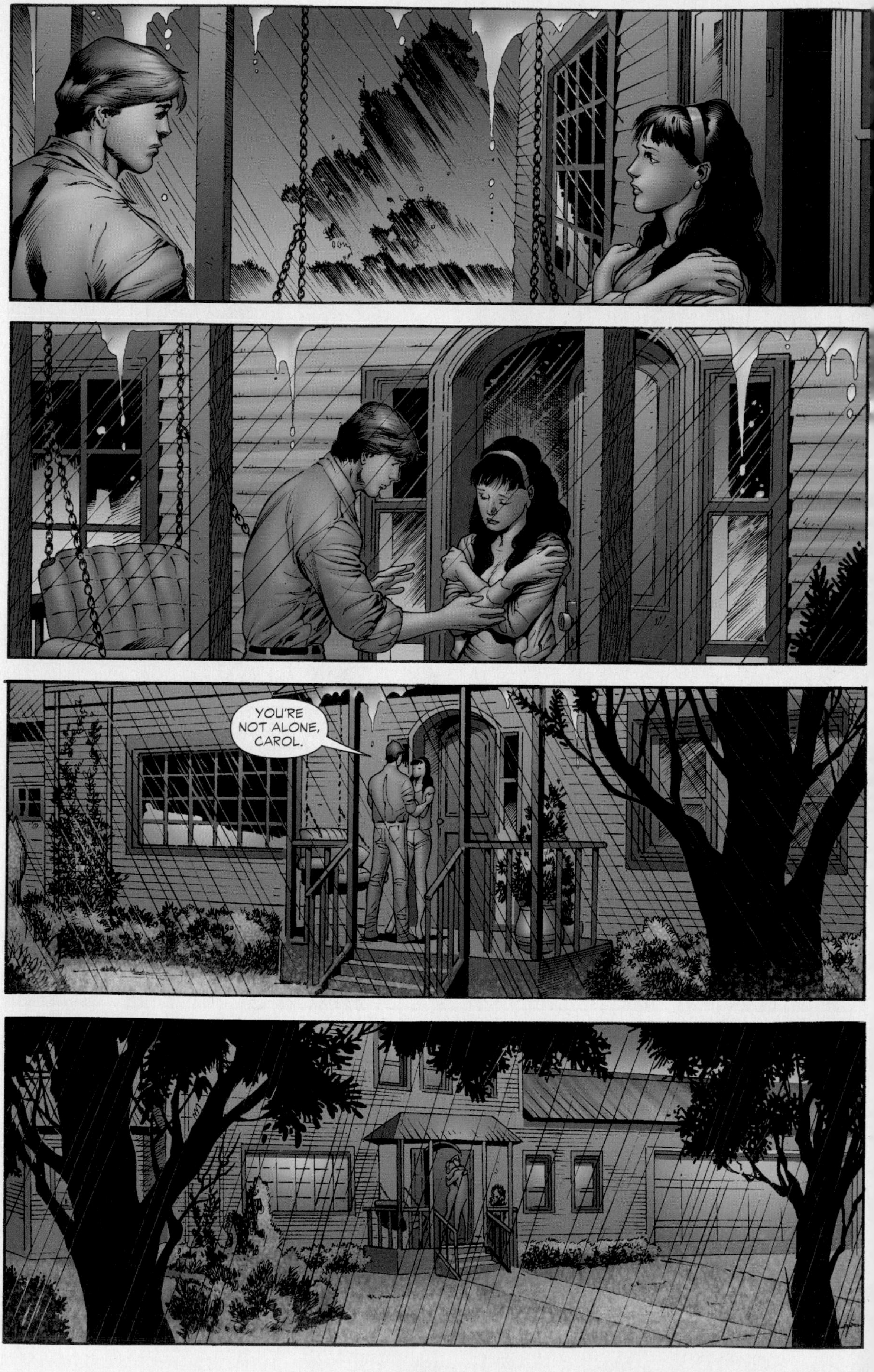
YOU'RE NOT ALONE, CAROL.

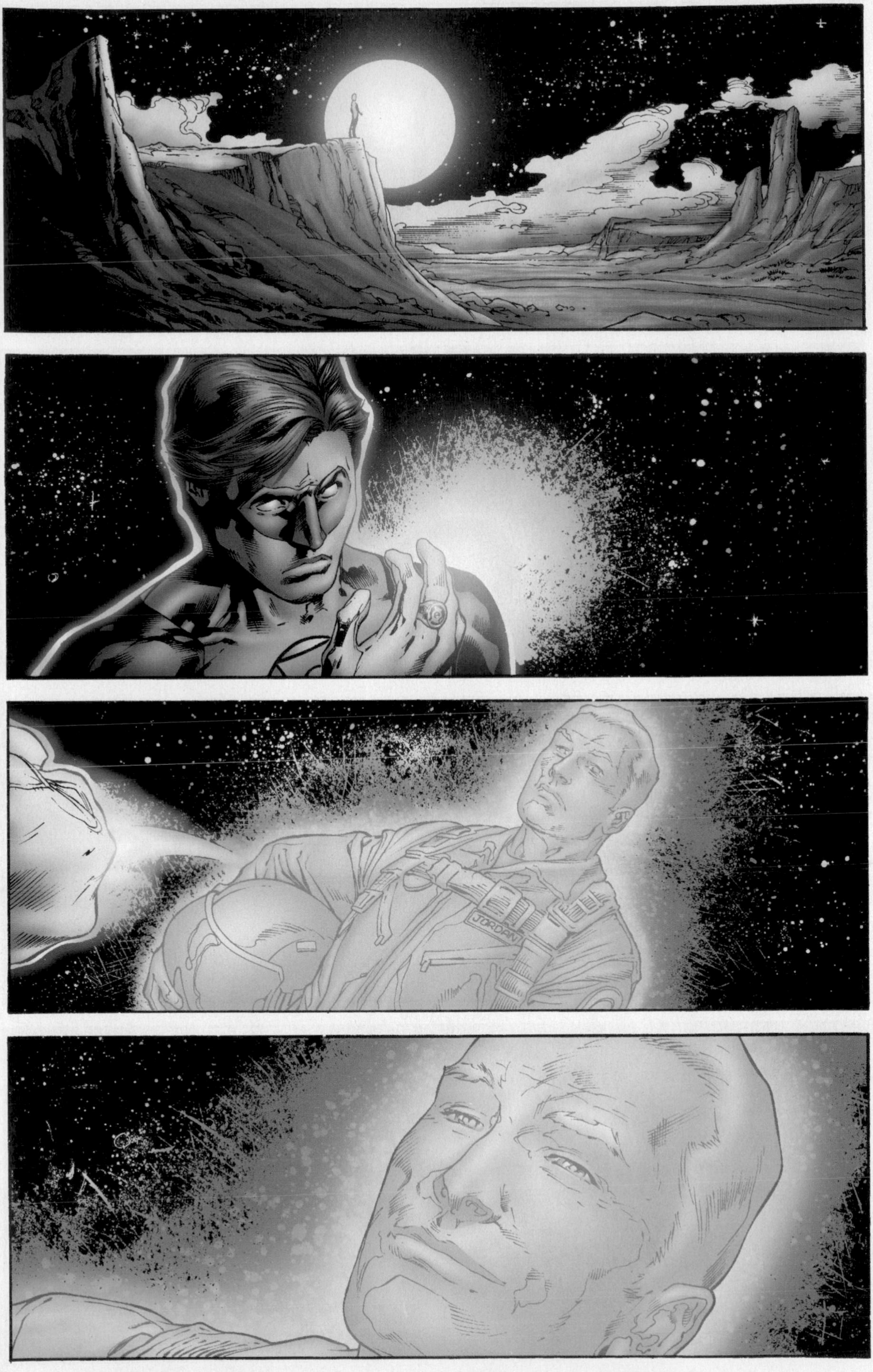
JORDAN

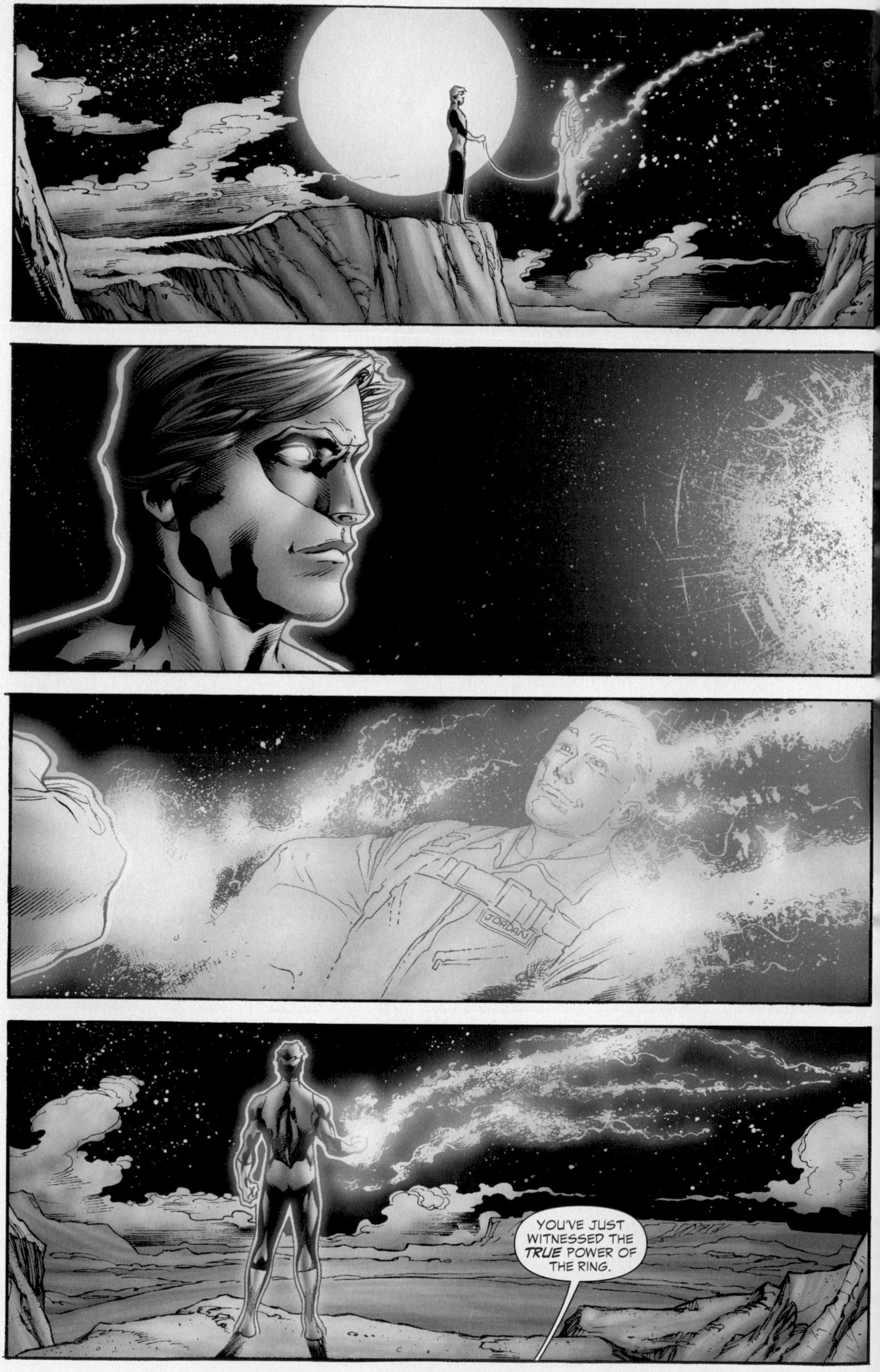
JORDAN
YOU'VE JUST WITNESSED THE *TRUE* POWER OF THE RING.

IT HAS HELPED YOU FIND THE *WILL* TO *LIVE.*

IT IS THE MOST *BASIC* ELEMENT WITHIN ONE'S WILLPOWER.

YOU WERE RIGHT.

I KNOW.

YOU AREN'T RIGHT ABOUT *EVERYTHING.*

BUT THE ANGER... THE ANGER I'VE HELD ONTO SINCE I WAS A *KID*...

...THAT'S BEEN FOR *NOTHING.* THAT HASN'T HELPED ANYONE.

BERATING YOU IS *MY* JOB, NOT *YOURS.*

I MYSELF HAVE SUFFERED LOSS, JORDAN. *GREAT* LOSS.

WITHOUT ABIN THERE TO HELP ME, I DOUBT THIS RING WOULD STILL BE *MINE.*

FOR BEINGS LIKE US, OVERCOMING FEAR IS WHAT WE DO BEST. BUT WHEN IT COMES TO GUILT, REGRET... *LOSS*...

...EVEN *GREEN LANTERNS* STRUGGLE WITH THOSE.

NEVER *FORGET* THAT, JORDAN.

ONE DAY YOU MAY NEED TO PASS THAT ON TO A ROOKIE AS I HAVE. AS ABIN *DID*.

SO YOU THINK I'LL MAKE IT AS LANTERN NOW?

YOU WILL, IF YOU COME TO UNDERSTAND THE *HONOR* THAT YOU'VE BEEN BESTOWED WITH. IF YOU LEARN THE TRUE *MEANING* BEHIND THE OATH WE RECITE.

AND IF YOU SPEND SOME TIME *OFF* THIS BALL OF MUD AND PRIMITIVE CULTURES AND EXPERIENCE THE WONDER OF THE OTHERS IN YOUR SECTOR.

PERHAPS EVEN IN *MINE*.

THANKS.

YOU ARE WELCOME--

--GREEN LANTERN.

TIME ALLOTMENT EXCEEDED. ILLEGAL FRATERNIZING BETWEEN OFFICERS REGISTERED.

WHAT?

LANTERN 1417.

LANTERN 2814.

YOU HAVE DISOBEYED OUR TERRITORIAL EDICT. YOU WILL REPORT TO OA--

--FOR IMMEDIATE DISCIPLINE.

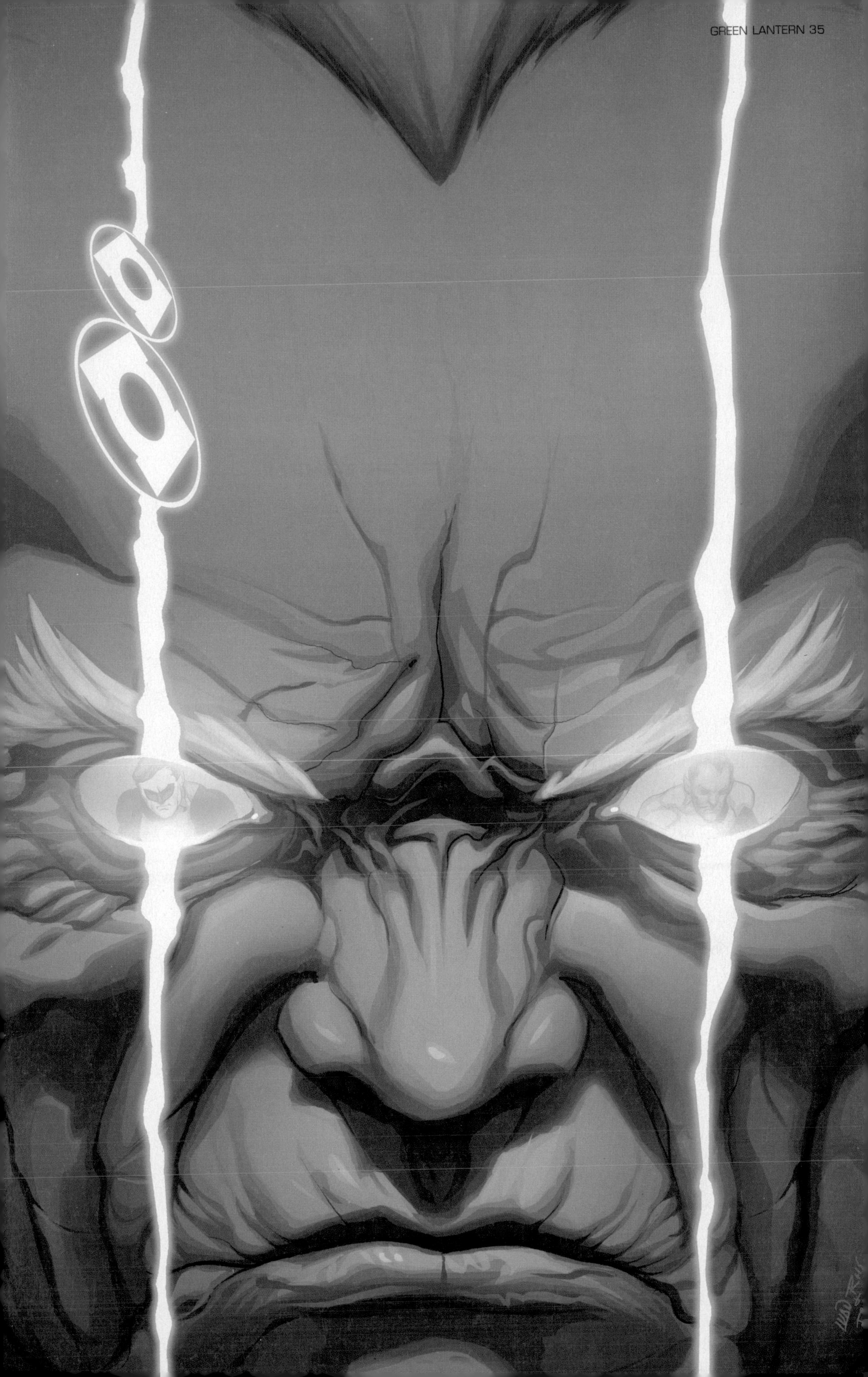

SECRET ORIGIN

BOOK SEVEN

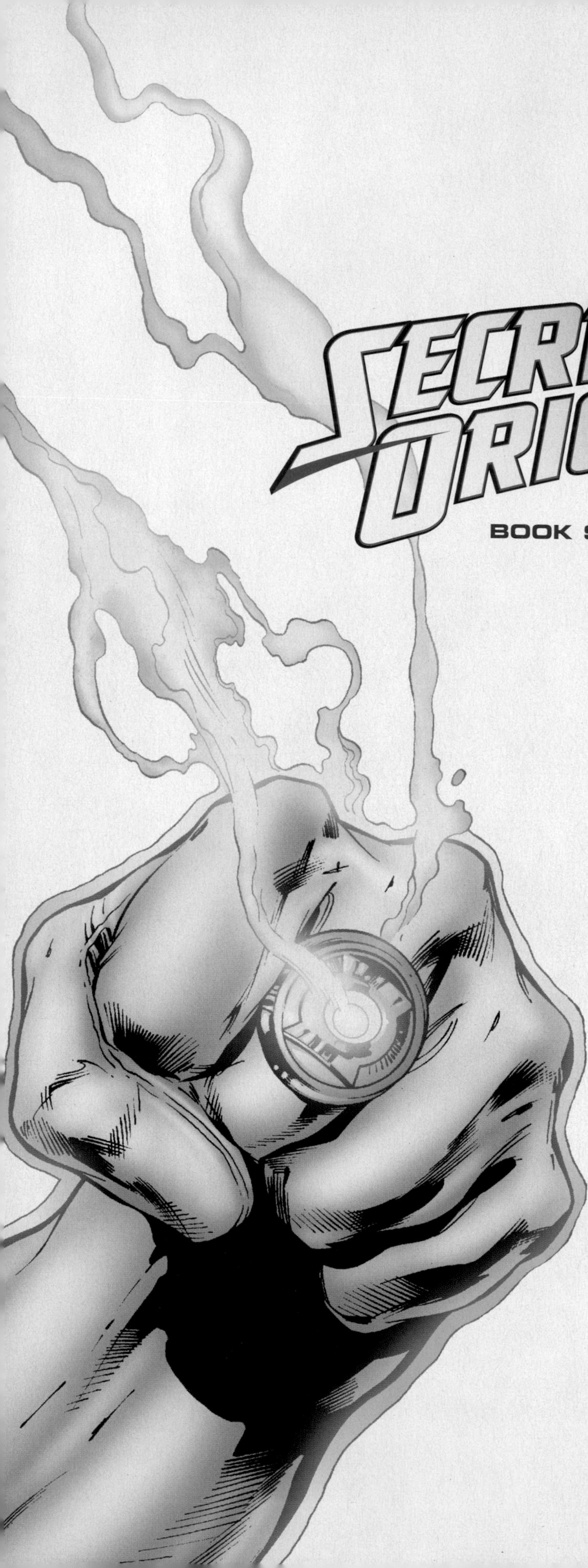

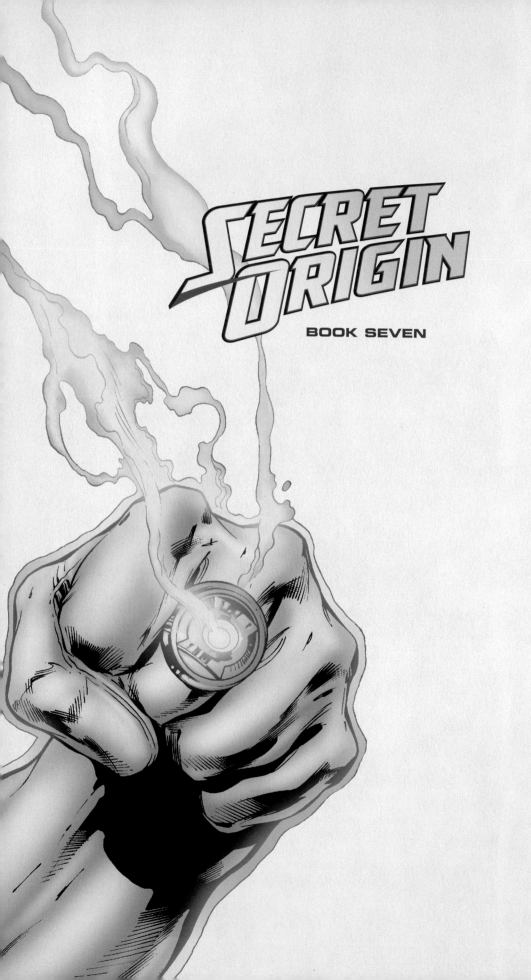

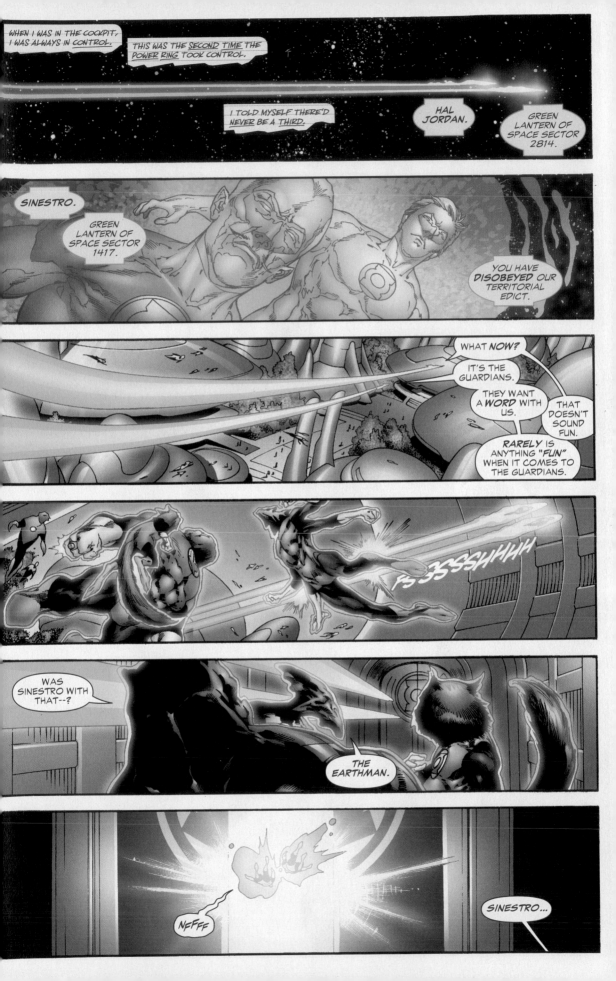

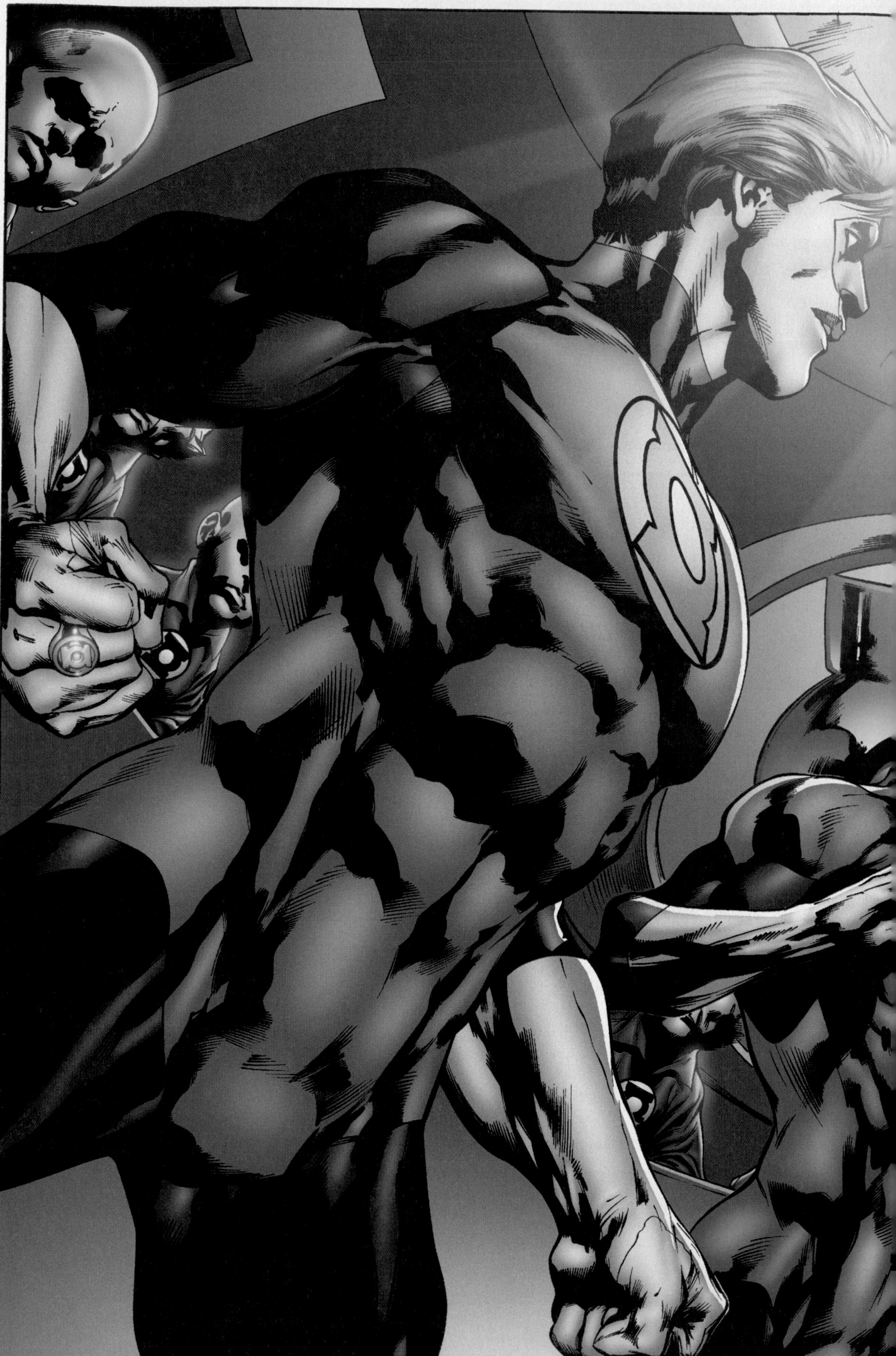

YOU ARE WELL AWARE OF THE *LIMITS* WE HAVE PUT ON THE CONGREGATION OF OUR OFFICERS *OFF* THE PLANET OA.

THESE ARE THE *GUARDIANS* OF THE *UNIVERSE?* THEY'RE SO *SMALL*--

SHUT UP.

THIS IS THE *SECOND TIME* YOU HAVE *DISOBEYED* US. AND *AGAIN* WITH THE GREEN LANTERN OF SECTOR 2814.

ALBEIT IT A *DIFFERENT* ONE. THIS IS NOT *ABIN SUR.*

MY NAME'S HAL JORDAN.

THEY *KNOW* THAT.

SINESTRO--?

EXPLAIN YOURSELF.

I WAS SIMPLY ASSISTING THIS OFFICER IN *LOCATING* AND *ARRESTING* THE *KILLER* WHO ENDED THE LIFE OF ABIN SUR.

ATROCITUS OF THE FIVE INVERSIONS.

AND BEFORE YOU SO *ARROGANTLY* RIPPED ME AWAY FROM THAT BACKWARDS BALL OF *DIRT*, I HAD HIM IN *CUSTODY*.

WE ARE WELL *AWARE*.

ATROCITUS WAS *TETHERED* TO YOUR RING.

THIS *TERRORIST* WILL BE RETURNED TO YSMAULT WHERE HE WILL CONTINUE HIS *SENTENCE*--

--AN *ETERNITY* OF IMPRISONMENT.

HOWEVER, THIS ARREST DOES NOT *EXCUSE YOU* FROM BREAKING OUR TERRITORIAL EDICT, SINESTRO.

GREEN LANTERNS MUST ONLY OPERATE IN THEIR *RESPECTIVE* SECTORS. THEY MUST PATROL *INDEPENDENTLY*. THEY MUST *FLY* ON THEIR OWN--

WHY?

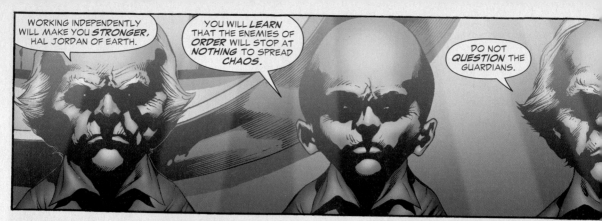

WORKING INDEPENDENTLY WILL MAKE YOU *STRONGER*, HAL JORDAN OF EARTH.

YOU WILL *LEARN* THAT THE ENEMIES OF *ORDER* WILL STOP AT *NOTHING* TO SPREAD *CHAOS*.

DO NOT *QUESTION* THE GUARDIANS.

WHY?

WE HAVE LIVED FOR *BILLIONS* OF YEARS.

WHAT WE DO, WE DO FOR THE *WELL-BEING* OF THE *ENTIRE* UNIVERSE.

LIKE THE *MANHUNTERS?*

JORDAN--

THE ANDROIDS THAT DID OUR JOB BEFORE THEY WENT "*GLITCHY*" AND SLAUGHTERED *EVERY* LIVING BEING IN SECTOR 666 BUT THE FIVE INVERSIONS--?

THEY ARE *LIES* FROM ATROCITUS--

IT *WASN'T* ATROCITUS THAT TOLD US ABOUT THE *MASSACRE*. IT WAS *ABIN SUR*. A MESSAGE--

MORE FABLES TO INSTILL *FEAR* AMONG YOU.

INSTILL FEAR IN *US?* YOU KNOW WHAT *I* THINK?

I THINK *YOU'RE* AFRAID.

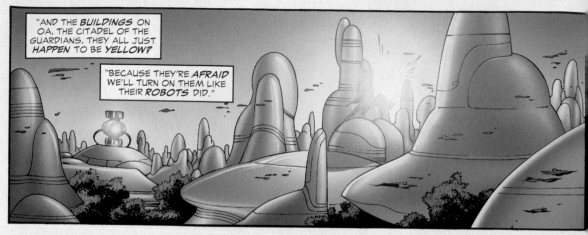

"AND THE *BUILDINGS* ON OA, THE CITADEL OF THE GUARDIANS, THEY ALL JUST *HAPPEN* TO BE *YELLOW?*

"BECAUSE THEY'RE *AFRAID* WE'LL TURN ON THEM LIKE THEIR *ROBOTS* DID."

THEY EXPECT *US* TO OVERCOME OUR FEARS.

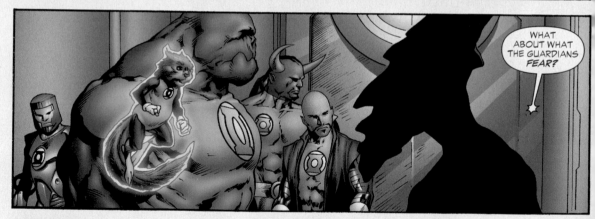

WHAT ABOUT WHAT THE GUARDIANS *FEAR?*

AND THAT *TERRITORIAL EDICT?*

THAT EDICT IS $#%?!$%#.

UNABLE TO TRANSLATE.

ENOUGH. YOUR ACCUSATIONS AND DISRESPECT CAUSE US *GREAT* CONCERN.

YOU ARE ON THE VERGE OF *EXPULSION*, HAL JORDAN OF EARTH.

GUARDIANS. YOU EXPEL JORDAN, YOU CAN HAVE *MY* RING AS WELL.

OA *HELP* ME, THE EARTHMAN IS *RIGHT*.

I AM?

QUIET. *PLEASE*.

WE *CAN* BE STRONGER *TOGETHER*.

THE CORPS *SHOULD* WORK IN UNISON WHEN NECESSARY.

AND IT SHOULD BE UP TO *US* TO NOT ONLY HELP OUR FELLOW OFFICERS *GROW*, BUT TO KEEP THEM IN *CHECK*. TO INSURE THAT THE TRAGEDY THAT HAPPENED IN SECTOR 666 *NEVER* HAPPENS AGAIN.

ALL OF *THIS*. THIS STARTED BECAUSE ONE OF YOU *SENT* ME TO ASSIST ABIN SUR'S REPLACEMENT.

ONE OF *US*?

THE ONE WHO CALLS HIMSELF "*GANTHET*."

"GANTHET"?

WE TAKE **NO** NAMES.

ONE OF YOU **HAS**.

WHICH ONE?

I BELIEVE WE HAVE HEARD **MUCH** TO CONSIDER, SINESTRO. FOR NOW, WE LEAVE THE EARTHMAN WITH HIS RING.

AND OBVIOUSLY, **YOU** WITH **YOURS**.

YES. BUT HE IS NOW AS MUCH **YOUR** RESPONSIBILITY AS KORUGAR AND THE REST OF SECTOR 1417.

WE **TRUST** THAT IS **ACCEPTABLE**, SINESTRO...

...GREATEST OF THE **GREEN** LANTERNS.

Hr.

YES.

"THAT IS ACCEPTABLE."

HNNN!!

FSSSSSS

I *DID* DO IT.

YOU *DIDN'T* DO IT.

I *DID*.

NO ONE CAN BREAK THROUGH YELLOW, JORDAN. NOT EVEN SINESTRO.

I CAN--

YOU ONLY TRIED LIKE *TWENTY* TIMES, HUMAN! YOU CAN TRY ANOTHER *THOUSAND* AND IT WON'T MAKE A DIFFERENCE.

I BELIEVE HIM.

YOU, TOMAR-RE? YOU ALWAYS HAD FAITH *FAR* TOO READILY.

I SUPPOSE THAT IS ONE THING ABIN TAUGHT ME THAT HE NEVER TAUGHT YOU.

I SUPPOSE...

...I MUST *GO.*

I DO NOT HAVE TIME FOR ANY MORE *GAMES*...

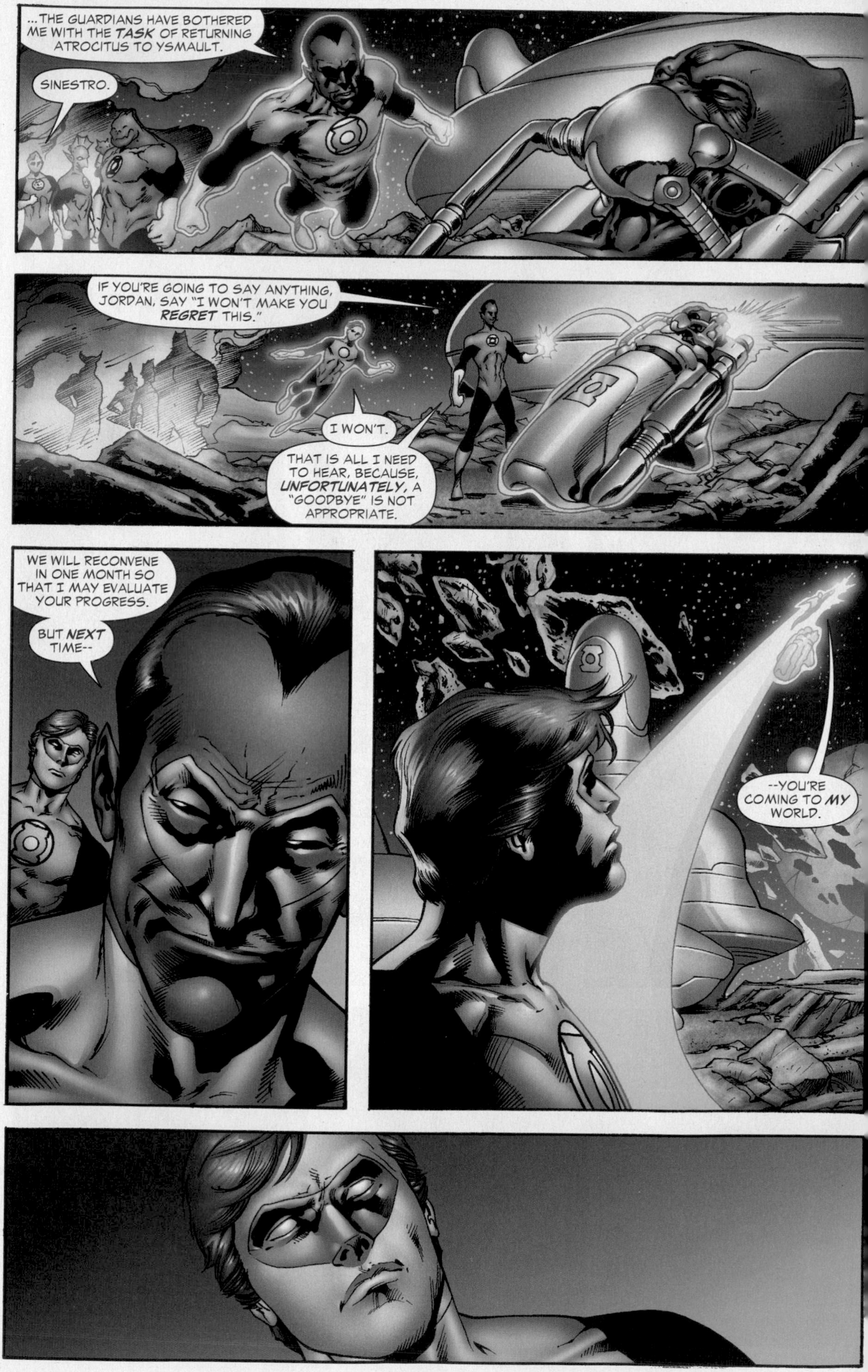
...THE GUARDIANS HAVE BOTHERED ME WITH THE *TASK* OF RETURNING ATROCITUS TO YSMAULT.
SINESTRO.
IF YOU'RE GOING TO SAY ANYTHING, JORDAN, SAY "I WON'T MAKE YOU *REGRET* THIS."
I WON'T.
THAT IS ALL I NEED TO HEAR, BECAUSE, *UNFORTUNATELY*, A "GOODBYE" IS NOT APPROPRIATE.
WE WILL RECONVENE IN ONE MONTH SO THAT I MAY EVALUATE YOUR PROGRESS.
BUT *NEXT* TIME--
--YOU'RE COMING TO *MY* WORLD.

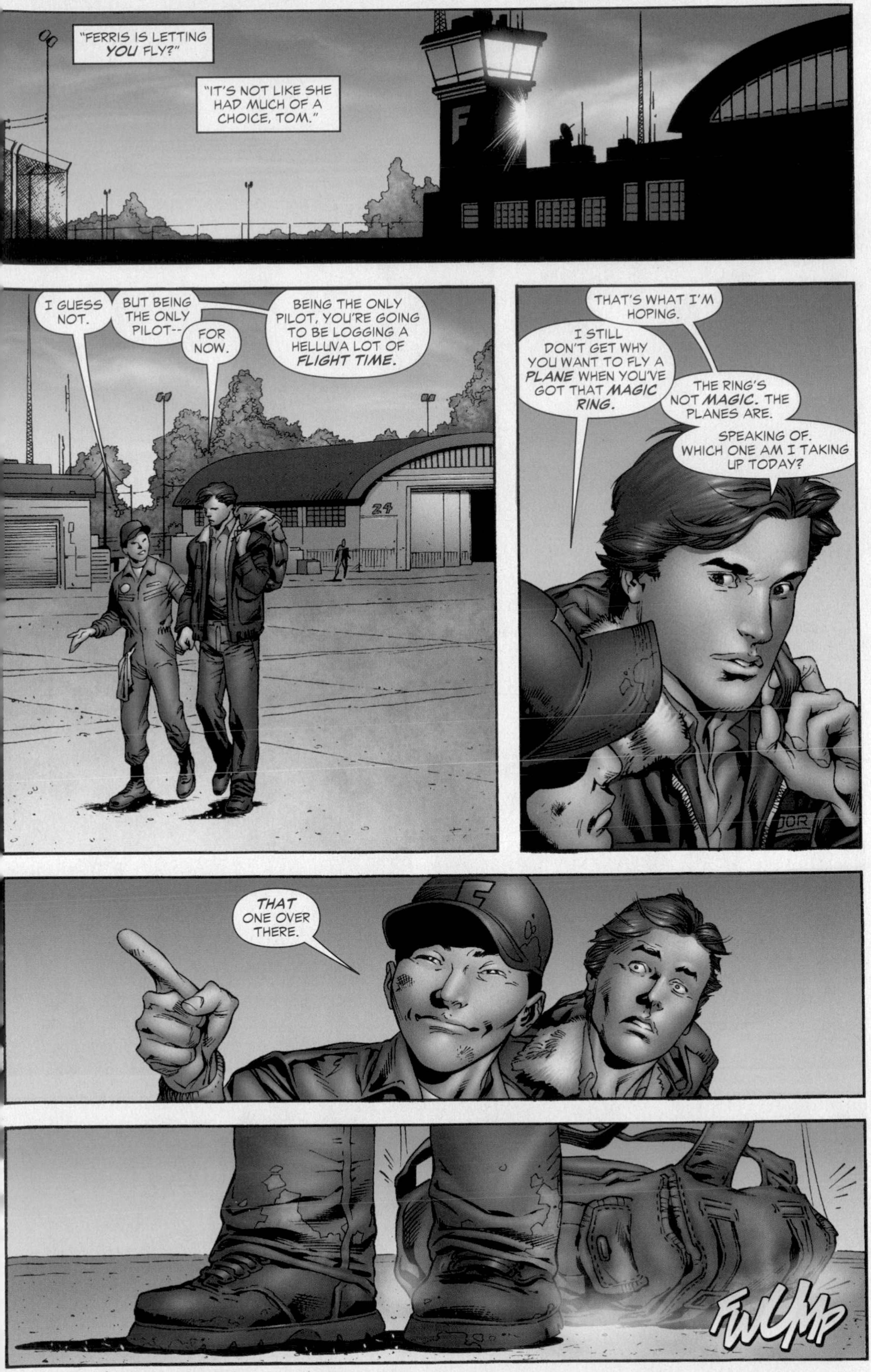
"FERRIS IS LETTING YOU FLY?"
"IT'S NOT LIKE SHE HAD MUCH OF A CHOICE, TOM."
I GUESS NOT.
BUT BEING THE ONLY PILOT--
FOR NOW.
BEING THE ONLY PILOT, YOU'RE GOING TO BE LOGGING A HELLUVA LOT OF FLIGHT TIME.
THAT'S WHAT I'M HOPING.
I STILL DON'T GET WHY YOU WANT TO FLY A PLANE WHEN YOU'VE GOT THAT MAGIC RING.
THE RING'S NOT MAGIC. THE PLANES ARE.
SPEAKING OF. WHICH ONE AM I TAKING UP TODAY?
THAT ONE OVER THERE.
FWUMP

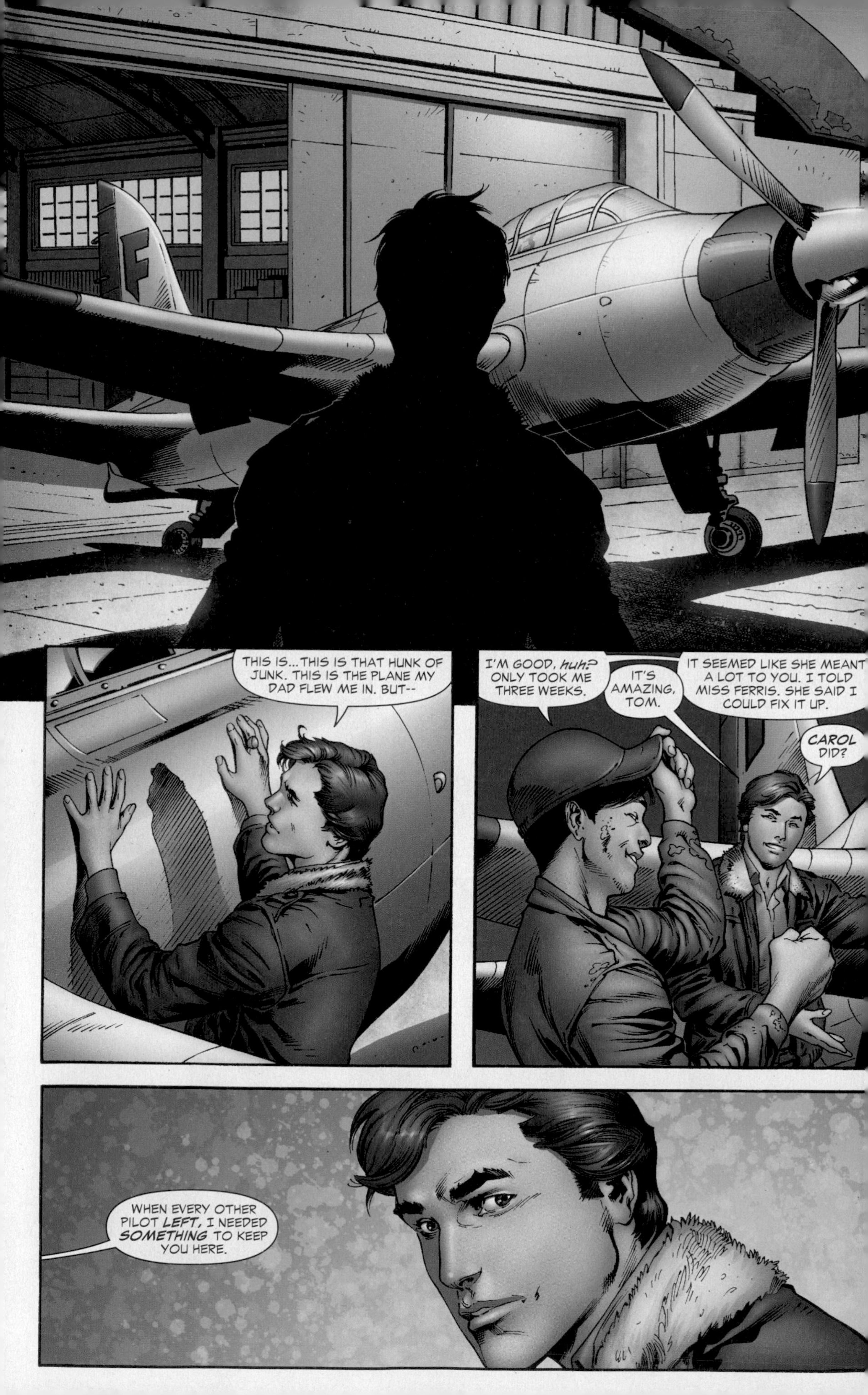
THIS IS... THIS IS THAT HUNK OF JUNK. THIS IS THE PLANE MY DAD FLEW ME IN. BUT--
I'M GOOD, *huh?* ONLY TOOK ME THREE WEEKS.
IT'S AMAZING, TOM.
IT SEEMED LIKE SHE MEANT A LOT TO YOU. I TOLD MISS FERRIS. SHE SAID I COULD FIX IT UP.
CAROL DID?
WHEN EVERY OTHER PILOT *LEFT,* I NEEDED *SOMETHING* TO KEEP YOU HERE.

...REPORTS OF MORE **STRANGE LIGHTS** IN THE SKY ARE POURING IN.

COAST CITY HOSPITAL CCH

U.F.O.'S? SECRET AIR FORCE TEST FLIGHTS? OR ARE THESE RUMORS OF A GLOWING GREEN **MAN** TRUE?

IS THE **GREEN LANTERN** REAL?

WITH THE RECENT APPEARANCE OF **SUPERMAN** IN METROPOLIS, COULD COAST CITY HAVE ITS VERY OWN PROTECTOR? AN EMERALD WARRIOR--?

KLANK

KLK

CHRIST.

I D-D-DIDN'T DO ANYTHING **WRONG.**

STAND **UP.** STAND UP AND GET AWAY FROM THAT--

AAAIEE!

WAAESSSH

IT'S OKAY. DEAD IS G-G-GOOD.

DEAD IS GOOD.

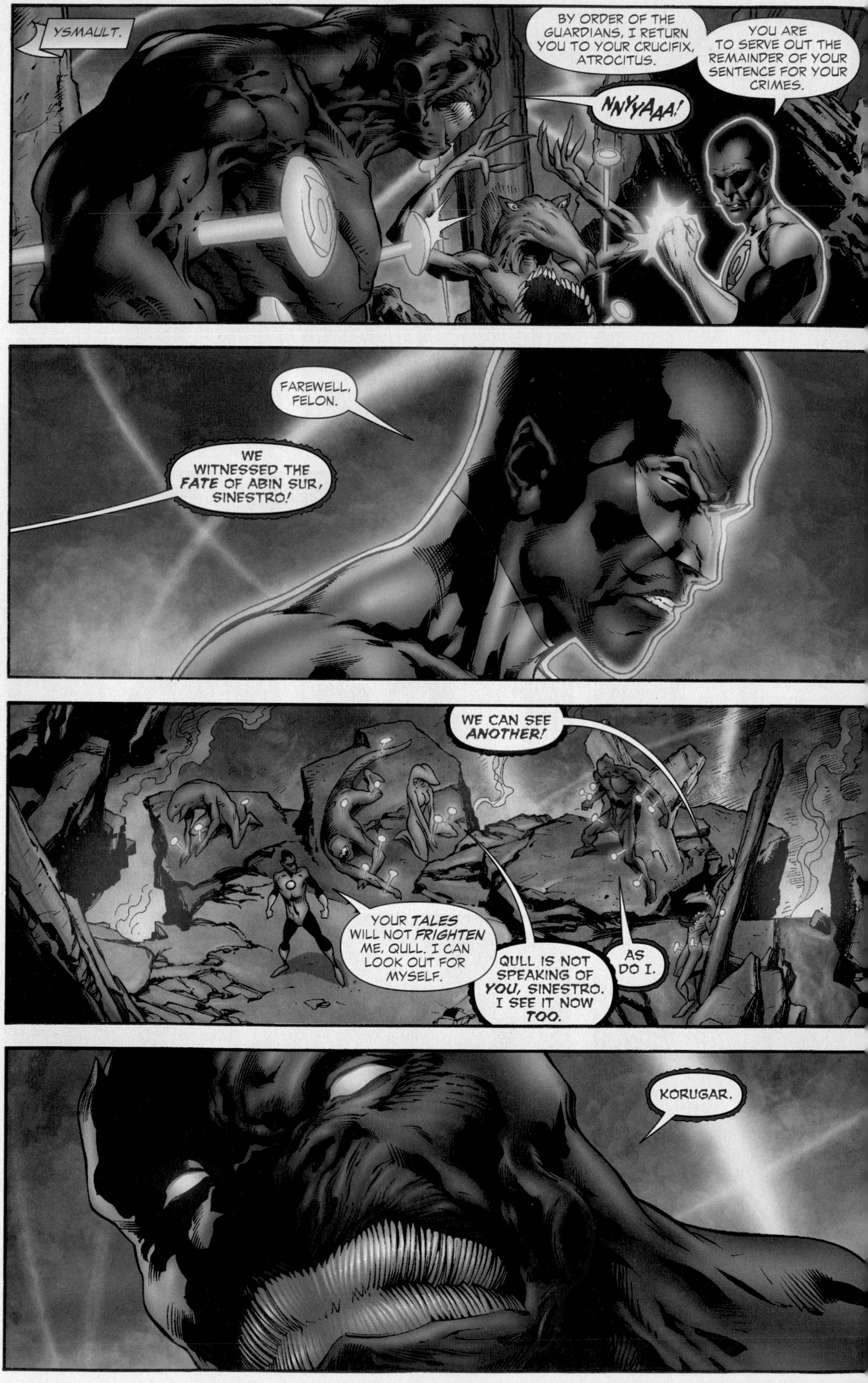
YSMAULT.
BY ORDER OF THE GUARDIANS, I RETURN YOU TO YOUR CRUCIFIX, ATROCITUS.
YOU ARE TO SERVE OUT THE REMAINDER OF YOUR SENTENCE FOR YOUR CRIMES.
NNYYAAA!
FAREWELL, FELON.
WE WITNESSED THE FATE OF ABIN SUR, SINESTRO!
WE CAN SEE ANOTHER!
YOUR TALES WILL NOT FRIGHTEN ME, QULL. I CAN LOOK OUT FOR MYSELF.
QULL IS NOT SPEAKING OF YOU, SINESTRO. I SEE IT NOW TOO.
AS DO I.
KORUGAR.

YOUR HOMEWORLD WILL SOON DESCEND INTO CIVIL *UNREST.* *VIOLENT* RIOTS. A *BLOODY* COUP.

YOUR PEOPLE WILL PLUNGE INTO *MADNESS* AS YOU SAVE WORLDS *NOT* YOUR OWN.

CHAOS WILL SPIN IT OUT OF YOUR *CONTROL.*

YOU THINK ME A *FOOL,* ATROCITUS?

KORUGAR WILL *NEVER* EMBRACE CHAOS. NOT AS LONG AS I AM AROUND TO INSTILL *ORDER.*

I FEEL *NO* FEAR, DEMONS.

NO FEAR OF *ANY* KIND.

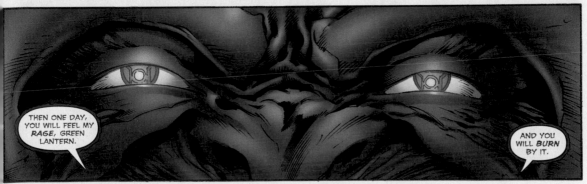

THEN ONE DAY, YOU WILL FEEL MY *RAGE,* GREEN LANTERN.

AND YOU WILL *BURN* BY IT.